The **MICHELIN** Guide

Chicago

RESTAURANTS
2011

W9-BVK-699

MICHELIN

Manufacture française des pneumatiques Michelin

Société en commandite par actions au capital de 304 000 000 EUR
Place des Carmes-Déchaux — 63000 Clermont-Ferrand (France)
R.C.S. Clermont-Fd B 855 200 507
No part of this publication may be reproduced in any form without the prior
permission of the publisher.

© Michelin, Propriétaires-éditeurs
Dépot légal Octobre 2010
Made in Canada
Published in 2010

The MICHELIN Guide
One Parkway South
Greenville, SC 29615 USA
www.michelinguide.com
michelin.guides@us.michelin.com

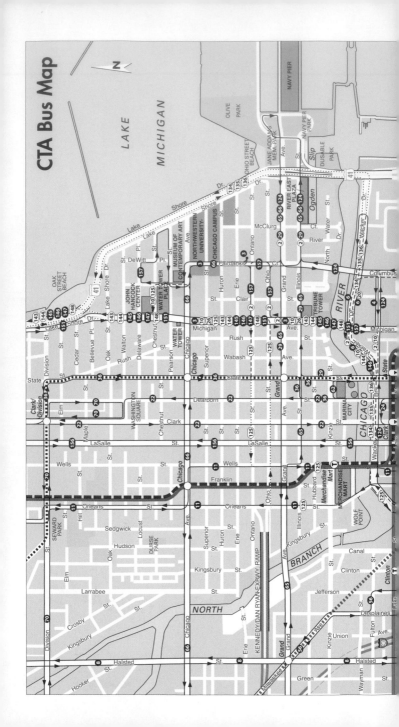

Dear Reader

W e are thrilled to finally present the very first edition of our MICHELIN Guide to Chicago.

Our dynamic team has spent this year updating our selection to wholly reflect the rich diversity of Chicago's restaurants and hotels. As part of our meticulous and highly confidential evaluation process, our inspectors have anonymously and methodically eaten through all of the city's neighborhoods and suburbs to compile the finest in each category for your enjoyment. While these inspectors are expertly trained food industry professionals, we remain consumer driven: our goal is to provide comprehensive choices to accommodate your comfort, tastes, and budget. Our Inspectors dine, drink, and lodge as 'regular' customers in order to experience and evaluate the same level of service and cuisine you would as a guest.

With the introduction of the Chicago guide, we have expanded our criteria to reflect some of the more current and unique elements of the city's dining scene. Don't miss the "Breakfasts" listing and our "Small Plates" category, highlighting those establishments with a distinct style of service, setting, and menu; and the comprehensive "Under $25" listings which also include a diverse and impressive choice at a very good value.

Additionally, you may now follow our Michelin Inspectors on Twitter @MichelinGuideCH as they chow their way around town. Our anonymous inspectors tweet daily about their unique and entertaining food experiences.

Our company's two founders, Édouard and André Michelin, published the first MICHELIN Guide in 1900, to provide motorists with practical information about where they could service and repair their cars, find quality accommodations, and a good meal. Later in 1926, the star-rating system for outstanding restaurants was introduced, and over the decades we have developed many new improvements to our guides. The local team here in Chicago enthusiastically carries on these traditions.

We sincerely hope that the MICHELIN Guide will remain your preferred reference to the city's restaurants and hotels.

Michel Rollier
Chief Executive Officer Michelin

Contents

© City of Chicago / GRC

© City of Chicago / GRC

Contents

The Michelin Guide

"This volume was created at the turn of the century and will last at least as long".

This foreword to the very first edition of the MICHELIN Guide, written in 1900, has become famous over the years and the Guide has lived up to the prediction. It is read across the world and the key to its popularity is the consistency in its commitment to its readers, which is based on the following promises.

→ Anonymous Inspections

Our inspectors make anonymous visits to hotels and restaurants to gauge the quality offered to the ordinary customer. They pay their own bill and make no indication of their presence. These visits are supplemented by comprehensive monitoring of information—our readers' comments are one valuable source, and are always taken into consideration.

→ Independence

Our choice of establishments is a completely independent one, made for the benefit of our readers alone. Decisions are discussed by the inspectors and the editor, with the most important decided at the global level. Inclusion in the guide is always free of charge.

→ The Selection

The Guide offers a selection of the best hotels and restaurants in each category of comfort and price. Inclusion in the guides is a commendable award in itself, and defines the establishment among the "best of the best."

The Michelin Guide

How the MICHELIN Guide Works

→ Annual Updates

All practical information, the classifications, and awards, are revised and updated every year to ensure the most reliable information possible.

→ Consistency & Classifications

The criteria for the classifications are the same in all countries covered by the Michelin Guides. Our system is used worldwide and is easy to apply when choosing a restaurant or hotel.

→ The Classifications

We classify our establishments using XXXXX-X and 🏨🏨🏨-🏠 to indicate the level of comfort. The ❀❀❀-❀ specifically designates an award for cuisine, unique from the classification. For hotels and restaurants, a symbol in red suggests a particularly charming spot with unique décor or ambiance.

→ Our Aim

As part of Michelin's ongoing commitment to improving travel and mobility, we do everything possible to make vacations and eating out a pleasure.

The Michelin Guide

How to Use This Guide

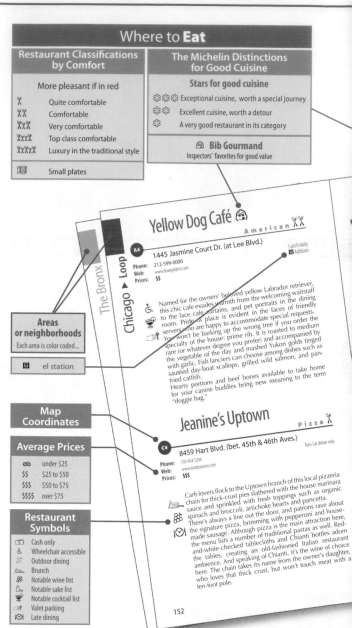

Where to **Eat**

Restaurant Classifications by Comfort

More pleasant if in red

X	Quite comfortable
XX	Comfortable
XxX	Very comfortable
XxxX	Top class comfortable
XxXxX	Luxury in the traditional style
▤	Small plates

The Michelin Distinctions for Good Cuisine

Stars for good cuisine

✿✿✿ Exceptional cuisine, worth a special journey

✿✿ Excellent cuisine, worth a detour

✿ A very good restaurant in its category

✿ Bib Gourmand
Inspectors' favorites for good value

Yellow Dog Café ✿

American XX

A4 1445 Jasmine Court Dr. (at Lee Blvd.)

Lunch daily
🚇 Addison

Phone: 212-599-0000
Web: www.ilovegoldens.com
Prices: $$

Named for the owners' beloved yellow Labrador retriever, this chic cafe exudes warmth from the welcoming waitstaff to the lace cafe curtains, and pet portraits in the dining room. Pride of place is evident in the faces of friendly servers who are happy to accommodate special requests. You won't be barking up the wrong tree if you order the specialty of the house: prime rib. It is roasted to medium rare (or whatever degree you prefer) and accompanied by the vegetable of the day and mashed Yukon golds tinged with garlic. Fish fanciers can choose among dishes such as sautéed day-boat scallops, grilled wild salmon, and pan-fried catfish.

Hearty portions and beef bones available to take home for your canine buddies bring new meaning to the term "doggie bag."

Jeanine's Uptown

Pizza X

C4 8459 Hart Blvd. (bet. 45th & 46th Aves.)

Tues-Sat dinner only

Phone: 310-454-5294
Web: www.eatatjeanines.com
Prices: $$$

Carb lovers flock to the Uptown branch of this local pizzeria chain for thick-crust pies slathered with the house marinara sauce and sprinkled with fresh toppings such as organic spinach and broccoli, artichoke hearts and pancetta. There's always a line out the door, and patrons rave about the signature pizza, brimming with pepperoni and house-made sausage. Although pizza is the main attraction here, the menu lists a number of traditional pastas as well. Red-and-white-checked tablecloths and Chianti bottles adorn the tables, creating an old-fashioned Italian restaurant ambience. And speaking of Chianti, it's the wine of choice here. The chain takes its name from the owner's daughter, who loves that thick crust, but won't touch meat with a ten-foot pole.

152

The Bronx

Chicago ▶ Loop

Areas or neighborhoods
Each area is color coded...

🚇 el station

Map Coordinates

Average Prices

☜	under $25
$$	$25 to $50
$$$	$50 to $75
$$$$	over $75

Restaurant Symbols

🕾	Cash only
♿	Wheelchair accessible
🍽	Outdoor dining
☕	Brunch
🍷	Notable wine list
🍶	Notable sake list
🍸	Notable cocktail list
🚗	Valet parking
☾	Late dining

How to Use This Guide

8

Where to **Stay**

Average Prices	Hotel Symbols	Hotel Classifications by Comfort
Prices do not include applicable taxes	**149 rooms** Number of rooms & suites	More pleasant if in red
$ under $200	♿ Wheelchair accessible	Quite comfortable
$$ $200 to $300	𝄞 Exercise room	Comfortable
$$$ $300 to $400	Spa	Very comfortable
$$$$ over $400	Swimming pool	Top class comfortable
Map Coordinates	Conference room	Luxury in the traditional style
	Pet friendly	

...alace ✿ ✿

Italian ✗✗✗✗

Manhattan ▸ Chelsea

...t. (at 39th Street)   Dinner only

...louspalace.com

...ine cooked Italian never tasted so good than at this ...retentious little place. The simple décor claims no big-...me designers, and while the Murano glass light fixtures ...e chic and the velveteen-covered chairs are comfortable, ...is isn't a restaurant where millions of dollars were spent ...n the interior.

...nstead, food is the focus here. The restaurant's name may ...not be Italian, but it nonetheless serves some of the best ...pasta in the city, made fresh in-house. Dishes follow the ...seasons, thus ravioli may be stuffed with fresh ricotta and ...herbs in summer, and pumpkin in fall. Most everything ...is liberally dusted with Parmigiano Reggiano, a favorite ...ingredient of the chef.

For dessert, you'll have to deliberate between the likes ...of creamy tiramisu, ricotta cheesecake, and homemade ...gelato. One thing's for sure: you'll never miss your nonna's ...cooking when you eat at Sonya's.

153

The Fan Inn

D1

135 Shanghai Street, Oakland

Phone: 650-345-1440 or 888-222-2424
Web: www.superfaninnoaklandf.com
Prices: $$

𝍄
Rooms
5
Suites
🏋
Spa

San Francisco ▸ Civic Center

...Housed in an Art Deco-era building, the venerable Fan Inn ...ecently underwent a complete facelift. The hotel now hits ...with the new generation of sleekly understated hotels ...ering a Zen-inspired aesthetic, despite its 1930s origins.

...oothing neutral palette runs throughout the property, ...ctuated with exotic woods, bamboo, and fine fabrics. ...he lobby, the sultry lounge makes a relaxing place for ...-mixed cocktail or a glass of wine.

...linens and down pillows cater to your comfort, while ...en TVs, DVD players with iPod docking stations, ...eless Internet access satisfy the need for modern ...s. For business travelers, nightstands convert to ...ables and credenzas morph into flip-out desks. ...inter, fax or scanner? It's just a phone call away. ...est, the hotel will even provide office supplies.

...half of the accommodations here are suites, ...uxury factor ratchets up with marble baths, ...ting areas, and fully equipped kitchens. ...inn doesn't have a restaurant, the nearby ...arly everything you could want in terms of ...o dumplings to haute cuisine.

315

How to Use This Guide

Where to Eat

Chicago

River North

Art galleries, hopping nightlife, well-known restaurants and chefs, swanky shopping, great views, even a head-turning fast-food chain: almost everything that Chicago offers is offered here. Perhaps because River North offers so much it also attracts so many. From ladies who lunch to office workers to tour bus-style tourists, most folks who pass through the Windy City make a stop here.

BEYOND THE ORDINARY

River North (which, it stands to reason, is located north of the Chicago River) has no shortage of food and drink attractions. True, as you pull up to Ontario and Clark streets, you might just think, "chain restaurant central," but even the chains in River North have their charm.

Among them is the **Rock 'n' Roll McDonald's**, a block-long, music-themed outpost of the ubiquitous burger chain. One of the busiest **MickeyD's** in the world, this one has an expanded menu, music memorabilia, and bragging rights to the first two-lane drive-through. (Remember: McDonald's is a local chain, still headquartered in the suburbs.) **The Rainforest Café**, **Hard Rock Café**, and **The Melting Pot** are popular tourist draws here, too. Speaking of drive-through chains, River North is the flagship location

of **Portillo's**, a local, beloved hot dog, burger, and beer chain. Its large exterior belies its efficient service and better-than-expected food.

When it comes to size, few buildings can top the mammoth **Merchandise Mart** (so large it has its own ZIP code). Along with its history and drool-worthy kitchen showrooms, it is home to two great food shops. At **Artisan Cellar**, in addition to boutique wines, panini, and specialty cheeses, you can purchase Katherine Anne Confections' fresh-cream caramels.

Locals also love **The Chopping Block** for its expert-taught, themed cooking courses and well-edited wine selections. (There's another location in Lincoln Square for north side courses.) Nearby, the Cooking Hospitality Institute of Chicago, known as **CHIC**, has a student-run restaurant where diners can get a glimpse of the next big thing in Chicago kitchens. Open Books, a used bookstore that relies on its proceeds to fund literacy programs, has plenty of cookbooks on its shelves. Outfit any kitchen with finds from the Bloomingdale's Home store in the 1912 Medinah Temple. You'll smell the **Blommer Chocolate Outlet Store** before you see it. Late at night and early in the morning, the tempting chocolate

14

aroma wreaks down the river beckoning city dwellers to its Willy Wonka-esque confines. This is where to stock up on sweets from the 70-plus-year-old brand. Blommer's also boasts a specialty cocoa collection ranging from such fabulous (and sinful) flavors as black cocoa, cake-based cocoa powders, and Dutch specialty varieties.

Deep-Dish Pizza

River North is as good a place as any to indulge in the local phenomenon of Chicago-style, deep-dish pizza. Also called stuffed pizza (referring to the pie, but it could also refer to the way you'll feel after you snarf it down), deep-dish pizza was created in the Windy City in the 1940s. Closer to a casserole (or, as they say in the Midwest, "hot dish,") than an Italian-style pizza, it is a thick, doughy crust, holding abundant cheese, sauce, and toppings inside.

Some say it is Chicago water in the dough that makes that crust so distinctive. Deep-dish pies take awhile to prepare, so be prepared to wait wherever you go. **Pizzeria Uno** (and its sister **Pizzeria Due**), **Giordano's,** and **Lou Malnati's** are some of the best known pie makers.

Street Stuff

If a little indigestion isn't a concern, follow that priceless pizza with another Chicago-style specialty: the Italian beef sandwich. Sort of like a very messy, yet very tasty, French dip, an Italian beef isn't Italian, but is all Chicago. Dating back to the 1930s, it features seasoned, thinly sliced beef on a hoagie roll, with either hot or sweet peppers on top. If you order it "wet," both the meat and the bread will be dipped in pan juices. You could also add cheese, but this isn't Philly! Two of the biggest contenders in the Italian beef wars are in this 'hood: **Al's Italian Beef** and **Mr. Beef**. Both eateries have high-quality sausages and hot dogs on the menu as well.

Get Your Groove On

Nightlife in River North is a scene, with everything from authentic Chicago Irish pubs, to cocktail lounges for those who like to see-and-be-seen. **Martini Ranch** is all about velvet ropes, house music, and an epic drink list.

Nestled in the landmark Chicago Historical Society Building, **Excalibur** is a multi-floor dance club. **Pops for Champagne** boasts several levels of champagne-tasting fun, plus live music inside the historic Tree Studios. Buy any gift for that bubbly drinker on your list here. **Blue Chicago** is a civilized place to sit, get a drink, and listen to that world-famous Chicago sound, the Blues. **English**, an aptly named British bar, is a popular watering hole for watching soccer and other sports, not usually broadcasted at your typical Chicago sports bar. English is also home to "Top Chef" alumna, Radhika Desai. Finally, don't skip the **Green Door Tavern**, which gets its name from the fact that its colored front told Prohibition-era customers where to enter for a drink.

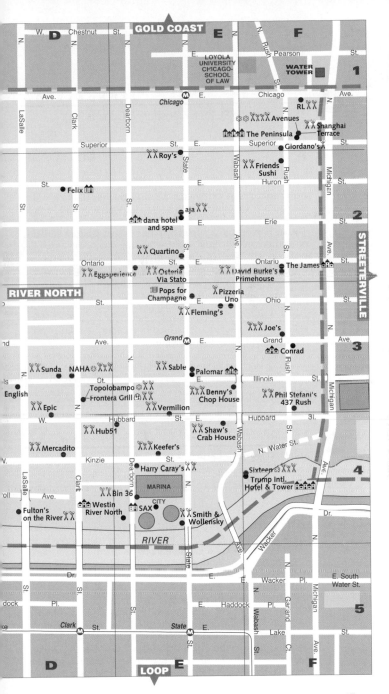

Ai

B2

Japanese XX

358 W. Ontario St. (bet. Kingsbury & Orleans Sts.)

Phone: 312-335-9888
Web: www.aichicago.us
Prices: $$

Lunch Mon – Fri
Dinner nightly
Chicago (Brown)

Ai is A+ when it comes to offering a Japanese dining experience. Bamboo-lined walls and touches of brick warm the room while tables, booths, and a sushi bar provide ample seating.

The sushi menu is arranged by type of fish, with four varieties of salmon; five of tuna; eight whitefish; seven shellfish; plus octopus, eel, and you name it. Sushi is neatly assembled, the fish good quality, and the flavor accents complementary. Maki are especially enjoyable; the signature *madai* ceviche maki is worth a shot, filled with avocado and cucumber then topped with Japanese red snapper and a piquant ceviche sauce. *Nabeyaki* udon is a wise choice for those who don't eat sushi: it bathes rich, marbled beef, udon noodles, and a firmly poached egg in a delicious broth.

aja

E2

Asian XX

660 N. State St. (at Erie St.)

Phone: 312-202-6050
Web: www.danahotelandspa.com
Prices: $$

Lunch & dinner daily
Chicago (Red)

While hotel dining may seem like a convenient choice for guests opting for ease over inspiration, the dana hotel's aja is a chic, urban-Asian café attracting as many area residents as it does temporary dwellers. It is debatable which is more attractive—the contemporary bi-level space or the fur coat-clad crowd that populates it.

The people watching and sexy space are worth a visit alone, but the bold flavors and pairings keep fashionistas coming back for more. The chef surprises palates with tasty creations such as sesame caramel chicken, tender five-spice short ribs, and crispy whole fish with black bean *nam pla* sauce. Rather than deciding on a single dish, know that the menu is designed to be shared, so go with a group and taste it all.

Avenues ✿✿

Contemporary ✕✕✕✕

F1

108 E. Superior St. (bet. Michigan Ave. & Rush St.)

Phone: 312-573-6695
Web: www.peninsula.com
Prices: $$$$

Dinner Tue – Sat
🅜 Chicago (Red)

Mark Wieland

I lead up to the second floor of the elegant Peninsula Hotel, located just off the Magnificent Mile, and you'll find a discreet, subtly marked entrance. Dress your best and be prepared for a night your stomach (and your date) will be thanking you for years to come—this is not your average hotel restaurant, but the posh, highly regarded Avenues.

Inside, you'll find an open exhibition kitchen—a bit of bustle in a room that is otherwise subdued and luxurious—with servers quickly, but quietly, humming back and forth as diners sink into plush chairs and soak in stunning views of the historic Chicago Water Tower.

Three tasting menus are offered nightly, each with a different number of courses, and though there is no à la carte, the kitchen handles special requests with grace. The haute, contemporary fare employs fine ingredients, prepared magnificently: a potato crisp with black truffle arrives floating atop delicate potato foam studded with bacon, mustard seeds, and lovage leaves. Also magical is Alaskan king crab poached in citrus sitting in a martini glass with cucumber, mounds of golden shad roe, floral and tangerine lace, curls of chili, and a *kalamansi* purée.

19

Benny's Chop House

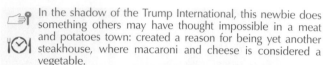

S t e a k h o u s e XXX

444 N. Wabash Ave. (bet. Hubbard & Illinois Sts.)

Phone: 312-626-2444
Web: www.bennyschophouse.com
Prices: $$$

Lunch & dinner daily
Grand (Red)

In the shadow of the Trump International, this newbie does something others may have thought impossible in a meat and potatoes town: created a reason for being yet another steakhouse, where macaroni and cheese is considered a vegetable.

The splendid service in particular is what makes Benny's a standout. Unsure what cut of steak will appease your appetite? Trust the waiters' wise words for they are well-versed in the caliber and characteristics of the different cuts. Should you order a fish that needs filleting, of course they will be happy to strut their stuff with trolley service at your table. Classic sides and even less expensive dishes (budget-friendly burgers) round out the menu, but the rational and ravenous know to go for steak and seafood.

Bin 36

A m e r i c a n XX

339 N. Dearborn St. (bet. Kinzie St. & the Chicago River)

Phone: 312-755-9463
Web: www.bin36.com
Prices: $$$

Lunch & dinner daily
Lake

Bin 36 is many things: a wine emporium, cheese shop, American restaurant; and, it also happens to be a school, offering courses like Wine 101. There are many balls in the air, but Bin 36 juggles them all smoothly, in a space that captures the essence of industrial chic with its cool vibe and sleek design. Grab a seat in one of the bar areas or make friends at the communal table with views of the cheese cave (there are 50 different types).

Surprisingly good seafood figures largely on the dinner menu; lunch tends toward sandwiches and salads. Breakfast is even offered, when the bar transforms into a coffee bar. However, wine is the star here, and you're encouraged to sample while you sip, whether as half or full glasses, flights, or bottles.

Coco Pazzo

Italian ✗✗

C3-4

300 W. Hubbard St. (at Franklin St.)

Phone: 312-836-0900
Web: www.cocopazzochicago.com
Prices: $$

Lunch Mon – Fri
Dinner nightly
▣ Merchandise Mart

Near the mammoth Merchandise Mart, this nearly 20 year-old mainstay attracts a steady crowd for both business lunches and after-work dinners. The rumble of the El and the hustle and bustle of the neighborhood contribute to the obvious energy here with a chatty and buzzy ambience. A simple, unfussy, Tuscan menu explains the repeat business and wide appeal.

Lunch and dinner menus differ slightly, with lunch featuring wood-burning oven pizzas and entrée salads; and dinner skewed toward more satisfying entrées. Try the creamy risotto with spinach and Taleggio, or the crispy veal Milanese accompanied by a crunchy arugula, tomato, and onion salad. The wine list has a strong Italian focus and is a good mix of well and lesser known winemakers and varietals.

David Burke's Primehouse

Steakhouse ✗✗

F2

616 N. Rush St. (bet. Ohio & Ontario Sts.)

Phone: 312-660-6000
Web: www.davidburkeprimehouse.com
Prices: $$$

Lunch & dinner daily
▣ Grand (Red)

David Burke's Primehouse is true to its name and focus: these steaks come from a bull named "Prime" raised on Creekstone Farm in Kentucky, before being aged in their Himalayan salt-tiled room, and, finally, wheeled on a cart to your table.

Inside the James Chicago Hotel, this is a comfortable, attractive, and suitably masculine space in which to enjoy an impressive steak—perhaps complemented by their two privately labeled bottles, a sauce called 207L, named after Prime's ear tag, and another spicy-sweet variation.

Appetites are whet with fluffy cheese-topped popovers, and then sated with surf and turf dumplings (a mixture of chopped lobster and braised short rib). Skip the sides to leave room for a s'mores-inspired slice of Prime cake.

Crofton on Wells ✿

Contemporary ✗✗

535 N. Wells St. (bet. Grand Ave. & Ohio St.)

Phone: 312-755-1790
Web: www.croftononwells.com
Prices: $$$

Dinner Mon – Sat
🚇 Grand (Red)

Crofton On Wells

For a solid, reliable affair, Suzy Crofton is your girl; and though she may have steered her eponymous restaurant for more than a decade, it still feels fresh and on-point. Crofton on Wells is an attractive space that invites intimacy and rejects stuffy. The refreshingly cool interior presents a comfortably arranged bar and sophisticated meal presentations. Servers may seem relaxed, but don't be fooled as they are in fact immensely attentive and completely competent.

Kick things off with a basket of hot crusty rolls anointed with melting butter before moving on to a simple, tender duck confit risotto with foie gras butter, winter squash, and truffle oil. Other front-runners like the Lake Superior whitefish, made über flavorful with chickpea panisse, lemon, and curried lentils; and a de-constructed German chocolate cake with malted vanilla ice cream showcase a pleasurable combination of textures.

The show begins with unpretentious picks like rabbit sausage served with potatoes and pickles; and ends with a clementine-rosemary curd. Crofton's California-meets-Midwest-meets-France menu bespeaks confidence, and her largely American wine list is marked with much flair and finesse.

Eggsperience

American ✕✕

E2

35 W. Ontario St. (at Dearborn St.)

Phone: 312-870-6773
Web: www.eggsperiencecafe.com
Prices: ⊜⊜

Lunch & dinner daily
🚇 Grand (Red)

When only a 24-hour diner will do, Eggsperience delights with an egg at the ready. This spacious, dressed-up diner offers a multitude of seating options, including a lengthy counter. Outside, you may find fast-moving lines, inside it is a bright, cheery spot, with natural light and many representations of the almighty egg.

Find it also on the plate, in omelets, skillets, and frittatas, just to name a few dishes. The cast-iron skillets are chock-full of ingredients, such as the "mmmmmushroom skillet" made with mushrooms, spinach, two kinds of cheeses, potatoes, and onions. With that order are sides of pancakes, which are mercifully light and fluffy. Caffeine addicts rejoice: a whole tasty pot of coffee is placed on your table.

English

Gastropub ✕

D3

444 N. LaSalle St. (at Illinois St.)

Phone: 312-222-6200
Web: www.englishchicago.com
Prices: $$

Lunch & dinner Mon – Sat
🚇 Merchandise Mart

An art deco façade gives way to a throwback interior of decorative ironwork, old timey photographs, and Victorian felt wallpaper, setting the mood for an evening of eating well and drinking better at this three-story gastropub. The room, with amber wagon wheel light fixtures, serves tasty plates of pub fare, plus artisanal cocktails for office workers and sports fans who appreciate the TVs above the bar.

"Between Bread" options like a fried egg BLT or Angus burger on a pretzel bun are popular, as are the array of sliders featuring Guinness-braised pork belly, Buffalo chicken, or lobster cakes. Substantial English pub fare like shepherd's pie, fish and chips, or bangers and mash are smart options if your initial reason to visit is for the booze.

23

Epic

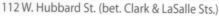

D3-4

Contemporary 🗙🗙

112 W. Hubbard St. (bet. Clark & LaSalle Sts.)

Phone: 312-222-4940
Web: www.epicrestaurantchicago.com
Prices: $$$

Lunch Mon – Fri
Dinner Mon – Sat
🚇 Grand (Red)

Epic is like nothing you anticipated; this isn't your run-of-the-mill restaurant. Instead, it delivers a powerfully "epic" performance with its catch-all attitude. You can come for drinks, stay for dinner, and then dance the night away in the lounge of this former 20th century mill, which now shines with its industrial chic design. Dark glossy floors, filament light fixtures, and gorgeous brick walls contribute to the flirtatious vibe of this lofty space. It's big, energetic, and bewitching with a serious buzz, but you'll never have to shout at your posse while at this party.

The Med-influenced food–halibut *en croute* with potato purée and Serrano ham-wrapped veal tenderloin with fricassee of fava beans–looms large for its textures and lush flavors.

Fleming's

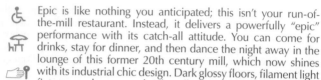

E3

Steakhouse 🗙🗙

25 E. Ohio St. (bet. State St. & Wabash Ave.)

Phone: 312-329-9463
Web: www.flemingssteakhouse.com
Prices: $$$

Dinner nightly
🚇 Grand (Red)

In many ways Chicago is still a meat and potatoes town, and the famous Fleming's chain is as good a place as any to find these faves. A classic steakhouse, Fleming's lounge is painted a rich burgundy and shows off redwood-stained furnishings. The crowd may be a confusing blend of corporates, pre-theater touristas, and gaggles celebrating a special occasion, but they all flock here for staples like an iceberg wedge served with gooey, blue cheese dressing and crowned with cherry tomatoes; and potatoes, sliced paper-thin and served gratinée, with layers of cheese and jalapeños. A simply seasoned USDA prime filet is served tender and enriched with spicy peppercorn sauce. More than 100 wines by the glass make it easy to sip the right vintage with your meal.

Friends Sushi

Japanese ✕✕

F2

710 N. Rush St. (bet. Huron & Superior Sts.)

Phone: 312-787-8998
Web: www.friendssushi.com
Prices: $$

Lunch & dinner daily
🚇 Chicago (Red)

This updated spot is yet another sushi shop, with the surprising twist of offering a moderate tab in a cool setting. Befitting its name, the funky décor has turned this restaurant into a great place to hang out with friends who want to share it all.
This isn't your regular sushi. The rice isn't Japanese, rice wine isn't part of the recipe, and the technique isn't flawless. But what Friends Sushi lacks in accuracy it makes up for in quality and creativity, particularly with good fish. Toasted nori makes for crisp wrappers of sushi and maki. The tasty salsa maki with tuna, cilantro, scallion, and jalapeño is rolled in *tobiko*, and topped with tempura crumbs. The asparagus and crab meat appetizer (one of several) is a good way to jump-start your meal.

Frontera Grill 😊

Mexican ✕✕

D3

445 N. Clark St. (bet. Hubbard & Illinois Sts.)

Phone: 312-661-1434
Web: www.fronterakitchens.com
Prices: $$

Lunch & dinner Tue – Sat
🚇 Grand (Red)

Rick Bayless may have left the building, but Frontera Grill is no lesser for it. Let slide the impossible masses waiting for a table, and head straight to the bar and its small seating area. Here you can look forward to warm and easy service and the entire menu without the script.
Brunch is the only real savoir here not impossibly overrun by the TV-watching hoi polloi (rest assured the food remains all-around outstanding). The kitchen slings Mexican-infused creations like *huevos fronterizos*, a creamy-dreamy plate of sunny side up eggs *al ajillo* over Yucatecan achiote sausage and buttermilk biscuits. Paired with the aromatic *café de olla* or a perfect Topolo margarita, and a side of the amazing salsa habañera, *this* is the way to start a Saturday.

Fulton's on the River

D4

Seafood ✕✕

315 N. LaSalle St. (at the Chicago River)

Phone: 312-822-0100
Web: www.fultonsontheriver.com
Prices: $$$

Lunch Mon – Fri
Dinner nightly
Merchandise Mart

Of all Chicago's many charms, its skyline–built from one iconic skyscraper after the other–is among the best. What better way to appreciate this treasure than to dine on a terrace in the shadow of these architectural wonders? Arrive early (no reservations accepted) at this large restaurant in a rehabbed brick warehouse for tables on the terrace of the Chicago River, where you'll also find the most spectacular view.

From here enjoy a homemade lemonade or glass of Champagne and settle in for a full meal. Lunch is popular, thanks to the value-oriented soups, salads, fish and chips, burgers, and sandwiches. At night Fulton's becomes a classic steakhouse with seafood and steaks to the max, plus oysters, crab cakes, and all the usual trimmings.

Gene & Georgetti

C3

Steakhouse ✕✕

500 N. Franklin St. (at Illinois St.)

Phone: 312-527-3718
Web: www.geneandgeorgetti.com
Prices: $$$$

Lunch & dinner Mon – Sat
Merchandise Mart

With such wonderful consistency for decades (and surely, for decades to come), dining here is akin to stepping into a time machine. Outside, cab drivers deliver women with hairdos that are still "set" at the beauty parlor. Inside, find crowds of suit-clad regulars who still believe in the three-martini lunch. Upstairs is a quieter, more subdued place to dine near a wintery wood-burning fireplace. Nonetheless, everyone is welcome, from Chi-town politicos to Joe the Plumber.

The menu offers a hybrid of Italian-American classics and standard steakhouse fare. The steaks are huge (get ready for that doggie bag) and sides equally so. The veal Parmesan is decadent and delicious. Cocktails trump the wine list, sticking with the feeling of the era.

Gilt Bar

Gastropub 🍴🍴

C4

230 N. Kinzie St. (at Franklin St.)

Phone: 312-464-9544
Web: www.giltbarchicago.com
Prices: $$

Dinner Tue – Sat
🚇 Merchandise Mart

The rag tag bunch in the kitchen look like they could break into a jam session any minute, but they are a talented group of focused cooks that don't take themselves too seriously. Demurely lit, Gilt Bar may be rustic on roids–with worn wooden chairs and a dainty chandelier–but this old-timer also shows plush sofas, and a throwback bartender serving refined cocktails to boot.

The serious alchemy takes place in the kitchen, mixing magic with classic country cooking. Starters like bone marrow and red onion jam on toast; or steak tartare with soft-cooked yolk are mandatory for foodies of every rank. Unctuous pork belly with farro and shallot-raspberry glaze will have you singing the praises of this slightly rowdy but always rollicking good tavern.

Gino's East

Pizza 🍴

C2

633 N. Wells St. (at Ontario St.)

Phone: 312-943-1124
Web: www.ginoseast.com
Prices: 💲💲

Lunch & dinner daily
🚇 Grand (Red)

When Chicagoans introduce visitors to their deep dish and thin crust, they head for hallowed Gino's East. The angular façade looks like a Frank Gehry ode to pizza; and the ample room is layered with decades of graffiti. While defacing the walls is encouraged, some see the kitsch as cool, others say rundown. Wood booths and chairs are dressed in classic red checks.

The service sways from pleasant to brusque, but the stuff here is really good. Calamari and cheesy spinach sticks are fried just so, but coming here for just that is absurd. A flaky pastry cornmeal crust is used on both thin and deep dish varieties—the latter then adds cheese gobs, sautéed spinach, and chunky tomato sauce. Instead of dessert, opt for a baby aspirin to keep the blood flowing.

Giordano's

F1

Pizza ✗

730 N. Rush St. (at Superior St.)

Phone: 312-951-0747
Web: www.giordanos.com
Prices: 💰💰

Lunch & dinner daily
🚇 Chicago (Red)

Value, friendly service, and delicious deep-dish pizza make Giordano's a crowd sweetheart. With several locations dotting the the city and suburbs, this restaurant has been gratifying locals with comforting Italian-American fare for years. Come during the week–service picks up especially at dinner–to avoid the cacophony.

Giordano's menu includes your typical salads, pastas, et al., but you'd do well to save room for the real star: the deep-dish. Bring backup because this pie could feed a small country. The spinach pie arrives on a buttery pastry crust, filled with spreads of sautéed (or steamed) spinach and tomato sauce, and topped with mozzarella and Parmesan cheese. For those cold, windy nights, opt for delivery—their website sketches a detailed menu.

Harry Caray's

E4

Steakhouse ✗✗

33 W. Kinzie St. (at Dearborn St.)

Phone: 312-828-0966
Web: www.harrycarays.com
Prices: $$$

Lunch Mon – Sat
Dinner nightly
🚇 Grand (Red)

The gone-but-never-forgotten Chicago sportscaster Harry Caray was known for his trademark "Holy Cow!" Guests might feel the need to utter it as they see the famous broadcaster's bronze bust complete with giant glasses. As Harry Caray is iconic to the Windy City, so, too, are steakhouses, so it makes sense that the restaurant that sports his name is a classic steakhouse specializing in USDA prime corn-fed beef.

Show up hungry: the 18oz dry-aged bone-in ribeye or 23oz Porterhouse are on the hefty side of what is an ample selection on this meat-centric menu. Like most steakhouses, all the sides–classics including garlic mashed potatoes, creamed spinach, and sautéed mushrooms–are served à la carte, but cooked to perfection, not an afterthought.

graham elliot ✿

C2

217 W. Huron St. (bet. Franklin & Wells Sts.)

Phone:	312-624-9975	Dinner Mon – Sat
Web:	www.grahamelliot.com	Chicago (Brown)
Prices:	$$$	

Here is a fine dining restaurant where servers wear jeans and button-downs. Imagine a large open space—faithful to its industrial heritage—featuring soft lighting, floor-to-ceiling windows, exposed brick walls, and contemporary espresso toned furnishings. A plethora of open dining areas break up the interior, which in turn reverberates with thumping music, leather upholstered seats, and seasonal embellishments such as artichokes displayed in a glass case.

Starting a meal with the deconstructed Caesar salad is a good peek at what the kitchen does nightly. Gingerly perched atop each crunchy Romaine heart is a perfectly white and pickled anchovy and a mascarpone-filled block of toasted brioche—each layer reveals the flavor and texture of the classic. Great Lake whitefish is served with a delicious curried red lentil purée and *chai* foam. Desserts follow suit as in the slender almond financier, moist and buttery, crested with a quenelle of cream cheese ice cream, dark chocolate ganache, and salted caramel sauce. Even cocktails are mixed with care, using artisan and hard-to-find spirits.

In 2010 the eponymous Chef Graham Elliot Bowles cooked for the public and the bands at Lollapalooza.

Hub51

International ✕✕

51 W. Hubbard St. (at Dearborn St.)

Phone: 312-828-0051
Web: www.hub51chicago.com
Prices: $$

Lunch & dinner daily
Grand (Red)

HUB51 got a ton of buzz when it opened in 2008, because of the boys backing the bar. The twenty-something sons of legendary Chicago restaurateur Rich Melman are behind this large, crowded bar-slash-eatery and were determined to make it appeal to a hip, downtown crowd. Having a nightclub, SUB 51, right downstairs doesn't hurt.

The menu appeals to the under-40 set with a hybrid offering of Tex-Mex, sushi, sandwiches, salads, and other things folks order when they get off of work. Fish tacos are well-conceived; the popular *shakishaki* tuna, crunchy and tangy; and the carrot cake super decadent with extra scoops of whipped cream and cream cheese icing. Drunker appetites can choose a green chile cheeseburger or the Dude, an aged 18oz ribeye with the works.

Japonais

Fusion ✕✕✕

600 W. Chicago Ave. (bet. Larrabee St. & the Chicago River)

Phone: 312-822-9600
Web: www.japonaischicago.com
Prices: $$$

Lunch Mon – Fri
Dinner nightly
Chicago (Blue)

Japonais isn't new, but is still mighty hip and trendy, and attracts its fair share of cute couples, fashionistas, and foodies. On the banks of the Chicago River, the sexy, bi-level space exudes elegance, and wears a décor that matches its Asian-accented menu–picture dark paneling, low seating, billowing silks, and large lanterns.

The menu spotlights a juxtaposition of flavors and textures, where a tuna flatbread–made green from wakame–gets a salty kick with the addition of *mochi*, cheese, olives, and anchovies. A seaweed salad is lightly dressed with lemon; while the *kabocha* cheesecake, made from a Japanese squash and served with a pineapple mousse, exemplifies the fusion aesthetic. The ever so efficient staff seems well-acquainted with large crowds.

Joe's

F3

American XXX

60 E. Grand Ave. (at Rush St.)

Phone: 312-379-5637
Web: www.joes.net
Prices: $$$$

Lunch & dinner daily
 Grand (Red)

An outpost of the Miami landmark, this Joe's may not be a Chicago original, but it certainly feels like one. It appears like it's been here forever, due in large part to the clubby ambience and the crew of golf shirt-wearing regulars. It's always jumping, especially with the business boys at lunch.

File it under the "when in Rome" rule, so yes, you should start with the stone crabs. But there's a flood more to this menu with steakhouse faves like oysters Rockefeller; ribeyes aside creamed spinach; some southern-flecked dishes (fried chicken); as well as odes to Florida (did you guess grouper?). Desserts like coconut cream and peanut butter cream pie are American through and through, but for the classic Joe's finish, get the Key lime pie.

Keefer's

E4

Steakhouse XXX

20 W. Kinzie St. (bet. Dearborn & State Sts.)

Phone: 312-467-9525
Web: www.keefersrestaurant.com
Prices: $$$$

Lunch Mon – Fri
Dinner Mon – Sat
 Grand (Red)

From the warm welcome and efficient service to the contemporary menu, everything Keefer's does, it does well. While Chicago has no shortage of steakhouses, this one distinguishes itself with a friendly bar area showing bistro-style booths and menu, and a vibe that is updated and upscale in the main dining room–this is a modern classic whose menu follows suit.

Find all the anticipated cuts of meat, sauces, and sides to feast on in an à la carte style. But also try the chef's signature items for something a little different: sides like the potato croquettes (imagine deep-fried mashed potatoes with all the toppings inside); braised endive in sauce Mornay; and broccoli salad combining florets, fennel, apple, and cheese with a lemon vinaigrette.

Mercadito

D4

Mexican 🍴

108 W. Kinzie St. (bet. Clark & LaSalle Sts.)

Phone: 312-329-9555
Web: www.mercaditorestaurants.com
Prices: $$

Lunch & dinner daily
🚇 Merchandise Mart

It's Mexican, but if you're thinking mariachi bands and sombrero-donning staff, you've got it all wrong. Mercadito, just steps from the Merchandise Mart in the design-centric River North, is a far cry from the usual haunts. Instead, it's the very definition of urban-chic with its funky light fixtures and specially commissioned art from graffiti artist, Erni Vales.

The Sandoval brothers got it right times three in New York, this is their fourth offspring. The menu pinpoints a plethora of small dishes that build a tasty Mexican meal. With six varieties of guac and salsa, three ceviches, luscious *botanas*, and ten differing tacos, something is bound to catch your eye. Steering off the main road are pork tacos with grilled pineapple and goat's milk flan.

Osteria Via Stato

E2

Italian 🍴

620 N. State St. (at Ontario St.)

Phone: 312-642-8450
Web: www.osteriaviastato.com
Prices: $$

Dinner nightly
🚇 Grand (Red)

Tucked inside the downtown Embassy Suites is a little taste of Italy. Osteria Via Stato's dark and cozy décor fashions the quintessential charming Italian trattoria. Inside, the space is halved, with a pizzeria in the front and dining room toward the back, though there is minimal difference between these menus.

Come hungry, since the restaurant's portions (and prices) are generous. The à la carte menu has it all, with pastas in half or full portions. The best way to sample the fare is to arrive with friends and order the Italian dinner party. This family-style meal comes with antipasti, two pastas, an entrée, sides, and you can even ask for seconds. Confused about wine? Fuggedaboutit and go with "just bring me wine," at three different price points.

NAHA

D3

American 🍴🍴🍴

500 N. Clark St. (at Illinois St.)

Phone:	312-321-6242	Lunch Mon – Fri
Web:	www.naha-chicago.com	Dinner Mon – Sat
Prices:	$$$	🚇 Grand (Red)

Lara Kastner

Appearances *are* deceptive. Sure, the dark gray cement façade reads hip, but there's nothing too cool for school about NAHA. Rather, she is all Midwestern-mod, blending good looks with good manners and deadly down-home charm.

Low lighting, large windows, and an industrial-esque mien give this magnet a decidedly current feel, but it is thankfully free of any pretension. The staff greets you with a warm smile and a professional, yet friendly, demeanor. Treasured by an army of admirers, NAHA tempts a trendy crowd who regard her as their beloved (and best) go-to spot for dinners and dates alike.

The menu introduces an esoteric mix of creative and complex dishes. From Hudson Valley foie gras and Nantucket Bay scallops to Quilcene oysters from Washington State, the appetizers are just the tip of the iceberg. Focused on farm fresh American products, the entrées span the states to source stunners like Rhode Island striped bass, Michigan cherries, Great Lakes' whitefish, and Alaskan halibut. All of them are dressed to the nines with unique textures and flavor combinations. Desserts go out on a limb–turtle sundae is a mod version of the classic that is at once elegant and decadent.

Phil Stefani's 437 Rush

F3

Italian ✗✗

437 N. Rush St. (bet. Hubbard & Illinois Sts.)

Phone: 312-222-0101
Web: www.stefanirestaurants.com
Prices: $$$

Lunch Mon – Fri
Dinner Mon – Sat
🔲 Grand (Red)

Phil Stefani's 437 Rush offers an Italian-themed menu, bolstered by steakhouse fare. This lone structure brings a bar (dressed with a painted mural) up front, where diners can lull when they first enter. Then, let the cordial waitstaff lead you to one of two dining rooms, each with a similar décor–wood accents, paneled-and-tile floors, and warm walls.

White-clothed tables carry a foray of food, presented in fine white china. Italian-born Federico Comacchio brings his native's sensibility to a tandem of treats including *tonno sott'olio*–tuna loin dramatically prepared (in a bath of olive oil and garlic), and presented (with blanched veggies) on a cutting board for slicing. Less theatrical, but as tasty, are the Caesar salad, steaks, seafood, and sweets.

Pizzeria Uno

E3

Pizza ✗

29 E. Ohio St. (at Wabash Ave.)

Phone: 312-321-1000
Web: www.unos.com
Prices: 💱💱

Lunch & dinner daily
🔲 Grand (Red)

Since 1943, this establishment has been laying claim to the (somewhat disputed) title of creating the original Chicago-style pizza. Its tiny booths and wood tables wear their years of graffiti etchings like a badge of honor. Nonetheless, an intricate pressed-tin ceiling reflects the cheery atmosphere as everyone counts down the 40 or so minutes it takes for these deep-dish pies to bake.

Of course, the main attraction here is, was, and always will be the flaky, buttery crust generously layered with mozzarella cheese, toppings, and tangy tomato sauce that comprise this belly-busting pizza. The menu also includes a selection of good, basic bar food like Buffalo wings, and a simple complementary salad, but most just save the room for an extra slice.

Pops for Champagne

E3

Contemporary

601 N. State St. (at Ohio St.)

Phone: 312-266-7677
Web: www.popsforchampagne.com
Prices: $$

Lunch Sat
Dinner nightly
Grand (Red)

Pops for Champagne has been a Windy City fixture for 25 years, although in its current location for just a handful. Lively groups, including happy hour hordes, couples looking for a romantic retreat, and even bachelorette parties, convene here for a tandem of small plates, and of course, the eponymous beverage.

The dining room is attractively donned with crackled green glass-topped tables, large windows, and an onyx-amber bar filled with choices. Best with your bevy–and providing a tasty tune of textures–is crawfish, accessorized with firm black-eyed peas and a few slices of pickled okra. But you're here for the bubbly (stocked in glass refrigerators), and maybe a few unusual indulgences like the Quebecois, with apple ice wine and brut Champagne.

Prosecco

C2

Italian

710 N, Wells St. (bet. Huron & Superior Sts.)

Phone: 312-951-9500
Web: www.prosecco.us.com
Prices: $$

Lunch Mon – Fri
Dinner Mon – Sat
Chicago (Brown)

Champagne hues and vintage-Venice inspired style create an atmosphere of casual elegance here at Prosecco, where bountiful portions of sumptuous Italian satiate adoring locals. Of course, the namesake sparkling beverage is offered in fifty different varieties. But first let the friendly and efficient staff guide you through a luscious *zuppa* seasoned with oregano, basil, rosemary, and finely minced black truffle, drizzled with truffle oil and served with Parmesan-topped bread for sopping. For a bit of spice, the *spaghetti alla diavola* gets things right–al dente pasta and fresh shrimp, tossed in herb-packed tomato sauce kicked up with red pepper flakes.

In the warmer months, enjoy a seat under the black and gold awning of the spacious patio out front.

Quartino

E2

Italian

626 N. State St. (at Ontario St.)

Phone: 312-698-5000
Web: www.quartinochicago.com
Prices: 💰

Lunch & dinner daily
🚇 Grand (Red)

Nobody feels left out in the cold at Quartino, the inviting Italian spot that has group dining down to a science. It earns its accolades catering to crowds with reasonably priced food and lots of it. Colleagues get to know each other better over heaping plates of pasta, while best buddies enjoy sampling small plates of short ribs and roasted sausage.

You can try a little bit of everything here, where even the all-Italian wine list (available in ¼, ½, and full carafes, as well as bottles) is meant to be divvied up. The menu dances across Italy for its inspiration, striving to represent the best of its culinary regions. Find a great selection of Neapolitan thin-crust pizzas, house-made salumi, tempting small plates, freshly made pastas, and risottos.

RL

F1

American

115 E. Chicago Ave. (bet. Michigan Ave. & Rush St.)

Phone: 312-475-1100
Web: www.rlrestaurant.com
Prices: $$$

Lunch & dinner daily
🚇 Chicago (Red)

Book a table at RL and you'll instantly feel like a member of the pedigreed elite. This place looks like a stage set for the American dream, so it's no surprise that Ralph Lauren is behind it. The ambience is clubby and posh (think rich mahogany paneled walls, leather banquettes, gleaming crystal) and the crowd is equally attractive. Thanks to the friendly staff, you'll never feel like an outcast. However, if you're lacking the natty uniform, its location inside the Ralph Lauren store is a boon.

A hot spot for brunch, the perennially packed RL echoes the brand's traditional American sensibility with its tried-and-true burgers; popular salads, like the "riff raff"; classic seafood dishes, like crab louis; and a tasty crème brûlée to finish.

Roy's

E1-2

Hawaiian

720 N. State St. (at Superior St.)

Phone: 312-787-7599
Web: www.roysrestaurant.com
Prices: $$

Dinner nightly
Chicago (Red)

Roy's may celebrate its Hawaiian roots in its food and background music, but this sophisticated spot with floor-to-ceiling windows and elegant seating does not play to any clichés.

This extremely popular outpost of the nationwide chain has many of the signature dishes (like macadamia nut-crusted mahi mahi or hibachi grilled salmon) found at all locations, but it also includes selections created specifically by the on-site chef. The Hawaiian fusion cuisine that Roy's is known for focuses heavily on simply prepared, quality seafood, as in blackened ahi tuna with spicy soy mustard, or the huge teppanyaki-seared tiger prawns served in a bowl with udon, sweet Chinese sausage, and Penang curry broth.

The bar attracts a sizable crowd for post-work cocktails.

Sable

E3

American

505 N. State St. (at Illinois St.)

Phone: 312 755 9704
Web: www.sablechicago.com
Prices: $$

Lunch & dinner daily
Grand (Red)

Chicago hotel restaurants have a knack for making a name for themselves, separate from the hotel, thus appealing to locals as well as guests. Sable, inside the Palomar, is no exception. She has a sleek, cosmopolitan, and contemporary look, and the outside garden patio that runs the length of the restaurant is a big bonus.

From an open kitchen, diners are presented with an eclectic American menu that has something for everyone and plenty of items that are easy to share. Dishes may include sweet corn crème brûlée, red lentil cake; bison short rib sliders; ricotta-herb ravioli; and roasted chicken with buttermilk dumplings. The brick oven flatbread pizzas are one of the best in this increasingly beloved category; and the bar's cocktail list is impressive.

Chicago ▶ River North

37

Shanghai Terrace

F1

Chinese ♟♟

108 E. Superior St. (bet. Michigan Ave. & Rush St.)

Phone: 312-573-6695

Web: www.peninsula.com

Prices: $$$

Lunch & dinner Mon – Sat

🚇 Chicago (Red)

When sporting a chinoiserie design, there is a fine line between setting a theme and looking like a Disneyfied cliché. But, Shanghai Terrace carries off the ethereal Asian look with *mucho* class and distinction. Set inside the posh Peninsula Hotel, this svelte sanctum draws an affluent crowd who come as much for the setting (adorned with Chinese antiques and furnishings and staff accoutered sharply in red Mandarin jackets), as they do for the food.

This isn't your shrimp fried rice kinda place, so await a nice medley of Asian-accented entrées like sea bass with Chinese sausage, golden and red beets, and wild ginseng; Dungeness crab sticky rice flavored with ginger, garlic, and ham; and curried slow-roasted lamb with root veggies and lemongrass.

Shaw's Crab House

E4

Seafood ♟♟

21 E. Hubbard St. (bet. State St. & Wabash Ave.)

Phone: 312-527-2722

Web: www.shawscrabhouse.com

Prices: $$$

Lunch Sun – Fri

Dinner nightly

🚇 Grand (Red)

There aren't that many restaurants that have tuxedoed waiters welcoming guests in jeans, as well as a kid-friendly menu. But that's the story at Shaw's, a mainstay for both locals and visitors. The ambience is old-school with black patent leather booths and big band music.

Crab is always on the menu, though it varies by season: Dungeness, king, stone, soft shell, and blue. The crab cakes are as simple a presentation as imaginable, yet tasty. The single round patty is all large lump Maryland crab with very little filler, served golden brown and kissed with spiced mayonnaise. For a non-crab option, try the horseradish-crusted grouper, prepared simply, but just right. Tuesdays, Thursdays, and Sundays the joint is jumping with live music at the oyster bar.

Sixteen ✿

F4

Contemporary 🍴🍴🍴

401 N. Wabash Ave. (bet. Hubbard St. & the Chicago River)

Phone: 312-588-8030
Web: www.trumpchicagohotel.com
Prices: $$$$

Lunch & dinner daily
🚇 State/Lake

Bill Haber

Even in a city teeming with stunning architecture, Sixteen–housed in the glittering Trump International Hotel & Tower, just north of the Chicago River–is home to some seriously jaw-dropping digs.

From the minute you enter the lobby, you'll be treated like royalty. Make your way up to the restaurant, and find glossy 30-foot ceilings with views of the Wrigley Clock Tower and the Chicago Tribune building. The inside is not half bad either—with an ethereal dining room featuring an enormous glass wine gallery; a 14-foot Swarovski crystal chandelier; and fresh orchids dotting every table.

With all this attention to design, can the fare possibly stack up? Absolutely, as long as Australian-born Chef Frank Brunacci has something to say about it. Witness a plate of crispy Columbia River sturgeon, paired with tender morels, a smoked potato purée studded with chives, baby fennel, crème fraîche, American caviar, and a savory meat jus; creamy, melt-in-your-mouth squares of pork belly piled over a tangle of vermicelli-thin strands of braised green cabbage and nuggets of crisped spaetzle laced with whole grain mustard; or pristine *loup de mer* with creamy lemon risotto and artichoke relish.

Smith & Wollensky

Steakhouse ✗✗

E4

318 N. State St. (at the Chicago River)

Phone: 312-670-9900
Web: www.smithandwollensky.com
Prices: $$$

Lunch & dinner daily
🚇 State/Lake

Chicago crawls with mighty steakhouses, but this babe (of the famed national chain) sits gorgeously on the Chicago River banks, and thus, lures all. Inside forever loved Smith & Wollensky, find handsome décor details like dark wood furniture, polished brass, and other accoutrements. The crowds are large (a common sight here), but the staff navigates them with little trouble.

The kitchen churns out steakhouse classics like dry-aged steaks with heaping sides of mashed potatoes and onion rings; and shrimp cocktail—three prawns lying beside three (mustard, tomato, and avocado) sauces. But you're here for the steaks, and they are well charred and perfectly cooked. Don't skip their signature steak sauce—it adds a great kick to the meat.

Sunda

Asian ✗✗

D3

110 W. Illinois St. (bet. Clark & LaSalle Sts.)

Phone: 312-644-0500
Web: www.sundachicago.com
Prices: $$

Lunch Sun – Fri
Dinner nightly
🚇 Grand (Red)

A large, bustling pan-Asian funhouse, Sunda is a trendy place to be seen as much as it is a place to dine. The sprawling, chic dining room boasts high ceilings, an earthy color palette, polished bamboo, and carved stonework housing plenty of beautiful people.

The menu is presented family-style and roams the Asian continent, stopping to pick up salads, appetizers (dumplings, tempura, and rolls), sushi, rice, noodles, and an assortment of larger entrées. Charsiu barbecue pork is a must, presented as a lean boneless pork chop with a red tinged glaze made from honey, miso, and palm sugar, accompanied by tender pieces of bok choy. Rock shrimp tempura isn't bad either with the crispy critters bathed in a sweet, honey aïoli with glazed walnuts.

SUSHISAMBA rio

C3

Fusion XX

504 N. Wells St. (bet. Grand Ave. & Illinois St.)

Phone: 312-595-3200
Web: www.sushisamba.com
Prices: $$$

Lunch & dinner daily
Merchandise Mart

From its stylized interior to the attractive staff and the Japanese-Brazilian-Cuban dishes themselves, tasting here happens with the eyes as well as the mouth. This is a fun fusion hot spot that prefers music to conversation, where even the restrooms are a social (co-mingled) experience. The space feels as much a nightclub as a restaurant, despite the fact that these tables are likely holding downtown business meetings—the seriously trendy have already moved on to a new scene.

The menu is a fusion of Latin American and Asian cuisines, with focus on ceviche, tempura, and sashimi all artfully arranged on the plate. The four-part lunch specials are a good bargain and way to taste a cross-section of the unusual flavor combinations that the chef concocts.

Vermilion

E3-4

Indian XX

10 W. Hubbard St. (bet. Dearborn & State Sts.)

Phone: 312-527-4060
Web: www.thevermilionrestaurant.com
Prices: $$

Lunch Mon – Fri
Dinner nightly
Grand (Red)

The sleek, sultry, and sexy room is the first clue that this is no ordinary Indian restaurant. From the stunning oversized photographs to the innovative culinary philosophy, everything here is new territory. While it may be a modern, Indian-ish restaurant, Vermilion is more an amalgam of the best of Indian and Latino tastes, emphasizing the ways in which ingredients and traditions overlap.

At street level, find a lounge with communal dining options—an ideal spot to sample the "heat" menu of pure Indian cuisine, inspired by the owner's own childhood memories. Or, try their upscale version of *chaat*, with fried dough, yogurt, spices, chutneys, and the intriguing addition of jalapeño. Braised lamb shank is hearty yet wonderfully heady with spices.

Topolobampo ✿

Mexican ✕✕

445 N. Clark St. (bet. Hubbard & Illinois Sts.)

Phone:	312-661-1434	Lunch Tue – Fri
Web:	www.rickbayless.com	Dinner Tue – Sat
Prices:	$$$	Grand (Red)

Brendan Lekan

Here's a fun rule to follow with Mexican restaurants: the harder it is to say, the tastier the food is likely to be. This colorful Rick Bayless number, attached to the more casual Frontera Grill in the heart of River North, fits the notion to a tee. But with the critically acclaimed father of Mexican cooking in North America helming the ship, was there any doubt?

Opened in November of 1989, Topolobampo was doing its thing long before the recent boom in Mexican fine dining hit hard—just one more thing to ponder as you settle into your cushy rose banquette, soaking in the bright turquoise ceilings and colorful Mexican art.

Diners can order à la carte or choose one of the clever tasting menus, divvied up into fun themes like adventurous food or house favorites. It's hard to go wrong here—Bayless didn't get famous hawking cheese nachos, after all. A walk with the master might unearth sweet Alaskan King crab laced with a rustic chili, peanut, and pumpkin seed mole, then paired with tequila-infused chayote, roasted fennel, young coconut, and Iroquois white corn croutons; or juicy, roasted lamb in a satiny Oaxacan black mole, paired with whipped jicama and black bean *tamalón*.

Zealous

B1

C o n t e m p o r a r y XXX

419 W. Superior St. (bet. Hudson Ave. & Sedgwick St.)

Phone: 312-475-9112

Web: www.zealousrestaurant.com

Prices: $$$

Dinner Tue – Sat

Chicago (Brown)

Set off the beaten path in a quiet neighborhood, find this serene and accommodating home of impressive and creative contemporary cuisine.

Culinary pleasures here are courtesy of Chef/owner Michael Taus (a Charlie Trotter protégé), who prepares a seasonal menu that is as ambitious as it is whimsical—be sure to ask about the creative offerings on the Spontaneous seven-course menu. From the single, crisp sweetbread to Prime filet of beef grilled to perfect medium rare, food here is tasty and well-executed.

The space is as contemporary as the food, with soaring ceilings, deep purple chairs, and a large glass-enclosed wine cellar that cradles the restaurant's impressive selection. This is a great date night spot, and is also hugely popular among locals.

Good food without spending a fortune? Look for the Bib Gourmand 😋.

 Chicago ▲ River North

43

Streeterville

If you simply had to pick a neighborhood that truly recapitulates Chicago, it would be Streeterville. Home to the Magnificent Mile, the iconic John Hancock Building, and the fun-loving Navy Pier, skyscraping and stirring Streeterville takes the cake.

Absorb the sights and smells of the stunning surroundings, especially upon arrival at Water

Tower Place's **foodlife**—a simple food court elevated to an art form, located on the mezzanine floor of the shopping mall. Before going further, know that this isn't your average mall or airport food court. Instead, this United Nations of food courts satiates with 14 different kitchens whipping up everything from Chinese potstickers and deep-dish pizza to fried chicken. **Wow Bao** (also located within

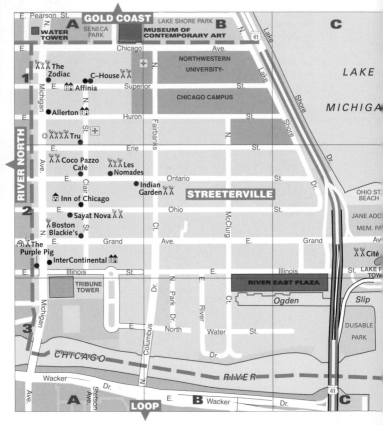

the landmark building), doles out some of the best handheld treats in town, like steamed veggie-and-meat-filled buns; and is so popular, they had to open a second spot in the Loop. The really cool part? Buy a card that gives you access to the many stands.

FOOD COURT FUN

Prefer panini and pastry? Stop by the legendary **Hancock Building**, otherwise known as food lovers paradise. The Italian deli **L'Appetito** is divine for yummy breakfasts, Italian and American style sandwiches, baked goods, and other classic delights. Lucky locals and office types can shop for groceries with sky-high prices to match the staggering view at **Potash Brothers**, a supermarket stunningly set on the 44th floor of the Hancock Building.

MUSEUMS AND MARKETS

The Museum of Contemporary Art houses one of the world's leading collections of contemporary art; but it's also the peppers and potatoes that lure gaggles, far and wide, to the farmer's market held here on Tuesdays from June through October. Those with money to burn should hit up posh gourmet supermarket **Fox & Obel** for gorgeous groceries year-round. This European-style bazaar also has a delightful café with scrumptious treats for all day dining. Carry on this darling adventure at **Teuscher**, **Godiva**, and **Lindt**—they all have boutiques here; but it is Chicago's own **Vosges Haut-Chocolat** that has made a name for itself by rocking taste buds with exotic ingredients—curry and chocolate anyone?

TASTY TREATS

Sure, it's crowded and a little bit carnival-like, but that's why we love it. Navy Pier can be tourist central, but it's also a dreamy junk food paradise. Begin with one of 27 different flavors of popcorn available at **The Popcorn Palace & Candy Emporium**. With a food philosophy as simple as crafting the finest and most fresh ingredients into delightful treats, this popcorn paradise

D
Streeterville

N

1

E. Ohio St.

JARDINE
WATER PURIFICATION
PLANT

OLIVE
PARK

E. Ohio St.

2

Park

E. Grand Ave.

NAVY PIER

Dr.

Riva

LAKE
MICHIGAN

NAVY PIER
PARK

3

• Hotels
• Restaurants

D

remains beloved and bustling all year-round. After popcorn prowling, move on to more substantial chow by grabbing an all-natural Chicago-style dog (with mustard, onion, relish, sport peppers, tomato, pickle, and celery salt) from **America's Dog**. This dog heaven boasts a gargantuan repertoire of city-style dogs from Houston, New York, and Philadelphia, to Detroit, Kansas City, and San Francisco.

In the mood for some crunch? Venture towards world-famous **Jiminy Chips** for some of the most fabulous kettle-cooked made-to-order potato chips. Also on the menu and prepared with top-notch techniques are sweet potato chips, pita chips, and tortilla chips. The choices are plenty, so make your pick and settle down for a crunchy feast.

STREETERVILLE FAITHFULS

The **Billy Goat Tavern** is a Streeterville institution. Now known more for its famous "cheezeborger, cheezeborger" Saturday Night Live skit, it's a "buy the tee-shirt" type of place with a spot in Navy Pier, and the original just off Michigan Avenue. The tavern's menu which includes breakfast specials, an array of steaks, and sandwiches galore is sure to please all who may enter its hallowed portals.

Jonesing for a juicy burger? Hit up **M Burger**, along with the hordes of business lunchers, tourists, and shoppers. It should be renamed "mmm" burger for its tasty, meaty treats. Bacon, cheese, and secret sauce comprise the signature M burger, but if you're feeling guilty, you can always order the all-veggie Nurse Betty.

SIP AND SAVOR

And for those whose tastes run more toward champagne and cocktails than cheeseburgers and crinkle-cut fries, there's the **Signature Lounge**, located on the 96th floor of the John Hancock Center, an idyllic spot for nightcaps. While their creative concoctions are a touch pricey, one glimpse of the sparkling city scape will have you beaming. For some quintessential old-world elegance, don your Grandmother's pearls for afternoon tea at the refined **Drake's Palm Court**. Sip (not slurp!) your tea while listening to the gentle strains of a harp. If it's good enough for Queen Elizabeth, it will certainly do.

And finally, the Northwestern Hospital complex is another esteemed establishment that dominates the Streeterville scene. Besides its top medical and surgical services, also catering to the spectrum of staff and visitors, are a parade of dining gems (cafés, lounges, and ethnic canteens) that loom large over the neighborhood and lake.

Boston Blackie's

American 🍴

164 E. Grand Ave. (at St. Clair St.)

Phone: 312-938-8700
Web: www.bostonblackies.com
Prices: 💰

Lunch & dinner daily
🚇 Grand (Red)

With more than a few locations now downtown and in the 'burbs, Boston Blackie's is a long-time favorite of Chicagoans for a burger and some beers in a casual and hospitable setting. This location is one of the older ones and has the worn-in charm of a local favorite with its comfy booths and bouncing bar. The warm waitresses treat you like a regular if it's your first time or 100th.

Don't mess around here; go for the burger. Maybe throw on some cheese, bacon, or Carson's barbecue sauce, and of course, add on a side of their crispy steak fries. If you're super-hungry, start with the tasty stuffed potato skins or a basket of onion rings; and if cow isn't your thing, the fried smelts or fish-n-chips make an equally satisfying alternative.

C-House

Contemporary 🍴🍴

166 E. Superior St. (at St. Clair St.)

Phone: 312-523-0923
Web: www.c-houserestaurant.com
Prices: $$

Lunch & dinner daily
🚇 Chicago (Red)

Housed in the Affinia Chicago hotel, C-House has made a name for itself since opening in 2008. The striking contemporary space was designed by Brazilian architect Arthur Casas, and that kind of attention to detail is applied to everything at this stylish, yet casual, seafood joint.

Every diner is served a freshly-baked Wisconsin cheese curd bread to get the taste buds salivating. Oysters and chilled seafood starters have developed a loyal following (there's even an oyster station with counter seating), but the short list of entrées (fish and chips, poached sturgeon, and grilled trout) should not be skipped. The dessert menu offers a whimsical "Candy Bar" selection of chocolate to satisfy one kind of vice. The beer and wine lists satisfy another.

Cité

Contemporary ✗✗

505 N. Lake Shore Dr. (entrance on Grand Ave.)

Phone: 312-644-4050   Dinner nightly
Web: www.citechicago.com
Prices: $$$

Any restaurant with 360-degree views of a magnificent city skyline and the expanse of Lake Michigan has to know that what's outside is likely to detract from what's inside. That's true at this 70th floor establishment atop Lake Point Tower, where the views of Navy Pier and the lake are particularly breathtaking.

The outdated continental menu and décor might not make for a destination on its own, but since you're here for the view, you might as well try a few things. The four-course chef's tasting menu tends to be more seasonally focused than the regular menu, and all of the dishes are hearty and filling. The lobster gnocchi is well made, the service polite, and the wine list and cocktail menu adequate. With these views, that's all you need.

Coco Pazzo Café

Italian ✗✗

636 N. St. Clair St. (at Ontario St.)

Phone: 312-664-2777   Lunch Mon – Fri
Web: www.cocopazzocafe.com   Dinner nightly
Prices: $$ Grand (Red)

Doctors finding time between rounds at nearby Northwestern Hospital, tourists, and local denizens all take in the cheery atmosphere at Coco Pazzo Café. This restaurant is proof that a nice setting with good service and tasty food does not have to be high-priced or high-minded. The warm, sunny colors of Italy create a relaxing ambience, while the outdoor seating is in demand during warmer months.

This kitchen delivers a crowd-pleasing mix of Italian-American cuisine that creates a nostalgic reflection of Tuscany. Their menu of simple preparations and presentations, like chicken Milanese, as well as daily specials appeal to a wide variety of diners. Despite the area's deep-pocketed competitors, Coco Pazzo Café delivers surprisingly good value.

Indian Garden

Indian 🍴🍴

A2

247 E. Ontario St. (bet. Fairbanks Ct. & St. Clair St.)

Phone: 312-280-4910
Web: www.indiangardenchicago.com
Prices: $$

Lunch & dinner daily
🚇 Grand (Red)

A few steps above the Streeterville graduate school bustle is a little oasis by the name of Indian Garden. Packed with those who work, teach, and study in the neighborhood, this popular spot gets more crowded during weekends, and the staff often struggles to keep up.

Yet its demand is thanks to consistently solid, traditional Northern Indian dishes, served at reasonable prices in a fun (if cliché) atmosphere. Favorites include classics such as the *dahi aloo poori*, served with tamarind chutney and *chat masala*, and the chicken *vindaloo*—spicy, decadent, and rich with ghee, served family style in copper vessels. A full bar and the requisite variety of *lassi* help wash down these classics. Budget-seekers can try the traditional Indian buffet at lunch.

Les Nomades

French 🍴🍴🍴

A2

222 E. Ontario St. (bet. Fairbanks Ct. & St. Clair St.)

Phone: 312-649-9010
Web: www.lesnomades.net
Prices: $$$$

Dinner Tue – Sat
🚇 Grand (Red)

If planning to pop the question, celebrate a special birthday, or toast to making partner, pick up the phone and dial Les Nomades straight away. This elegant French restaurant was made for special occasions.

Tucked inside a brownstone, Les Nomades was once an exclusive private club. This is no surprise, given the first-rate fuss they make over you from start to finish. It's all very proper, leaving guests feeling privileged and pampered.

The posh setting and spot-on service set the tone for the sophisticated French cuisine, served as a four or five-course prix-fixe menu, also available with wine pairings. Classic dishes, like roasted sturgeon or apple tart, are comprised of delicate flavors and are as beautifully plated as they are prepared.

The Purple Pig

Mediterranean

A2

500 N. Michigan Ave. (at Illinois St.)

Phone: 312-464-1744
Web: www.thepurplepigchicago.com
Prices: $$

Lunch & dinner daily
Grand (Red)

Just because it's on Michigan Avenue doesn't mean you have to spend mucho moolah to get a good meal. Walk away from the glittering jewels at Cartier and head straight for the down-home digs of this wonderful place.

Simply decorated with wood floors, exposed pipes, communal tables, and a marble-topped bar, The Purple Pig puts on the ritz with its amped-up Mediterranean small plates. Choose from parts of the pig—crispy pigs ears, pork-fried almonds, dried hams, and salamis—or go for cheeses and other tangy treats. The prices are good, but flavors are better; and the plates may be small, but after sampling a few, you won't go home hungry. Wine is a big deal (glimpse the sayings chalked on the walls) and selections available by the glass are excellent.

Riva

Seafood

D2

700 E. Grand Ave. (on Navy Pier)

Phone: 312-644-7482
Web: www.rivanavypier.com
Prices: $$

Lunch & dinner daily

Navy Pier may be loaded with dining choices, but Riva stands out for its seafood-driven menu and unrivaled views of Lake Michigan. Yachts and tall sailing ships serve as an idyllic backdrop for this nautical-themed restaurant run by the ever-expanding Phil Stephani Group. Escape the hustle and bustle to this stylish dining room with soaring windows featuring the cityscape at sunset.

The menu is rich with seafood favorites and brings together the usual classics, such as lobster bisque, fresh oysters, and jumbo lump crab cakes. Entrées are creatively enhanced, as in the blackened whitefish set in a pool of ancho-chile sauce with creamy, horseradish-mashed potatoes. Landlubbers need not fear, since prime steaks and meats are featured as well.

Sayat Nova

A2

Middle Eastern ✗✗

157 E. Ohio St. (bet. Michigan Ave. & St. Clair St.)

Phone: 312-644-9159
Web: www.sayatnovachicago.com
Prices: $$

Lunch Mon – Sat
Dinner nightly
🚇 Grand (Red)

Streeterville's business crowd knows a good deal; that's why they flock to Sayat Nova. Here generous portions and reasonable prices are always on the menu. Also adding to its lure is a sidewalk patio, perfect for family feasting on warm days. Inside, find tables tucked intimately along the wall, while intricately designed metal luminaries lend a pleasant exoticism to the space.

The menu is made up of tasty, boldly spiced Armenian and Middle Eastern treats. Perhaps begin with creamy *hommos*, heaped with tahini, garlic, and olive oil and finished with a spike of paprika and parsley. Follow it up with a satisfying entrée: choose from a variety of kebabs, or go for a lesser-known dish like ground lamb *kibbee* served with *jajik*, a refreshing yogurt sauce.

The Zodiac

A1

American ✗✗✗

737 N. Michigan Ave. (at Superior St.)

Phone: 312-694-4050
Web: www.neimanmarcus.com
Prices: $$

Lunch Mon – Sat
🚇 Chicago (Red)

Nestled inside the Neiman Marcus department store, this fourth-floor restaurant (different than the third-floor quick-service café) offers exactly what you'd expect of a restaurant that bears the Neiman Marcus imprimatur. It is elegant, but refined and not ostentatious, with a contemporary décor.

Each meal starts with a Neiman Marcus signature a complimentary serving of a demitasse cup of chicken broth and a warm, well-executed popover with strawberry butter. From there, choose from soups, salads, and sandwiches, the kind of light fare you'd want during a break from shopping or sightseeing. The menu items themselves may not be particularly innovative (such as an Asian chicken salad), but everything is presented in the style you'd expect of Neiman's.

Tru ✿

A1

676 N. St. Clair St. (bet. Erie & Huron Sts.)

Phone: 312-202-0001
Web: www.trurestaurant.com
Prices: $$$$

Dinner Mon – Sat
🚇 Chicago (Red)

Mark Ballogg/Tru

You'll have to don a jacket to enter this hallowed house of fine dining, but it's a tiny price to pay for a night of culinary perfection. Long considered one of the top restaurants in Chicago, Tru has been wowing Windy City locals and in-the-know tourists for a decade now—practically a lifetime in restaurant years.

Tucked into a Streeterville nook set a few blocks back from the Magnificent Mile hubbub, Tru's décor reads lofty and elegant with white walls broken up by modern artwork snuggled under low lighting, slate gray floors, and dark fabric banquettes.

The menu is progressive French, with an impressive, well-thought-out wine list and a nightly parade of dishes that are as pretty to look at as they are to eat. A three-course prix-fixe (with several choices available for each course), or two nightly tasting menus might reveal a soft, fragrant bouillabaisse bobbing with fresh langoustine, quenelles of lobster mousse, and saffron-infused potato; succulent herb-crusted lamb loin served with favas and lemon and tomato confitures; or a wickedly good bitter almond cake nestled between creamy scoops of milk chocolate ice cream, vanilla custard, and a bright streak of cherry sauce.

Travel your own way with the NEW MICHELIN GREEN GUIDES

More than 50 destinations
around the world
In-depth coverage
Easy to use

MICHELIN

CHICAGO

THE GREEN GUIDE

Available wherever books are sold.

www.michelintravel.com

MICHELIN
A better way forward

Loop

The hustle and bustle of Chicago's main business district is named after the El train tracks that make a loop around the area. Their clickety-clack noise is an instrinsic part of the soundtrack of the Windy City.

TODAY'S LOOP

This neighborhood has a culinary soundtrack as well, one that is constantly evolving with the region. It wasn't that long ago that the Loop locked up at night. When offices, housed in the great iconic Chicago skyscrapers, closed at 5:00 P.M., so did the surrounding businesses, and the area remained quiet and deserted. Thanks to a revitalized Theater District, new residential living, hotels, and student dorms, there are now renewed restaurants, thrilling wine shops, and gorgeous grocery stores open past dusk. Local foodies and visitors with queries can now contact the Chicago Cultural Center's "culinary concierges" with any food tourism question.

SENSATIONAL SPREADS

Start your voyage and begin exploring at **Block 37**, one of the city's original 58 blocks. It took decades of work, and several political dynasties, but the block is now home to a new five-story atrium with shopping, restaurants, and entrances to public transportation lines.

Here, you'll find Japanese cream puff sensation **Beard Papa**, with its mochi ice cream, *fondant au chocolat*, mango showers, and vanilla-filled baked obsessions. Probiotic **Starfruit** with a spectrum of flavorful frozen yogurts also has an outpost here, as does **Andy's Frozen Custard**, a more decadent choice for travelers thirsty for a treat.

There are several quick food options on the Pedway level that are popular for office lunches. (The Pedway system of tunnels links crucial downtown buildings underground, which is essential during those cruel Chicago winters.) More restaurants, including one from Chicago's own Lettuce Entertain You, are in the works.

EAT YOUR WAY THROUGH THE LOOP

Chicago Chocolate Tours gives two-plus hour tastes of downtown's candy and baked icons' sites on Thursdays and Fridays. These delicious walking tours leave from Macy's State Street location.

Another preference is **Tastebud Tours** which has a Loop option on its daily tour menu. Stops include hot dogs, pizza, and **The Berghoff**, the city's oldest restaurant. Check out the historic Berghoff bar for lunch, dinner, dessert, and of course, steins of beer. Also terrific is Berghoff's pre-theater, prix-fixe menu that may reveal juicy eats like *sauerbraten*, potato pierogies, and Thai codfish cake. Their bevy of beers such as the Berghoff Seasonal Special, Prairie Lager, and Sundown Dark will keep you boisterous and quenched; and if you're in the mood for something lighter, root for the root beer.

When strolling these grounds, don't miss the public art that pops up in many of the government plazas and other open spaces across the Loop. Summer brings a melange of musical performances to Millennium Park, Grant Park, and the Petrillo Music Shell, that is just begging for a picnic *en plein air*.

FARMER'S MARKETS AND COFFEE CAROUSING

During warmer months, several farmers' markets cater to the downtown crowd, including the ones at Federal Plaza on Tuesdays and Daley Plaza on Thursdays. Concession carts freckle the streets of various locations in nearby Millennium Park, and are simply perfect for grabbing a snack whilst sauntering. In 2008, produce options increased with the opening of **Chicago's Downtown Farmstand**, a locally-focused vegetable purveyor on Randolph Street, that showcases a spectrum of colorful produce. Lake Street's **Pastoral Artisan Cheese** (a favorite of both *Saveur* Magazine and locals alike) is the go-to, made-to-order sandwich spot for the Loop's lunch crowd.

The city is filled with caffeine addicts and coffee connoisseurs. Sightseeing is tiring, so make sure you get a pick-me-up at **Intelligentsia Coffee**, a local coffee chain with an emphasis on direct trade. Locations can be found all over town, but the **Millennium Park Coffeebar** is particularly convenient. Caffeine addicts also appreciate the several **Torrefazione Italia** locations dotting maps of the Loop.

No trip to Chicago, much less the Loop, would be complete without munching on **Garrett Popcorn**. Head to one of the three Loop locations (follow the aroma for directions) for cheese, caramel, pecan, and other uniquely flavored popcorn.

TASTE OF CHICAGO

The Taste of Chicago is one of the city's biggest events. This 10-day summer fête in Grant Park draws hoards of eaters from near and far. (The park itself was incorporated before the city was founded.) For the last 30 years, local restaurants have set up scores of food booths featuring delicacies from around the globe. The place is packed for the 10-day duration, thanks to the food and live music, but come July 4th weekend, it's a bit of a madhouse! This free festival is now the second-largest attraction in the state. The beloved local **Eli's Cheesecake** is the sole remaining original Taste of Chicago exhibitor. In 2010, it celebrated its 30th anniversary with a giant, creamy cheesecake.

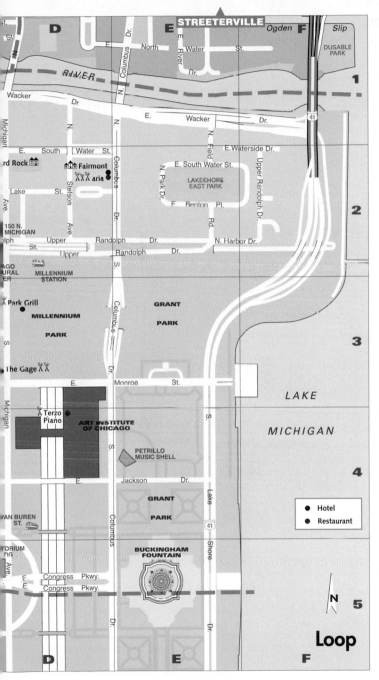

aria

D2

Asian 🍴🍴🍴

200 N. Columbus Dr. (bet. Lake & Water Sts.)

Phone: 312-444-9494
Web: www.ariachicago.com
Prices: $$$

Lunch & dinner daily
🚇 Washington

Current and luxurious, aria (the famed restaurant for the Fairmont in Chicago) satiates guests with a parade of breakfast, lunch, and dinner. But, thanks to the mighty mod sushi bar, dinner may be your best bet at this Asian-inspired arena.

With the recent arrival of Chef Chad Starling, aria's menu has upped the fusion ante, serving delicacies like buckwheat soba noodles, served at just the right cool temperature; and seared *madai* snapper delivered on a bed of rice cooked in prawn stock, and dotted with porky chorizo.

The lounge is a great place for a signature drink—maybe a take on the classic Tom (chive and pepper) Collins? But, leaving aside her tried-and-true blends, aria's selection of spirits (and bar service) is purely premium.

Atwood Café

C3

Contemporary 🍴🍴

1 W. Washington St. (at State St.)

Phone: 312-368-1900
Web: www.atwoodcafe.com
Prices: $$

Lunch & dinner daily
🚇 Washington

Tucked inside the Hotel Burnham, elegant Atwood Café provides both style and substance. Soaring windows showcase fantastic views while the dining room, complete with red velvet seating and glittering chandeliers, is both grand and graciously attended.

The look may be old-world, but the menu is modern, with inspired culinary creations like subtly sweet fried calamari coated in graham cracker, or scallops with pumpkin flan. Globally influenced, the dishes are also rooted in comfort food (chicken pot pie, goat cheese and macaroni), and are as artfully presented as they are prepared. Rich, warming desserts may include the pear and brown butter clafouti.

All-day dining is a bonus in this highly trafficked location, just blocks from the Theater District.

Bella Bacinos

C1

Italian ✗✗

75 E. Wacker Dr. (bet. Michigan Ave. & State St.)

Phone: 312-263-2350
Web: www.bellabacinos.com
Prices: $$

Lunch & dinner daily
🚇 State/Lake

Deep-dish, thin crust, or stuffed, Chicagoans love their pizza no matter how it is sliced and Bella Bacinos, one of four in the city, dishes up some fantastic pizza with top ingredients. It all started over 30 years ago when Dan Bacin decided to throw a curve ball into pizza making. No more canned ingredients and sauces. Instead, Bacin used the freshest meats, cheeses, and vegetables he could find. The result? Some of the best pizza in town.

You can have it any way you want it at Bella Bacinos, but the stuffed pizza is always a pleaser. This location, in the landmark Mather Tower, has a swanky décor with a lively bar. It's more than just pizza (hearty pastas and entrées round out the menu), but really, why would you want anything else?

Cibo Matto

C2

Italian ✗✗✗

201 N. State St. (at Lake St.)

Phone: 312-239-9500
Web: www.thewithotel.com
Prices: $$$

Dinner Mon – Sat
🚇 State/Lake

Literally, *cibo matto* means "crazy food," but this restaurant is more like crazy good. Located inside the suave Wit Hotel, this Italian respite ups the ante in the Theater District and its cache of delicious dishes will surely have you rethinking pre-theater dining. From the pretty butterfly theme, plush styling, and requisite hot waiters, it's all very Sex and the City in here. The menu brings an appealing mix of American and Italian flavors. Starters (ricotta cheese-filled zucchini blossoms or soft shell crab with wild garlic sauce) tantalize; pastas (bucatini carbonara) please; but you can't go wrong with entrées like tender braised short rib; or lamb chops atop Mediterranean farro. Save room for a sophisticated chocolate tart with banana gelato.

Everest ✿

B5

French 🍴🍴🍴🍴

440 S. LaSalle St. (bet. Congress Pkwy. & Van Buren St.)

Phone:	312-663-8920	Dinner Tue – Sat
Web:	www.everestrestaurant.com	🚇 LaSalle/Van Buren
Prices:	$$$$	

Everest

Tucked into the 40th floor of the Chicago Stock Exchange, celebrated chef Jean Joho's most renowned restaurant opened in the fall of 1986 to thunderous applause and hasn't looked back since.

The art deco penthouse space calls to mind a lavish 20's film set with curved booths, a big expanse of windows overlooking the city, and lacquered ivory walls hung with original paintings by Chicago artists Adam Siegel and Tim Anderson. Service is equally charming, and you can count on the perfectly polished, often humorous, staff to help you navigate the impressive wine list.

Joho's Alsatian background pops up throughout the New French menu: oysters are accented with Riesling, and sautéed foie gras is garnished with endive and apples and caressed with a velvety jus and deglaze of Picon Bière. Dinner revolves around the season but may reveal perfectly poached beef tenderloin and root vegetables, paired with tender bone marrow dumplings; creamy, Carnaroli risotto (the most exquisite variety of the stuff) studded with winter vegetables and topped with a sheet of gold; or melt-in-your-mouth wild sturgeon in a glistening wine reduction with whole chestnuts and braised Savoy cabbage.

The Gage

D3

Gastropub ✗✗

24 S. Michigan Ave. (bet. Madison & Monroe Sts.)

Phone: 312-372-42743
Web: www.thegagechicago.com
Prices: $$

Lunch & dinner daily
Madison

A superb location opposite Millennium Park with an impressive patio offering views across the street would be enough to pack this place, regardless of the food. To The Gage's credit, it doesn't rest on its location's laurels. This massive place pleases locals and tourists alike, with its solid gastropub menu, reasonable prices, and popular post-work bar.

The pan-roasted Great Lakes whitefish is indicative of what one can expect here: a fresh, locally sourced piece of fish, cooked to perfection, served with Brussels sprouts leaves and a roasted beet vinaigrette. Scoop up the to-die-for N-17 "fondue," of Butter Kaase, brie, and spinach; or chomp the upmarket "Gage" burger with local Camembert and melted onion marmalade on a toasted malt roll.

Lockwood

C3

Contemporary ✗✗✗

17 E. Monroe St. (at State St.)

Phone: 312-917-3404
Web: www.lockwoodrestaurant.com
Prices: $$$

Lunch & dinner daily
Monroe

Nestled in the Palmer House Hilton, Lockwood is set off the timeless and ornate lobby, rubbing shoulders with the hotel bars. While its layout may feel choppy, that is part of the cozy charm of being located in an 1870s building, as is the hotel's magnificent frescoed ceiling.

The upscale dining room is matched by the contemporary American menu. Clever appetizers include the "buffalo-ed" chicken wings, served lollipop-style with Great Hills blue cheese and fiery *sriracha* sauce. While perhaps not as fun, the roasted chicken is equally inventive: the free-range bird is served with chestnut purée, wild mushrooms, and a compressed gratin of Jerusalem artichokes. Some desserts may not be worth the calories, but the star anise ice cream is a showstopper.

One North Kitchen & Bar

American ✕✕

1 N. Wacker Dr. (bet. Madison & Washington Sts.)

Phone: 312-750-9700
Web: www.restaurants-america.com
Prices: $$

Lunch Mon – Fri
Dinner Mon – Sat
🚇 Washington

Both on street level and within the USB Tower, One North Kitchen & Bar is a hub of activity, albeit different kinds depending on the time of day. When the clock strikes noon, the ballast is abuzz with financial industry types who come in droves over their lunch hour. Things calm down until pre-theater, after which One North's dinner rush heralds a changed clientele.

FiDi folk love the lunches because they star generously sized sandwiches made with luscious ingredients, and sided with pomme frites. Grilled shrimp, pork chops, and macaroni and cheese are some of the other big hits among the 9-to-5'ers. For those looking to lull, enjoy a homemade and daring dessert of the day on the terrace, also idyllic for a drink before or after city sightseeing.

Park Grill

American ✕✕

11 N. Michigan Ave. (at Millennium Park)

Phone: 312-521-7275
Web: www.parkgrillchicago.com
Prices: $$

Lunch & dinner daily
🚇 Madison

Located next to the shining Cloud Gate inside Millennium Park, appealing and approachable Park Grill affords views of would-be medalists hitting the winter ice rink and just about every other tourist in town walking by during warmer months. No matter the season, diners find a dressed up American cuisine to please the masses.

The wide-ranging menu has everything from salads big and small to burgers of Kobe beef, salmon, or Berkshire pork. Ambitious dishes like thyme-roasted scallops please the sophisticated palate, while contemporary desserts like the peanut butter tart served with roasted banana purée are worth the caloric splurge. Budget diners like the two-course power business lunch during the week and the children's specials on the weekends.

Rhapsody

American ✕✕

C4

65 E. Adams St. (bet. Michigan & Wabash Aves.)

Phone: 312-786-9911
Web: www.rhapsodychicago.com
Prices: $$

Lunch Mon – Fri
Dinner nightly
🚇 Monroe

From its charmingly whimsical exterior and its large patio nestled in a blooming flower garden to its friendly and timely service, Rhapsody delivers a virtuoso performance. Attached to the Symphony Center, it is a natural choice for pre- or post-performance breaks, but the beautiful, contemporary setting makes it a destination at any time.

Open to the bar and dining room, the kitchen's performance is equally impressive. Dishes, such as a fillet of salmon topped with kumquat-ginger relish and served with Asian pear and snow pea salad, blend unusual pairings, interesting textures, and distinct flavors. Even dessert shows off a flair for the unexpected: sweet spices of warm apple cake are counterbalanced with the tang of goat cheese ice cream.

Rosebud Prime

Steakhouse ✕✕✕

C3

1 S. Dearborn St. (at Madison St.)

Phone: 312-384-1900
Web: www.rosebudrestaurants.com
Prices: $$$

Lunch Mon – Fri
Dinner nightly
🚇 Monroe

Class and elegance drift through the striking bi-level dining space, where luxurious rose banquettes, soaring ceilings, and a gorgeous mezzanine create an air of sophistication. Knowledgeable, tuxedo clad servers rapidly fire off daily specials, though still maintain passion and sincerity. Thin, crispy salted raisin bread and fresh rolls with honey butter start things off right, while scrumptious starters like peppercorn ahi tuna with ginger soy, coconut shrimp, and smoked salmon pastrami please the palate.

Slice into a juicy *petit* filet, seared just so and served with a side of jus. Complete the decadence with fresh blueberries, raspberries, and strawberries served with velvety *sabayon*—whipped with a touch of cream and spiked with Grand Marnier.

Shikago

B4

190 S. LaSalle St. (at Adams St.)

Phone: 312-781-7300
Web: www.shikagorestaurant.com
Prices: $$

Lunch & dinner Mon – Sat
🚇 Quincy

Shikago may not be unique in attracting its lunchtime loopers and the happy hour set, but few dining rooms are so alluring that one imagines the tables could be pushed aside so an art show could begin. Inside this contemporary, gallery-like space (with an inviting bar for that martini lunch), find wispy metallic sculptures set against stark walls, oversized fixtures with ginko-embossed tissue, and tables of salvaged wood.

At midday, find business folks flocking in for bento boxes, sizzle plates, and a selection of *bahn mi.* At dinner, nigiri sushi, maki, and more substantial entrées, with influences from Korea, Japan, China, and Vietnam, replace the lighter lunch fare. Green tea crème brûlée is a tasty, signature pan-Asian twist on dessert.

State & Lake

C2

201 N. State St. (at Lake St.)

Phone: 312-239-9400
Web: www.thewithotel.com
Prices: $$

Lunch & dinner daily
🚇 State/Lake

Its name says it all, so don't fret if you forgot to write down the address of this restaurant before setting sail. State & Lake, nestled into the ground floor of the sleek Wit Hotel, is draped in dark leather padded walls, cork floors, and intimate, soft lighting that give the space a seductive sophistication. The dining room is perpetually packed with corporates over lunch and groups—destined for the nearby Theater District—for dinner. Start the day with a sausage and egg casserole, break midday for a short rib panino, and come dusk, tuck into potato gnocchi or roasted salmon. Channel your inner frat boy and go for the kegs and eggs (on weekends only), or for the oblong bar that also boasts frosty taps (literally) pouring around a dozen beers.

Terzo Piano

D4

Italian ✕

159 E. Monroe St. (bet. Columbus Dr. & Michigan Ave.)

Phone: 312-443-8650
Web: www.terzopianochicago.com
Prices: $$$

Lunch daily
Dinner Thu
🚇 Monroe

With a dash of urban-sophistication, this luminous space befits its larger digs displaying a crisp minimalist design and sleek outdoor terrace. Tucked into the west wing of the Art Institute of Chicago, this immaculate room shows off sweeping floor-to-ceiling windows, edgy artwork, and a fantastic view of the park.

Take a break from the galleries and refuel on delicious roasted pike, served atop a bed of *farro, cipollini* onions, and aromatic almond and herb purée; or fresh made *ravioletto*, stuffed with creamy mozzarella and porcini mushrooms floating in a rosemary scented broth. Chef Tony Mantuano of Spiaggia is at the helm, spinning out decadent offerings such as flat bread pizzas, antipastos, and artisanal cheeses. Dinner is served on Thursdays only.

Trattoria No. 10

C3

Italian ✕✕

10 N. Dearborn St. (bet. Madison & Washington Sts.)

Phone: 312-984-1718
Web: www.trattoriaten.com
Prices: $$

Lunch Mon – Fri
Dinner Mon – Sat
🚇 Washington

Trattoria No. 10 is something of a charming underworld. Located on the basement level (accessible through a sidewalk level foyer's staircase or elevator), this inviting and cozy restaurant feels like an intimate world away from the hustle and bustle of the Loop. Lunchtime is particularly busy at this Italian eatery, where a power-crowd of lawyers and financial advisors rub elbows and hold court—reservations are recommended.

However, the real draw is a menu of rustic Italian trattoria specialties that is far from fussy or formal. Expect good old-fashioned cooking in dishes that range from the tender grilled, slightly smoky calamari to the plump ravioli stuffed with homemade sausage and topped with perfectly thick and spicy *arrabbiata* sauce.

65

Vivere

Italian

71 W. Monroe St. (bet. Clark & Dearborn Sts.)

Phone: 312-332-4040
Web: www.vivere-chicago.com
Prices: $$

Lunch Mon – Fri
Dinner nightly
 Monroe

Vivere exalts in its curves, and has ample sexy, swirling shapes to give Sophia Loren a run for her money. Everything, from light fixtures to the sweeping staircase that leads to a buzzing mezzanine, shows off a rounded look. Rich dark colors and soft lighting make this old-school Italian charmer an especially romantic spot.

Outfitted in suits and ties, the staff is disciplined, formal, and delivers spot-on service with a courteous manner. Trust in their knowledge and ask for guidance while reviewing the extensive wine selection. The menu is concise and offers a variety of rustic Northern Italian dishes and handmade pastas. House specialties may include grilled sausage and peppers or pheasant-stuffed *agnolottini* in sage butter sauce.

The sun is out – let's eat alfresco! Look for 🏠.

West Loop
Greektown · Market District

NEIGHBORHOOD NOUVEAU

What a difference a century (or two) makes! The West Loop was once home to smoke-spewing factories and warehouses, but walk through this natty neighborhood now, and you'll find young professionals instead of struggling immigrants. Transformed into luxurious lofts, cool nightclubs, art galleries, and cutting-edge restaurants, the warehouses and factories are a far cry from their former existence.

Immigrants staked their claim to this neighborhood years ago, and traces of ethnic flavor are still found here. It's not as big as it once was, but Little Italy's Taylor Street still charms with its old-world, slightly kitschy

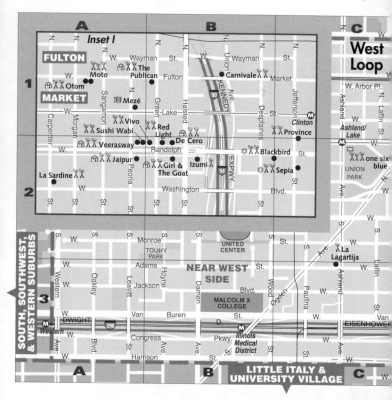

feel. It is delis, groceries, and restaurants galore.

A TASTE OF GREECE

Maintain this Mediterranean vibe by heading over to Greektown, where everybody's Greek, even if just for the day. Shout "oopa" at the Taste of Greece festival, held each August, or stop by the **Parthenon** for gyros and some serious showmanship – they even serve flaming *saganaki* cheese. A deluge of Greek restaurants line these blocks and are perfect for those looking to snack; as well as for groups who wish to linger over large spreads.

Speaking of "oopa," Chicago's favorite first lady of talk, Oprah Winfrey, is headquartered here. Harpo Studios, housed in a former armory, has been luring gaggles of fans since the late 80's. Tickets are free, lines are long, but who knows what she'll hand out to the audience? If Greek and Italian foods don't fit the bill, there's surely something to whet your appetite along Randolph Street, often referred to as "Restaurant Row." From sushi to subs, this street has it all. For those who enjoy binging at breakfast, head on over to **Dodo at Dino's**. This local

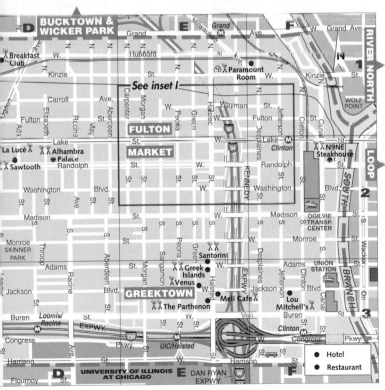

favorite satiates all and sundry with its daily brunch proffering of seasonal frittatas, French toast, and yes, Japanese pancakes!

For a magnificent night about town, you can even round up 1,000 of your closest peeps to dine together at **Alhambra**, an enormous Moroccan-Mediterranean restaurant showcasing a spectrum of treats from hummus, baba ghanoush, and *lebna*, to more faithful spreads like shrimp *charmoula*, *dolmeh*, and kibbeh. Further west on Randolph, find **The Tasting Room**, a two-level stop for excellent wines accompanied by a good selection of small plates.

CRAFTING CULINARY SKILLS

Rather whip it up than wolf it down? Beef up your kitchen skills at the Calphalon Culinary Center, where groups can arrange for private hands-on instruction. Mastered the bœuf Bourguignon? Get in line at **Olympic Meat Packers**. This old-school meatpacking joint is one of the last holdouts in the area. It's not for the squeamish, but the butchers slice and dice the perfect meat to order.

MARKET FEVER

Troll the stalls at the **Chicago French Market** for artisan cheeses, roasted nuts, gourmet pickles, flowers, and other specialty goods for your next dinner party. Don't have a ramekin or Dutch oven? Northwestern Cutlery Supply stocks everything a chef could need—even the requisite white coat.

Treasure hunters mark the spot at the Chicago Antique Market. This massive indoor/outdoor market is held the last Saturday of each month from May through October, and stocks everything from jewelry to furniture.

BEER AND THE BALLGAME

Hoops fans whoop it up at Bulls games at the United Center, which is also home to the Stanley Cup winners—the Blackhawks. Depending on the score, the most exciting part of the night might be post game, especially if over a beer at **Beer Bistro**. You'll need to bring your most decisive friends, since this place has 124 different types of bottled beer (and 21 on tap).

To nibble on the side, faithful pub grub such as spinach and artichoke dip, fried calamari, beer-battered chicken fingers, and mac & cheese are sure to satisfy. Another spot for those who like a little brawl with their beer is **Twisted Spoke**. The proverbial biker bar (serving shrimp Po'Boys, meatloaf sandwiches, BBQ Kobe brisket, and smut & eggs after midnight on Saturdays), is complete with tattoos and 'tudes to match. The music is loud, crowds are big, and drunks are plentiful, but it's all in good testosterone-and alcohol-fueled fun.

Switching gears, lovely ladies sip champagne at posh hot spot **Plush**. If you've indulged in one too many glasses of bubbly, grab a blanket and some fresh air, and head to Union Park for a much-needed al fresco nap.

Alhambra Palace

Middle Eastern ✗✗

D2

1240 W. Randolph St. (bet. Elizabeth St. & Racine Ave.)

Phone: 312-666-9555

Web: www.alhambrapalacerestaurant.com

Prices: $$

Lunch & dinner daily

Ashland (Green/Pink)

"Palace" aptly describes this mammoth restaurant. With a lounge, dining room, and even its own large sidewalk protected from the elements, everything here is on the larger-than-life scale.

The menu provides a fusion of different Middle Eastern dishes. The cream free lentil soup, served with freshly made, perfectly charred pita would be enough for a satisfying lunch. But if you stopped there you wouldn't get a chance to order the other standouts. The Mezza combo offers a sampling of well-seasoned baba ghanoush, hummus, falafel, and stuffed grape leaves. The Toshka is a Middle Eastern *panino* of sorts, grilled pita stuffed with ground beef and cheese. For dessert the baklava is well-made, topped with thick honey, crushed pistachio, and almonds.

Breakfast Club

American ✗

D1

1381 W. Hubbard St. (at Noble St.)

Phone: 312-666-2372

Web: www.chicagobreakfastclub.com

Prices: 🍪

Lunch daily

Ashland (Green/Pink)

It may share the name of one John Hughes' favorite teen flick, but inside, this "Breakfast Club" is totally "Pretty in Pink." The walls and furniture are dusty rose, and the servers wear hot pink polo shirts. There's even a pink canopy over the outdoor seats open in warm weather.

Those movie references may be dated, but the food here isn't stale. Classic breakfasts start the day off right with hearty choices like a chorizo-filled Mexican skillet; the crispy perfection of pan-fried potato pancakes; stuffed French toast; or biscuits and gravy. Side everything with some ham sliced off the bone. Lunch offers traditional fare, like burgers, club sandwiches, grilled cheese, and meatloaf.

The Breakfast Club has an early curfew—no dinner service here.

Blackbird ✥

B2

Contemporary 🍴🍴

619 W. Randolph St. (bet. Des Plaines & Jefferson Sts.)

Phone: 312-715-0708
Web: www.blackbirdrestaurant.com
Prices: $$$

Lunch Mon – Fri
Dinner Mon – Sat

🚇 Clinton (Green/Pink)

Douglas Reid Fogelson Photography

Like a triple threat performer tapping their way through a musical, Blackbird nails it on not one, not two, but three all-important fronts—killer food, spot-on service, and great atmosphere. If you can find all that in one spot, there's not a whole lot of reason to venture beyond Chef Paul Kahan's critically-acclaimed restaurant.

Situated next to sister establishment, avec, along a restaurant-strewn stretch of Randolph Street, Blackbird's space cuts a thoroughly sleek, minimalist line—its modish white-and-steel space broken up by curious art pieces, polished wood floors, and a semi-open kitchen.

Kahan's menu (available à la carte or prix-fixe) takes seasonal fare and pristine ingredients to inspired levels, and might include a tender confit of wood-grilled octopus treated to a flutter of petite lettuce leaves, pickled ramp stems, candied red onion, and malt-flavored sour cream; a silky fan of fresh Ahi tuna laced with a streak of smoked buttermilk and garnished with nutty clusters of candied wild rice, Picholine olives, green garbanzos, and a dash of cilantro; or a perfectly roasted Colorado lamb saddle matched with white asparagus, vermouth, fromage blanc, and spring pea falafel.

Carnivale

Latin American ✗✗

B1

702 W. Fulton Market (at Union Ave.)

Phone: 312-850-5005
Web: www.carnivalechicago.com
Prices: $$

Lunch Mon – Fri
Dinner nightly
🚇 Clinton (Green/Pink)

The exterior of Jerry Kleiner's latest hot spot obscures its mammoth size, but the name says it all. This colorful venue features a pan-Latin theme park of the cuisine and culture of the Caribbean, Central, and South America.

Carnivale's menu varies significantly between lunch and dinner, but the fusion style and tasty drink menu stays the same regardless of the time of day. At lunch try the *remolachas*, a tasty beet salad with goat cheese and a sharp sherry vinaigrette; or hit the tilapia fish tacos accompanied by a crunchy apple and avocado salad. In the evening, taste the artisan Spanish hams and cheeses, or opt for a cool ceviche, or smoky wood-grilled pork. Forget that diet and end with crispy churros, served with chocolate and caramel sauces.

De Cero 😊

Mexican ✗✗

B2

814 W. Randolph St. (at Halsted St.)

Phone: 312-455-8114
Web: www.decerotaqueria.com
Prices: $$

Lunch & dinner Tue – Sun
🚇 Clinton (Green/Pink)

The duo behind the super successful Sushi Wabi has done it again. This time, they've applied their creative, edgy formula to Mexico. As expected, it's a bit of a scene, with the loud music and a neat, natty vibe, but the amiable staff and laid-back locale help to keep things in check.

Thankfully, there are no native clichés in sight at this West Randolph gem. The menu may have numerous selections, but remember, this is light and simple Mexican. Come to relish in fine and fragrant fare and homemade tortillas holding 12 types of fresh tacos, so don't expect that food coma. Wash down a few shrimp tacos or the *huitlacoche* quesadilla with a Mexican beer, tequila, or better yet, a limey and lip-smacking margarita.

Girl & The Goat

B2

Contemporary 🍴🍴

809 W. Randolph St. (bet. Green & Halsted Sts.)

Phone: 312-492-6262
Web: www.girlandthegoat.com
Prices: $$

Dinner nightly
🚇 Clinton (Green/Pink)

 If you think this girl's menu is all about goat, think again. *Top Chef* winner, Stephanie Izard is now busy winning over Chicago's heart with her hugely hyped Girl & The Goat, whose funky and global menu floats fabulously between goat and garbanzo. In spring 2010, she swung open her doors unveiling a lofty, industrial space graced with wood floors, an alluring bar, and cushy sofas beneath big windows.

Blazing beyond, the open kitchen bestows a tandem of small plates like sautéed green beans with fish sauce; and escargot and goat cheese balls with *romesco*. The hip staff will be happy to initiate you into a lusty salad of fresh, fried, and puréed chickpeas united with Parmesan and shallot vinaigrette; and rabbit *rillette* rolled into golden crêpes.

Greek Islands

E3

Greek 🍴🍴

200 S. Halsted St. (at Adams St.)

Phone: 312-782-9855
Web: www.greekislands.net
Prices: 💰💰

Lunch & dinner daily
🚇 UIC-Halsted

This restaurant is as much a Chicago experience as a place to eat. For 40 years, Greek Islands has packed a mix of local business folks and tourists into its multiple dining rooms. This place is always buzzing, thanks to the crowds, the guitar-strumming background, and the bar's shouts of "Oopa!"

 The menu highlights traditional Greek (and Greek-American) fare such as grilled octopus, *pastichio*, *spanakotiropita*, flaming *saganaki* cheese, rotisseries of meat for gyros, and daily specials. Even simple sides are tasty, such as fluffy rice served with rich and thick yogurt. Focus is on the food and not the presentation, but portions are accommodating, with many favorites offered as family-sized entrées for sharing or half-orders for children.

Izumi

Japanese ✗

731 W. Randolph St. (bet. W. Court Pl & Halsted St.)

Phone: 312-207-5299
Web: www.izumisushi.com
Prices: $$

Lunch Tue – Fri
Dinner nightly
🚇 Clinton (Green/Pink)

The bright red paint around the front windows and on the front door alerts you to stop here. Fans of contemporary, westernized Japanese cuisine ought to heed that call, but traditionalists might want to walk on by.

The inventive and contemporary maki at Izumi may cause a classic sushi *itamae* to faint. But those who like bold flavor and innovative combinations will love to stretch their culinary minds here. Try the tasty Latin roll: a pipe of superwhite tuna, *kampyo*, and fresh cilantro, drizzled with hot sauce and crusted in red *tobiko*; or go really crazy with the strawberry roll: white tuna and tempura crunch, spicy tuna, strawberry slices, and *unagi* sauce.

Noodle dishes and bento boxes are decent options at lunch, but the maki are the stars here.

Jaipur

Indian ✗✗

847 W. Randolph St. (bet. Green & Peoria Sts.)

Phone: 312-526-3655
Web: www.jaipurchicago.com
Prices: $$

Lunch Mon – Sat
Dinner nightly
🚇 Clinton (Green/Pink)

Conveniently located on the West Randolph restaurant row, Jaipur is popular with the weekday Loop crowd at lunch, and the hip dinner crowd that loves the scene on the weekends. In general, the menu is a collection of hits at this standout among the many Indian restaurants in town. Kerala chicken is boldly flavorful, bathed in coconut milk, chilis, coriander, *garam masala*, turmeric, ginger, cloves, and onion. Traditional sides, like *saag paneer*, *chana masala*, and naan are well-executed. Skip the overcooked tandoori chicken, but don't miss the *rasmalai*, a disc of fresh cheese soaked in cardamom-sweetened milk, for an enjoyable finish.

Good value combination meals are offered at lunch, a refreshing break from the ubiquitous Indian buffets.

La Lagartija

 C2·3

Mexican

132 S. Ashland Ave. (bet. Adams & Monroe Sts.)

Phone: 312-733-7772
Web: N/A
Prices: 🍜

Lunch & dinner Mon – Sat
🚇 Ashland (Green/Pink)

May we take a moment to talk about the salsas? One, a tangy tomatillo verde with lime juice, cilantro, and green chiles; the other a smoky roasted red chile—both like harbingers of deliciousness. Pop into this jaunty joint, where prismatic walls shout out Spanish food words in funky fonts, and the namesake lizard shows up in artsy renditions about the room. Chef/owners Luis Perea and Laura-Cid Perea captain this operation, making it one of the best taquerias in all of Chi-town. Sink your chops into a juicy taco *al pastor*—pork, spit-roasted with pineapple, shaved, and then topped with onion and cilantro; or the heavenly shrimp taco—three lightly battered prawns, fried and tossed into a fluffy homemade corn tortilla with shredded lettuce and chile-mayo.

La Lucé

D2

Italian

1393 W. Lake St. (at Ogden Ave.)

Phone: 312-850-1900
Web: www.lalucewestloop.com
Prices: $$

Lunch Mon – Fri
Dinner nightly
🚇 Ashland (Green/Pink)

It should come as no surprise that La Lucé looks straight out of a Hollywood set. This restaurant, snuggled inside a Queen Anne Victorian dating back to 1892, is often used as a location for films and television series. From the exterior copper work and meat locker with original milk glass panels, to the wood-burning stove, La Lucé is the real deal.

The Italian-American cooking and that quintessential old-time vibe may have you looking over your shoulder for Vito Corleone, but at least your last meal will be a good one. Choose from classics like veal Parmesan, chicken Marsala, stuffed pork chops, spaghetti with meatballs, and homemade cannoli. Meat and cheese ravioli melt in your mouth, and the pizzas, served at lunch, are worth the 20-minute wait.

La Sardine

French 🍴🍴

A2

111 N. Carpenter St. (bet. Randolph St. & Washington Blvd.)

Phone: 312-421-2800
Web: www.lasardine.com
Prices: $$

Lunch Mon – Fri
Dinner Mon – Sat
🚇 Clinton (Green/Pink)

A dependable French-style bistro, La Sardine has one most American of claims to fame: it is located literally in front of the entrance to Harpo Studios, Oprah Winfrey's media empire. For years, live television tapings have fed audience-member diners into this eatery, although it is also popular with locals and staffers who appreciate its solid food and warm ambience.

Many bistro-goers expect French onion soup as a bellwether, and on this point La Sardine's rich, brothy, sweet, and cheesy stew brimming with onions cooked until tender but still recognizable, does not disappoint. Specials like the halibut are simple, well-priced, and made with the freshest ingredients. A nice wine list and excellent espresso finish off the meal with French flair.

Lou Mitchell's

American 🍴

F3

565 W. Jackson Blvd. (bet. Clinton & Jefferson Sts.)

Phone: 312-939-3111
Web: www.loumitchellsrestaurant.com
Prices: 🍪🍪

Lunch daily
🚇 Clinton (Blue)

At the top of Chicago's list of beloved names is Lou Mitchell. This eponymous diner is by no means an elegant affair, but thanks to its fluffy omelets and iconic crowd, it has been on the Windy City's must-eat list since 1923. Don't panic at the length of the lines; they are long but move fast, and free doughnut holes (one of the restaurant's signature baked goods) make the wait go faster.

Back to those omelets: they may be made with mere eggs, like everyone else's, but somehow these are lighter and fluffier, almost like a soufflé, stuffed with feta, spinach, onions, or any other ingredients of your choice. They arrive in skillets with an Idaho-sized helping of potatoes. Save room, because everyone gets a little soft serve ice cream at the meal's end.

Meli Cafe

American 🍴

E3

301 S. Halsted St. (bet. Jackson Blvd. & Van Buren St.)

Phone: 312-454-0748
Web: www.melicafe.com
Prices: ☕☕

Lunch daily
🚇 UIC-Halsted

Locals love Meli Cafe, not just for the food (back to that in a minute) but because it offers something other than the traditional Greek eats in the heart of Greektown. The proximity to UIC and the Loop packs folks into this yellow dining room decorated with rows of marmalades. Pick homemade apricot and grape or another favorite for your toast.

Meli is open through lunch, but breakfast is where it's at. The kitchen specializes in egg dishes made from organic eggs—omelettes, frittatas, and benedicts. The sundried tomato and basil frittata, for example, is made from cage-free eggs, and chock-full of ingredients. Waffles, French toast, and fancy sweet and savory pancakes and crêpes are alternatives for those who don't want eggs.

Mezé

International 🍽️

A1

205 N. Peoria St. (at Lake St.)

Phone: 312-666-6625
Web: www.mezechicago.com
Prices: ☕☕

Dinner Tue – Sat
🚇 Clinton (Green/Pink)

A newcomer to the Fulton Market area, Mezé (named for the Middle Eastern-style small plates relative) is a see-and-be-seen-type of joint, one that gets louder as the night goes on. While there are plenty of folks enjoying an adult beverage or two, the global menu doesn't play second fiddle to the high energy and luxurious ambience of the lounge.

The rich flavors from the Americas, Asia, the Mediterranean, and the Caribbean are evident in the dishes here. Seared tuna is served upon wonton chips and a pungent wasabi crema, creating a nice spicy-sweet snack. The chicken quesadilla is toasted just enough to melt the cheese and is served with a zippy chipotle dipping sauce. Happy hour is a bargain with discounted tapas and bottles of wine.

Moto

Contemporary 🍴🍴🍴

A1

945 W. Fulton Market (bet. Morgan & Sangamon Sts.)

Phone: 312-491-0058
Web: www.motorestaurant.com
Prices: $$$$

Dinner Tue – Sat
🚇 Clinton (Green/Pink)

Chef Homaro Cantu's Moto is understated on the outside. Inside is a statement: this is a special occasion place, with a molecular gastronomy wow factor that makes it a once-a-year, must-do experience. The first clue that this is not your father's celebratory spot? The whimsical food can favor form over flavor, but look forward to the edible menu on compressed pita, served with spinach purée and lava salt for dipping.

A menu (with either ten or 20 courses) guides diners through the evening, with no options. Selections from recent meals include a "Cuban" edible cigar of pulled pork served on an ashtray; and faux maki made with sous vide rabbit rubbed in beet powder to resemble crab. The wine list is limited, but pairs well with Cantu's creations.

N9NE Steakhouse

Steakhouse 🍴🍴

F2

440 W. Randolph St. (at Canal St.)

Phone: 312-575-9900
Web: www.n9ne.com
Prices: $$$

Lunch Mon – Fri
Dinner Mon – Sat
🚇 Clinton (Green/Pink)

"New" is typically the watchword that determines whether or not a night spot is trendy. But even after a decade N9NE Steakhouse still attracts the city's beautiful people for mingling, ogling, and, eating. The restaurant's name comes from the age the owners were when they first met. Those owners include Michael Morton, of Morton's steakhouse fame. So, it stands to reason that N9NE can serve a good steak. The food is taken seriously, and the menu is simple, but not staid. Also fitting the nightlife vibe are the surf and turf specials, prepared like sliders, with beef tenderloin on one tiny sandwich and Maine lobster on the other. The shrimp cocktail is a little pricey but worth it simply for the kick of the horseradish-tomato cocktail sauce.

one sixty blue

C2

Contemporary XXX

1400 W. Randolph St. (at Ogden Ave.)

Phone: 312-850-0303
Web: www.onesixtyblue.com
Prices: $$

Dinner Mon – Sat
🚇 Ashland (Green/Pink)

This West Loop winner, part of Michael Jordan's restaurant group, is a lay up with its creative Mediterranean-influenced food. Chef Michael McDonald whips up some serious artistry here. Unexpected combinations and preparations keep you on your toes in this retro place, where you can also peek in on the action of the open kitchen or jam to the beats of the vibey soundtrack.

Chef McDonald's riffs on the classics are all over the place. The bar menu's fried blue cheese olives and crispy hash brown foie gras burgers aren't your typical treats; but rest easy as charred octopus aside grilled squid and crisp rice-crusted shrimp on a bed of quinoa tabbouleh round out the main menu. For a cheat sheet version, come weeknights for the three-course prix-fixe.

Otom 😋

A1

Contemporary XX

951 W. Fulton Market (bet. Morgan & Sangamon Sts.)

Phone: 312-491-5804
Web: www.otomrestaurant.com
Prices: $$

Dinner Tue – Sat
🚇 Clinton (Green/Pink)

Otom—like its sister restaurant nearby, Moto–is beefing up the cool quotient in the Fulton Market District. This marvelous masterpiece has a fun, upbeat sense defined by brick and concrete walls, dark wood floors, bright orange chairs, and smart stripes inspired by designer Paul Smith. Fresh and funky with its sexy crowd and so-bad-it's-good beats, Otom is the very place to impress your out-of-towners with how hip you are.

The food is as artsy as its setting: there's everything from German potato salad gnocchi to mole chicken. The menu veers in some wacky directions, but who cares? Even the drinks are nouveau—the "pickles are made from cucumbers" cocktail mixes gin, dill, cucumber, Midori, lime, and seltzer for a refreshing libation.

Paramount Room

Gastropub

415 N. Milwaukee Ave. (bet. Hubbard & Kinzie Sts.)

Phone: 312-829-6300
Web: www.paramountroom.com
Prices: $$

Lunch Thu – Sun
Dinner nightly
 Grand (Blue)

In some ways, this popular gastropub merits multiple listings, because each of its levels has a different vibe, depending on your mood. Housed in a former speakeasy, Paramount Room offers the friendly American Tavern plus the resurrected Prohibition-era basement lounge.

Check out the beer list when thirsty. It includes Belgian, craft-brewed, domestic, and imported beers, such as the Obamagang, brewed in honor of President Barack Obama's Inauguration. The menu fits the nosh-style kind of eating that takes place at a tavern, such as ale-steamed mussels, onion soup, sandwiches, and decadent desserts that are all several steps above typical bar fare. The website lists daily specials, such as half-off fish and chips and discounted Kobe beef burgers.

The Parthenon

Greek

314 S. Halsted St. (bet. Jackson Blvd. & Van Buren St.)

Phone: 312-726-2407
Web: www.theparthenon.com
Prices:

Lunch & dinner daily
 UIC-Halsted

"Opaa!" From the signature shout, to the crowds, to the decor, to the size of the room, to the well-connected clientele, to the spits with gyros meat roasting in the front windows, this Greek mainstay is stereotypical Greektown. It is loud, bustling, and fun—the kind of place you'd go with a group of co-workers, not for a romantic tête-à-tête.

The menu is large and classic; all the traditional Greek favorites are here. Order the dolmades, tender grape leaves filled with a mixture of onion-scented ground beef and rice, and you'll have enough to share with friends or to munch on for lunch the next day. End the meal with the baklava, which has a lovely infusion of cinnamon in the filling, complemented by the well-browned flaky dough.

Province

C1·2

161 N. Jefferson St. (bet. Lake & Randolph Sts.)

Phone: 312-669-9900
Web: www.provincerestaurant.com
Prices: $$

Lunch Mon – Fri
Dinner Mon – Sat
🚇 Clinton (Green/Pink)

♿
🕐 Take a glance at the menu, playfully divided into categories like "bites" and "bigger," and you might think it relies on gimmicks, but a few tastes prove that a pro is running this show. Fuschia accented walls and tree branches suspended from the ceiling fashion a modern and cool space that looks and feels like a breath of fresh air.

Equally cool, the American cuisine has a unique Spanish/Latin bent and showcases artisanal ingredients from sources like Anson Mills and Gunthorp Farms. Fashion your own feast, building from "small" plates of goat cheese fondue to "big" portions of rabbit confit or even "bigger" entrées like the ten-hour barbecued lamb. Or enjoy the range by sticking to lots of little "bites" like squash and spring onion *taquitos*.

The Publican 🐶

B1

845 W. Fulton Market (bet. Green & Peoria Sts.)

Phone: 312-733-9555
Web: www.thepublicanrestaurant.com
Prices: $$

Lunch Sun
Dinner nightly
🚇 Clinton (Green/Pink)

♿
💺
☝
🕐 This hot spot from Blackbird and Avec was the 2009 see-and-be-seen foodie favorite. From the line outside, to the long bar, to the communal restroom sink, to the Scandinavian-design that is both stylish and very Viking, no detail of the visual experience has been overlooked. Happily, equal attention is paid to the culinary experience.

With a beer sommelier, the global and eclectic list offers 100 varieties of ales, ciders, and beers. The menu is heavy on pork dishes, such as pork rinds and aged ham, but also features a well-prepared chef's selection of terrific freshly shucked oysters, local vegetables with house-made aïoli, and Monterey Bay sardines. The provenance of the ingredients is all-important and duly emphasized on the menu.

Red Light

B2

Asian

820 W. Randolph St. (at Green St.)

Phone: 312-733-8880
Web: www.redlight-chicago.com
Prices: $$

Lunch Mon – Fri
Dinner nightly
Clinton (Green/Pink)

Despite its suggestive name, this Pan-Asian corner location is elegant rather than risqué—its name comes from the large trees that stand sentry outside the restaurant, strung with red lights. Inside, the bold, romantic décor is luxurious and sophisticated, complemented by red leather banquettes, velvet drapes, cherry wood paneling, and impressive service. Skilled Chef Jackie Shen finesses Asian flavors while adding her own brand of quirkiness to many of the dishes. Traditional dishes like Chinese Peking duck and Thai green curry with prawns and coconut rice are offered alongside more updated takes on classics. Expect the likes of Amish chicken apple curry or Asian riffs on European favorites such as paella or Bolognese with spicy ground pork.

Santorini

E3

Greek

800 W. Adams St. (at Halsted St.)

Phone: 312-829-8820
Web: www.santorinichicago.com
Prices:

Lunch & dinner daily
UIC-Halsted

Named for the idyllic Greek island, Chicago's Santorini honors its home country by serving some of the best Greek food this city has to offer. Its charming taverna-style dining room, amiable service, and authentic ambience likewise deserve accolades for being among the most pleasant to be found in Greektown. Whitewashed walls, copper pots, and wood-beamed ceilings define the look, while upbeat Greek music sets a lively tone. Everyone feels like family here—note the groups arriving in droves.

All of the usual classics are on the well-rounded menu, but pay attention to rotating specials, like the hearty lamb *stamnas*, roasted until tender, and tucked with sautéed vegetables inside fluffy crêpes, then blanketed in melted Greek cheeses.

Sawtooth

Vietnamese ✗✗

D2

1350 W. Randolph St. (at Alda St.)

Phone: 312-526-3320
Web: www.sawtoothrestaurant.com
Prices: $$

Lunch & dinner daily
Ashland (Green/Pink)

Hang with the cool kids at Sawtooth. This glassy, ultramodern restaurant opened in late 2010, and has already attracted a loyal following of trendy types who come as much for the scene as they do for the Vietnamese fare. With a space this sexy, it's certainly no wonder. Bright and airy, yet wearing an unmistakable lounge feel (with the requisite beats et al), Sawtooth is comfortably cutting edge.

The contemporary Vietnamese cuisine covers all of the bases. Begin with an appetizer such as sugar cane shrimp, charcuterie, or crispy, spicy Sawtooth wings before tucking into specialties like shaking beef, mushroom-stuffed roasted quail, grilled pork chop, and clay pot catfish. A nice selection of cocktails completes the swanky experience.

Sushi Wabi

Japanese ✗✗

A2

842 W. Randolph St. (bet. Green & Peoria Sts.)

Phone: 312-563-1224
Web: www.sushiwabi.com
Prices: $$$

Lunch Mon – Fri
Dinner nightly
Clinton (Green/Pink)

Others may come and go, but this trendy sushi-ya is still going strong and continues to be a mob scene, especially on weekends. Don't bother trying to wing it—reservations are essential most nights.

Sushi Wabi has that hip warehouse look typical of the West Loop. Loud mod music, attractive black-clad waitresses buzzing about, and a packed crowd make this a definite scene. While the sushi is not authentically Japanese and caters to a more Midwestern palate with its oversized rolls, fried elements, and delicious sauces, it nonetheless succeeds in playing to the crowd. Everyone loves these creative house rolls, which are as fun as they are fantastic, including the dragon roll with tempura shrimp or the fire roll drizzled with spicy *sriracha*.

Sepia ✿

Contemporary 🍴🍴

C2

123 N. Jefferson (bet. Randolph St. & Washington Blvd.)

Phone: 312-441-1920   Lunch Mon – Fri
Web: www.sepiachicago.com   Dinner nightly
Prices: $$ 🚇 Clinton (Green/Pink)

Doug Snower

Housed in an antique print shop, the vibe at this Warehouse District favorite is raw, urban, and sexy in a very current, rustic-industrial sort of way. Think art nouveau tile floors, antiqued mirror panels, raw brick walls and communal tables—all the sorts of things that make you want to drag your out-of-town guest here as soon as they land, slap a cocktail in their hand and say: "I can't wait to show you what's going on in Chicago."

And you'd be smart to start with Sepia, which opened in 2007, for Chef Andrew Zimmerman's modern American cooking makes wide use of local and seasonal products, spinning them into such simple, elegant fare that–when combined with the space's considerable charms–manages to appeal to all types: young, old, artsy, corporate, dates, and groups of friends.

Kick things off with one of the house's delicious flatbreads, like one sporting thick, applewood-smoked bacon, diced Bosc pears, and warm blue cheese; and then move on to golden sea scallops served over soft pillows of gnocchi and crispy, sautéed cabbage in a whole grain mustard sauce; or a juicy, perfectly grilled Berkshire pork chop wrapped in crispy bacon and paired with an apple and arugula salad.

Veerasway

Chicago ▶ West Loop

Indian ✕✕

A2

844 W. Randolph St. (at Peoria St.)

Phone: 312-491-0844
Web: www.veerasway.com
Prices: $$

Dinner Tue – Sun
Clinton (Green/Pink)

Part of co-owner Angela Hepler-Lee's trio of enticing Randolph Street eateries, the talented kitchen of this beloved Indian boutique has a unique way with traditional ingredients. The enchanting name is partly derived from the London-based chef who affected the lighthearted fare that follows at Veerasway.

The dining room wears a fresh and clean aura—pale wood furnishings and mustard walls are a fitting complement to meals that may start off with vibrant chutneys accompanying freshly fried *pappadams*. Market veggie samosas and savory Bollywood lollipops exude just the right spice, and precede tandoor and other delicacies including a vegetarian's delight of *masoor dal*, lentils decked with a confetti of curry leaf and dried red chilis.

Venus

Greek ✕

E3

820 W. Jackson Blvd. (bet. Green & Halsted Sts.)

Phone: 312-714-1001
Web: www.venuschicago.com
Prices: $$

Lunch Sun
Dinner nightly
UIC-Halsted

Take a vacation without breaking out the passport (or the piggy bank) at Venus. From its garden-style setting amid walls outfitted with shuttered windows, to its genial staff, this charming spot is as sunny and bright as a seascape and gives the impression of dining on a patio in the Mediterranean.

Venus dishes up traditional Greek and Cypriot cuisine in a menu that includes a generous listing of cold and hot appetizers; spreads like hummus and *taramasalata*; and *keftedes* (Cypriot meatballs with yogurt). The entrées feature a well-rounded selection of classic salads, grilled meats, chicken, and seafood, but the signature dishes from Crete or Cyprus are highlights, such as *afelia*—cubes of lean pork marinated in red wine and coriander.

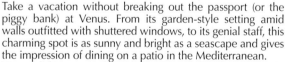

Vivo

Italian

B2

838 W. Randolph St. (bet. Green & Peoria Sts.)

Phone:	312-733-3379	Lunch Mon – Fri
Web:	www.vivo-chicago.com	Dinner nightly
Prices:	$$	Clinton (Green/Pink)

Life is cheery at the congenial Vivo, resting on Randolph Street's restaurant row. This Italian idol's engaging and casual vibe is palpable both outdoors on the patio, and inside the pleasant dining room capped with exposed ductwork and brick walls. Those in the know angle for the most desired table in the restaurant—perched in the converted elevator shaft with fantastic views. Expect well-prepared, rustic Italian cooking here, brought to you by informal yet attentive waiters. Appetizers like *caprese* salad and bruschetta signal the kitchen's dedication to the classics; and entrées like *conchiglie* with spicy chicken sausage, rapini, and tomato; and the fish of the day (ask for it) round out a traditional menu. It's nothing new but tasty all the same.

Look for our symbol ☌,
spotlighting restaurants
with a notable sake list.

Chinatown & South Loop

Chinatown and the South Loop were two neighborhoods that for years didn't have much linking them, besides the north-south running Red Line El. Geographically, they were close, but world's apart in terms of population, architecture, gentrification, and a gastronomic vibe.

Recent development here has allowed for the two to meet in the middle. While, they're still very distinct, both neighborhoods have managed to combine their old and new in ways that should appeal to any gastronome residing in the Windy City.

STROLLING THROUGH SOUTH LOOP

One of Chicago's oldest neighborhoods, the South Loop houses a number of buildings that were spared the Great Chicago Fire. Prairie Avenue, in particular, is a concentration of magnificent homes that were built by some of the wealthiest in the city. Glessner House and Clarke House are particular gems.

Glimpses of all sorts of history can be toured through time-tested churches; Willie Dixon's Blues Heaven Foundation, whose main mission is to preserve the blues legacy; National Vietnam Veterans Art Museum; and other impressive landmarks. In previous incarnations, the South Loop (which begins south of Roosevelt Road) housed Al Capone, Chess Records, and other buzzing industrial spaces. However, in the last 15 years this neighborhood has undergone quite a transformation; and it now includes new condos and shopping, which have helped fuel a rash of fresh restaurants.

Also home to Mayor Richard M. Daley, Columbia College, Museum Campus, and Soldier Field, almost anything (or anyone) can be found in the South Loop.

MAGNIFICENT MUNCHING

Nurse your sweet tooth at **Canady Le Chocolatier Ltd**. Want a glimpse of the way *real* natives eat? Nearby **Manny's Coffee Shop and Deli** is ground zero for local politicians. Pastrami, corned beef, and potato pancakes are solid here, and the speedy staff keeps the line moving. So follow suit, glimpse your pick, and grab it! Come to watch the wheeling and dealing, or just eat a giant pastrami on rye. Either way, you will feel satiated.

South Loop Wine Cellar arranges food and wine pairing classes, private tastings, and has well-stocked shelves. Looking to while away an afternoon? Visit the striking **Three Peas Art Lounge** which is an art gallery, coffee shop, and cupcake bakery united.

PRINTERS ROW

These historical printing lofts were converted into a hotel, condos, and related retail space (such as browse-worthy used bookstores) before the rest of the area was gentrified. Now this multi-block strip is bustling with restaurants, offices, and shops, and a Saturday farmers market June through October.

Just north of the district is the looming Harold Washington Library Center, which serves as a city resource and boasts a beautiful glass-top garden on the ninth floor. On the south end is the landmark Dearborn Station, the oldest remaining train depot in Chicago. It is now a multi-use space for retail, offices, and the like.

CHINATOWN

Chicago is home to the U.S.'s fourth largest Chinatown, with a population of about 15,000 ethnic Chinese, and offers a good combination of original Chinese-American history and contemporary Chinese-American life. At Wentworth Avenue and Cermak Road, you'll find the Chinatown Gate, an ornate, older icon for the neighborhood.

Outdoor mall **Chinatown Square** is the hub for much of the commercial activity; this two-story thrill houses restaurants,

retail spaces, boutiques, and banks. While strolling this neighborhood, don't miss St. Therese Chinese Catholic Church, an edifice that points to the area's pre-Chinatown Italian roots.

FOOD AND CULTURE

Much of the food served in restaurants here is Chinese-American, which is usually an amalgam of Sichuan, Cantonese, and Chinese-American favorites of the Midwest. Crab Rangoon anyone?

STELLAR SWEETS AND SPICY EATS

Locals come here, not just to eat out, but to stock up on a gamut of good eats in order to dine in. **Hong Kong Noodle Factory** is, in fact, a factory, and the place to go for wonton wrappers. **Mayflower Foods** also has one of the largest selections of fresh noodles. **Ten Ren Tea** is lauded for its extensive tea selection and unique tea-making gadgets.

To top off a day of fun feasting, don't forget to quench the adventure with a fresh-baked treat from **Golden Dragon Fortune Cookies**, or sweets from **Aji Ichiban**. Those who need guidance can pick up a cookbook from the Chinese Cultural Bookstore and all the necessary gear at **Woks 'n' Things**. After these ethnic delights, saunter over to U.S. Cellular Field, home of the Chicago White Sox, the rare baseball park that serves veggie dogs and house-made potato chips.

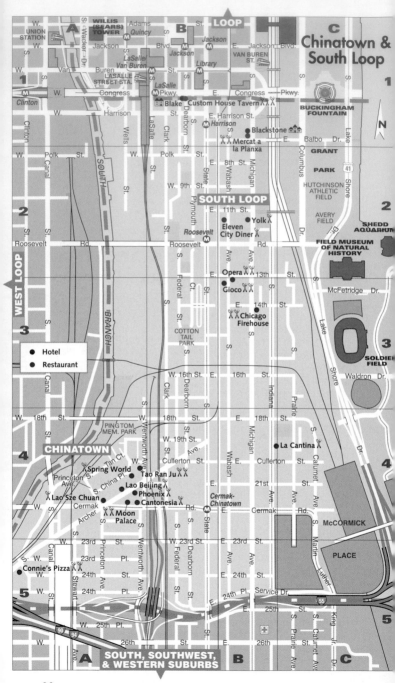

Chinatown & South Loop

SOUTH LOOP

WEST LOOP

CHINATOWN

SOUTH, SOUTHWEST,
& WESTERN SUBURBS

● Hotel
● Restaurant

Cantonesia

A4

Chinese ✕

204 W. Cermak Rd. (at Wentworth Ave.)

Phone: 312-225-0100
Web: www.cantonesia.com
Prices: 💰💰

Lunch & dinner daily
🚇 Cermak-Chinatown

The nondescript exterior of Cantonesia belies a more stylish interior, with dark wood, warm paint, and a brightly-lit back bar. The service is pleasant and efficient.

Dishes are served on enthrallingly-shaped contemporary white place settings. In some cases the plates are more interesting than the dishes themselves, which include a number of westernized Chinese favorites, including hot and sour soup; *kung pao* chicken; and *shiao long bao*, pork-ginger-scallion soup dumplings served in a bamboo steamer. None of these will win awards for creativity or authenticity, but for those who crave such pan-Chinese dishes, Cantonesia does the trick. The kitchen uses quality ingredients, such as fresh bamboo shoots, mushrooms, and handmade dumplings.

Chicago Firehouse

B3

American ✕✕

1401 S. Michigan Ave. (at 14th St.)

Phone: 312-786-1401
Web: www.mainstayhospitality.com
Prices: $$

Lunch Mon – Fri
Dinner nightly
🚇 Roosevelt

The shiny brass fire pole is your first clue (after the restaurant name) that this location was once a working firehouse. Today, the overall vibe is more 1940s sophistication, with cherrywood, leather, subway tiles, and other decorative elements of the era.

But firefighters are known for appreciating a good meal, and here nice work is done on American classics. Sautéed rainbow trout is fresh, moist, and delicate in a lemon-caper *beurre blanc*—its saltiness perfectly complements the natural sweetness of the fish. A classic onion soup arrives complete with melted Gruyere, both nutty and crispy, and caramelized onions in a rich beef broth with a splash of Port. The wedge of creamy raspberry cheesecake with chocolate-crumb crust is a lovely finale.

Connie's Pizza

A5

Pizza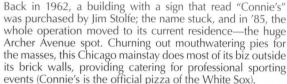

2373 S. Archer Ave. (at Normal Ave.)

Phone: 312-326-3443
Web: www.conniespizza.com
Prices: $$

Lunch & dinner daily
Halsted

Back in 1962, a building with a sign that read "Connie's" was purchased by Jim Stolfe; the name stuck, and in '85, the whole operation moved to its current residence—the huge Archer Avenue spot. Churning out mouthwatering pies for the masses, this Chicago mainstay does most of its biz outside its brick walls, providing catering for professional sporting events (Connie's is the official pizza of the White Sox).

Delish deep dish is a total Chi-town fave. Bursting with fillings of your choice (try the tender Italian sausage), these stuffed pies are sealed with a buttery bread-like crust and topped with garlicky tomato sauce (also available sans sauce). Call ahead to avoid cooking wait times, and pick up your pizza at the drive-through window.

Custom House Tavern

B1

American XXX

500 S. Dearborn St. (at Congress Pkwy.)

Phone: 312-523-0200
Web: www.customhouse.cc
Prices: $$

Lunch & dinner daily
Library

Inside the Hotel Blake, Custom House Tavern seems plucked straight out of California with its floor-to-ceiling windows and natural elements like stacked stone walls, stone floors, and polished wood. It's no surprise that many of the wines featured on the huge chalkboards hail from the Golden State. Everything seems easy, casual, and cool here, making it a perfect fit for both business lunches and intimate dinners alike. Also note the steady stream of hotel guests stopping in for the popular Custom House burger.

Gourmet American fare headlines the menu, which is as effortlessly chic as the setting. Find a nice variety of seafood: perhaps smoked trout treated with spicy oil and radicchio, or roasted Amish chicken with a caramelized chickpea spaetzle.

Eleven City Diner

B2

Deli ✗

1112 S. Wabash Ave. (bet. 11th St. & Roosevelt Rd.)

Phone: 312-212-1112
Web: www.elevencitydiner.com
Prices: ☉☉

Lunch & dinner daily
🚇 Roosevelt

What's old is new again at this reprise of the classic Jewish deli. The candy counter is stocked with sweets of yore, like Bazooka Joe, while another counter tempts with hanging salamis, smoked fish, and cured meats ready to eat or to go.
The extensive menu features ample servings of exactly what should be on a diner menu: big salads, burgers, and thick sandwiches piled high. Many dishes are a twist on the regulars, like the "Shappy" sandwich, which features thick-cut salami grilled and served on challah. The beef and pastrami is served grilled with mozzarella cheese on a French roll, making it clear that this is a Jewish-style deli and not a kosher joint.
Revisit your youth with thick malts, phosphates, and other drinks from the soda jerk.

Gioco

B3

Italian ✗✗

1312 S. Wabash Ave. (bet. 13th & 14th Sts.)

Phone: 312-939-3870
Web: www.gioco-chicago.com
Prices: $$

Lunch Sun – Fri
Dinner nightly
🚇 Roosevelt

From KDK Restaurants (of Opera and Red Light) comes this rustic Italian mainstay featuring a pleasant setting and tantalizing fragrance of a wood-fired pizza oven. Exposed, crumbling brick and arches leading to a second, sunken dining room are reminders that the space dates back to the 1890s.
The traditional menu and open kitchen reveal a taste for Tuscan and Umbrian specialties. Pastas may include fresh spaghetti–with squared off tips and a springy texture that boasts their handmade origins–sauced with chunky tomatoes, chili pepper, and very tender octopus. The menu includes a number of starters, pastas, and heartier entrées like *bistecca alla Fiorentina*. Budget-seekers come for the $10 lunchtime special that includes a soup or salad and an entrée.

La Cantina

B4

Mexican

1911 S. Michigan Ave. (bet. Cullerton & 18th Sts.)

Phone: 312-842-1911
Web: www.lacantinagrill.com
Prices:

Lunch & dinner daily
 Cermak-Chinatown

Whether taking a seat at the bar, snagging a spot on the patio, or dining indoors, the first order of business at La Cantina is to check the chalkboard for the tasty and thirst-quenching margarita menu.

Dark-tiled floors and terra-cotta-hued walls look straight out of Mexico, while the comprehensive menu of Mexican and Tex-Mex favorites is like a love letter to our neighbor to the south. Close your eyes and imagine a Mexican menu and you'll find it all here: burritos, quesadillas, fajitas, nachos, and tacos. Be sure to try a house specialty, like the steak topped with *charro* beans in the Zamora platter, served with a host of outstanding accompaniments. No matter the choice, plates are brimming with flavorful, well-prepared, and delicious food.

Lao Beijing

A4

Chinese

2138 S. Archer Ave. (in Chinatown Sq.)

Phone: 312-881-0168
Web: www.tonygourmetgroup.com
Prices:

Lunch & dinner daily
 Cermak-Chinatown

Just finding the door to this restaurant in the heart of Chinatown Square may work up an appetite. The address brings you to the back delivery entrance—follow the footpath to the opposite side for the front door.

Once inside the red-carpeted den, Lao Beijing offers a rather no-frills space in which to savor a bold and pungent array of Chinese dishes. The ample nine-page menu includes many classics, but the house specials highlighting the cuisine of Beijing separate it from other local restaurants. Dishes are tantalizing, with large pieces of meat or vegetables and distinctive spices, as in the Chengdu chicken made with ginger and fermented black bean paste.

Excellent lunchtime bargains bring in the local Asian business community.

Lao Sze Chuan

A4

Chinese 🍴

2172 S. Archer Ave. (at Princeton Ave.)

Phone: 312 326-5040
Web: www.tonygourmetgroup.com
Prices: $$

Lunch & dinner daily
🚇 Cermak-Chinatown

Inside Chinatown Square, this restaurant has all the hallmarks of success in its large offering of regional specialties made with quality ingredients, but with a little added wallop in the form of chilies. They hang from the ceiling, the walls, decorate the menu, and pack the plates.

Take advantage of Chef/owner Tony Hu's expertise by ordering something offbeat. One unusual option is a cold appetizer, the pig ear Sichuan, served as a terrine, slathered with chili oil, garlic, green hot chilies, and scallions; or lamb seasoned with cumin and more chili oil. A baby octopus dish includes sour pickles that cut the richness of the chili oil, but not the heat. The "hot pot deluxe" is served with flourish and more than 50 items to cook tableside.

Mercat a la Planxa

B1

Spanish 🍴🍴

638 S. Michigan Ave. (at Balbo Ave.)

Phone: 312-765-0524
Web: www.mercatchicago.com
Prices: $$

Lunch & dinner daily
🚇 Harrison

Iron Chef Jose Garces transforms this corner of the Blackstone Hotel, with its view of Grant Park, into a gem of Catalan cuisine with a certain sexy, Barthelonian appeal.

Flavorful, fun, and consistently delicious, these small plates may include the likes of salt cod (*bacalao*) croquettes with a tangy, traditional *Vizcaina* sauce or almond stuffed dates wrapped in bacon. This is a great place to splurge on imported specialty cheeses and sliced-to-order Spanish hams like the spendy *jamón Ibérico de Bellota*. Nowhere else will you find fried chocolate croquettes with *dulce de leche*, olive oil, and toasted marshmallow, so there's no excuse for not trying them here. A tasting menu is available for those who (understandably) want a little bit of everything.

Moon Palace

Chinese

A4

216 W. Cermak Rd. (bet. Princeton & Wentworth Aves.)

Phone: 312-225-4081
Web: www.moonpalacerestaurant.com
Prices: 😊😊

Lunch & dinner daily
🚇 Cermak-Chinatown

More stylish than your average Chinatown restaurant, Moon Palace also boasts particularly friendly, attentive service, and unexpectedly authentic food. Walk into a room of dark wood furnishings and wainscoting juxtaposed with buttery yellow walls, contemporary paintings, and a modern bar.

While the décor is updated, this Chinese menu has not been adjusted to suit the Western palate. The *kung pao* dishes are seriously spicy—tender pieces of chicken are deeply caramelized in a soy-chili oil glaze with peppers, roasted peanuts, and plenty of fried red chilis. Clearly hand-made soup dumplings (*xiao long bao*) filled with ground pork, ginger, scallions, and rich broth add to the charm here. The noodle soups are as delicious as they are authentic.

Opera

Asian

B3

1301 S. Wabash Ave. (at 13th St.)

Phone: 312-461-0161
Web: www.opera-chicago.com
Prices: $$

Lunch Mon – Fri
Dinner nightly
🚇 Roosevelt

Authenticity may not be the goal at this boisterous, contemporary Chinese spot, but the results are decidedly delicious. Housed in a former movie warehouse, the art deco façade and lofty interior is a riot of color that seems to complement its upbeat, group-friendly ambience.

Dishes may include starters of neatly arranged shrimp dumplings with spicy mustard, or heartier entrées like firecracker chicken—large morsels of white meat, chopped spinach, and a generous dose of chili peppers in a fermented bean sauce, arranged around an egg roll filled with mesclun greens. Desserts are likewise a hit, as in the crème brûlée infused with lemongrass. Keep with the festive spirit and indulge in a Pama cosmopolitan, made with pomegranate liqueur.

Phoenix

Chinese 🍴

A4

2131 S. Archer Ave. (bet. Princeton & Wentworth Aves.)

Phone: 312-328-0848
Web: www.chinatownphoenix.com
Prices:

Lunch & dinner daily
🚇 Cermak-Chinatown

Come to Phoenix armed with an appetite and a fun mix of people. This banquet-style dining room in the heart of Chinatown may lack an inspiring décor, and service may be efficient to the point of feeling rushed, but any shortfalls are forgotten over this tasty dim sum.

The requisite carts may be winding their way through the dining room, but a menu complete with photographs documents the made-to-order offerings. Get ready for a smorgasbord of Cantonese classics, from barbecue pork crêpes bursting with smoky and tasty meat; steamed shrimp and cilantro dumplings packed with flavor; melt-in-your-mouth spare ribs; and crispy fried rice balls coated in toasted sesame seeds. The á la carte menu offered in the evening showcases tasty traditional Chinese dishes.

Spring World

Chinese 🍴

A4

2109 South China Pl. (at Wells St.)

Phone: 312-326-9966
Web: N/A
Prices: $$

Lunch & dinner daily
🚇 Cermak-Chinatown

Despite its somewhat contrived appearance, Chicago's Chinatown Square houses some of the city's most authentic restaurants, including Spring World, the neighborhood's go-to spot for Hunanese cuisine.

Tables may begin with the complimentary cabbage appetizer—a sweet, lightly pickled, and wonderfully spicy prelude. The extensive menu is illustrated with photographs to help guide you through a language barrier and find your favorites. Highlights include the Sichuan tea smoked duck, which is marinated and seasoned with peppercorns, five spice, and soy sauce, then served with buns. The tender, crisp-skinned end result is at once a perfect balance of spice, heat, and smoke.

While the restaurant is BYOB, a liquor store is conveniently located next door.

Tao Ran Ju

Chinese ✗✗

2002 S. Wentworth Ave. #103 (bet. Archer Ave. & Cullerton St.)

Phone: 312-808-1111
Web: N/A
Prices: ⊜⊜

Lunch & dinner daily
🚇 Cermak-Chinatown

♿ Don't be confused by the sign in the window for "T Tasty House." There's also a sign reading, "Tao Ran Ju," and the servers sport this on their shirts. But you're not in this Chinatown staple to mince words. You're here to eat.

Good choice, too. The chef is said to have come from Din Tai Fung in Los Angeles, a mecca for those juicy, meaty delights, soup dumplings. These *xiao long bao* are potentially the best in the city, made with delicate wrappers, fragrant pork soup, and well-seasoned ground pork in the center. Accompanied by the traditional vinegar and julienned ginger sauce, it's tough to move beyond these and try anything else on the menu. Some skillful dishes from the kitchen should follow the dumplings; just pass on the hot pots.

Yolk

American ✗

1120 S. Michigan Ave. (bet. 11th St. & Roosevelt Rd.)

Phone: 312-789-9655
Web: www.yolk-online.com
Prices: ⊜⊜

Lunch daily
🚇 Roosevelt

♿ If walking through Grant Park works up your appetite, try Yolk for a solid, budget-friendly breakfast or lunch solution (until 3:00 P.M. daily). This bright and whimsical diner, with its sunny yellow awnings, sits just across from the park, serving up substantial daytime meals as well as carb-loaded desserts. Just about everything on the menu comes in ample portions alongside abundant diced red potatoes and fresh fruit. Favorites may include the "Irish Bennie," a toasted English muffin topped with sautéed tomatoes, grilled corned beef hash, and poached eggs with tangy hollandaise sauce. Nutella fans and newbies alike should order the chocolate-hazelnut nirvana that is a Nutella crêpe, served folded in quarters with powdered sugar, strawberries, or bananas.

Little Italy &
University Village
Pilsen

This cluster of neighborhoods packs a perfect punch, both in terms of food, spice, and sheer energy level. It lives up to every expectation and reputation, so get ready for a tour packed with literal, acoustic, and visual flavor. The Little Italy moniker applies to one stretch of Taylor Street. While it abuts the University (of Illinois at Chicago) Village neighborhood, Little Italy is bigger and more authentically Italian than it first appears. The streets are as stuffed with epicurean shops as an Italian

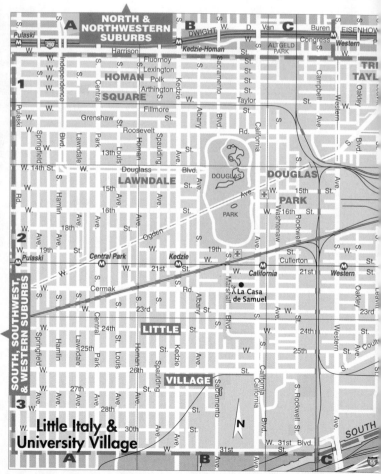

Little Italy &
University Village

beef sandwich is with meat. (Speaking of which, try a prime example of this iconic Chicago sandwich at the aptly named **Al's No. 1 Italian Beef**.)

Start with **Conte Di Savoia**, an Italian grocery and popular take-out lunch counter. In June, folks flock here for the Oakley Festa Pasta Vino festival. Wash this down with a frozen, fruit slush from **Mario's Italian Lemonade**. Lemon is the most popular flavor from the cash-only stand, but offbeat varieties like chocolate and banana are also refreshing. While strolling these vibrant grounds, make sure you glimpse the Christopher Columbus statue, which was originally commissioned for the 1893 World's Columbian Exposition.

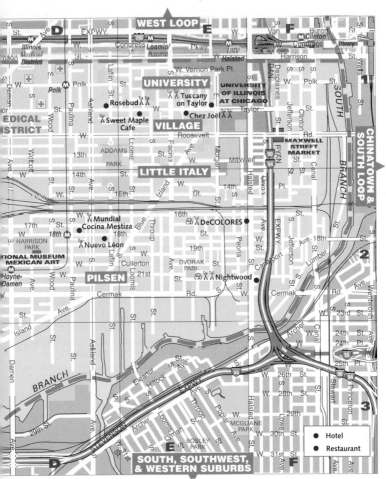

University Village

Like any good college "town," University Village houses a plethora of cozy coffee shops and cafés. A population of doctors, med students, nurses, and others working in the neighborhood hospital contributes to an always-on-the-move vibe. **Lush Wine & Spirits** sells the expected, plus local obsession **Salted Caramel** popcorn, including the bacon bourbon variety.

On Sundays, the destination is the legendary **Maxwell Street Market**. Relocated to Desplaines Street in 2008, the sprawling market welcomes more than 500 vendors selling produce, Mexican street food including tamales and tacos, and non-food miscellanea. Celebrity chef Rick Bayless and others shop here for locally grown tomatoes and tomatillos, while others buy ingredients for at-home culinary creations (not to mention tires, tube socks, and other flea market fare). Maxwell Street Market is also the choice for authentic Mexican eats.

Pilsen and Little Village

Chicago's large Mexican population (more than 500,000 per the last U.S. Census count) has built a patchwork of regional Mexican specialties, many of which are found in the south side's residential Pilsen and Little Village neighborhoods. Pilsen is home to the free National Museum of Mexican Art, the only Latino museum accredited by the American Association of Museums, as well as an abundance of authentic Mexican taquerias, bakeries, and other culturally relevant businesses. Everyone goes all out for Mexican Independence Day in September, including more than 25 participating area restaurants. The Little Village Arts Festival packs 'em in October.

Stop by the **Sabinas Food Products** factory for freshly made tortillas and chips to take home, followed by a trip to the Tuesday farmer's market at the Chicago Community Bank. Much of Pilsen's 26th Street is filled with auto chop shops and other workaday businesses. But the large-scale tortilla factories, where three or four women press and form corn tortillas, are an exception. Since 1950, **El Milagro** has offered a unique taste, with a cafeteria-style restaurant (presenting seven kinds of tamales on the menu), a store that sells burritos, spiced corn chips, maize, and those locally made tortillas. While feasting, don't forget to fix your eyes upon the mural on the wall! Pork lovers (and, well, that's most Chicagoans) can't resist the siren call of **Carnitas Uruapan**. Close to the pink line El, this storefront serves carnitas by the pound, accompanied by corn or flour tortillas and tangy salsas. Massive *chicharrónes*, fried pork skins, are also available for those craving more artery-blocking goodness.

Pilsen's low rents and eclectic vibe have for long now attracted artists and hipsters. They congregate at **Simone's Bar**, a certified green restaurant and place-to-be-seen.

Chez Joël

French 🍴🍴

E1

1119 W. Taylor St. (bet. Aberdeen & May Sts.)

Phone: 312-226-6479
Web: www.chezjoelbistro.com
Prices: $$

Lunch Tue – Fri & Sun
Dinner Tue – Sun

Why go for the expected in Little Italy when you can travel to France and maybe visit Chez Joël? Owned and managed by brothers Joël and Ahmed Kazouini, the utterly charming and authentic French bistro is a refreshing change in this red sauce mecca.

From its petite red brick structure and butter yellow walls to its brick-lined courtyard for breezy outdoor dining, Chez Joël is trés chic. Classic French tunes add to the transporting experience. It also tastes the part; after a few bites of the food you'll definitely feel like you've died and gone to Paris.

Classic bistro dishes deliver hit after hit. Onion soup gratinée, escargots with garlic butter, *steak au poivre*, duck à l'orange—you'll find them all neatly tucked in this traditional menu.

DeCOLORES

Mexican 🍴

E-F2

1626 S. Halsted St. (bet. 16th & 17th Sts.)

Phone: 312-226-9886
Web: N/A
Prices: $$

Dinner nightly

Looking for a side of culture with your main course? DeCOLORES is just the right spot. This art gallery-cum-restaurant feeds your soul and your stomach with its unique blend of culture and cuisine. From the unframed torn canvases lining the walls to the bright and festive skull that rests on the bar, art can be found throughout the space. The dining room's cool ambience is punctuated by ethnic reminders (white skulls and red votive candles).

But it's not just about the art—the kitchen also mixes up masterpieces of nouveau Mexican food. From a creamy and silky scallop and crawfish soup; flaky tilapia dotted with olives and paired with a salad of romaine, apples, walnuts, and cranberries; to a velvety, tart cheesecake flan, the meals here are works of art.

La Casa De Samuel

B2

Mexican

2834 W. Cermak Rd. (bet. California Ave. & Marshall Blvd.)

Phone: 773-376-7474
Web: N/A
Prices: 💰

Lunch & dinner daily
California (Pink)

 This Mexican jewel has been tossing tortillas since 1989, and it's still going strong. Packed with everyone from *familias* to couples, La Casa de Samuel draws them in with dishes piled high displaying tasty treats. From the chunky salsa made with toasted chiles to the crêpes flambé prepared tableside and doused with flaming Cointreau for added drama, everything is good from start to finish.

You can go with the usual suspects (chicken enchilada maybe?) or go all out and try something quirky, like grilled rattlesnake, grilled alligator, or marinated venison. No matter the choice, diners are forever rewarded with juicy, flavorful dishes topped with aromatic sauces. The best part? It won't scorch your wallet to feed your face and leave with a full belly.

Mundial Cocina Mestiza

D2

Mexican

1640 W. 18th St. (bet. Marshfield Ave. & Paulina St.)

Phone: 312-491-9908
Web: www.mundialcocinamestiza.com
Prices: $$

Lunch & dinner Tue – Sun
18th

 In a city with a good offering of creative Mexican cuisine, Mundial distinguishes itself with its unusual and delicious fusion menu. Those who want something beyond the tried and true will appreciate these efforts to combine new flavors and textures.

Start with the *croquetas de coliflor*—lightly battered and fried cauliflower florets served atop melted Asiago cheese. Accompanying the dish are shallots roasted in balsamic vinegar, which add just the right contrast to the richness of the cheese and batter. The *chile en nogada* is a perfectly roasted pepper, blistered skin and all, stuffed with chopped beef and pork, onions, cloves, raisins, almonds, and candied fruit. If the salty-sweet *dulce de leche* cheesecake is on the menu, order it.

Nightwood

Contemporary 🍴🍴

F2

2119 S. Halsted St. (at 21st St.)

Phone: 312-526-3385
Web: www.nightwoodrestaurant.com
Prices: $$

Lunch Sun
Dinner Mon – Sat

This Pilsen luminary hits all the right notes—chic, comfy, and gracious with a skilfully prepared and oft-changing menu that will have diners exclaiming (silently) OMG. The inviting and softly lit room is elevated by a charming patio area; and a counter is cunningly set in front of the rightly run kitchen with a glossy backdrop of black tile and glass block windows.

Nightwood's strictly seasonal ethos is crystallized in a delightful summer salad of vine-ripened melon cubes with whipped goat cheese, sweet corn, and habañeros. Handmade pastas like tasty rigatoni dressed with cherry tomato in a butter pan sauce; and entrées like the semolina-cloaked fried rabbit paired with grilled green beans and sweet and sour plums, are best described as a slam dunk.

Nuevo Léon

Mexican 🍴

D2

1515 W. 18th St. (bet. Ashland Ave. & Laflin St.)

Phone: 312-421-1517
Web: www.nuevoleonrestaurant.com
Prices: 🍜

Lunch & dinner daily
🚇 18th

From the minute your feet step on the clay tiles inside this Mexican eatery, you'll be transported into the ethnic ambience for which Pilsen is known. Take in the artifacts like hand-painted plates and murals on the walls, and Mexican music blasting.

Like any good Mexican joint, this cash-only spot has combination platters on the menu, and they're the best way to get a cross-section of the kitchen's best. The *carne a la Tampiqueña* includes simply-seasoned tender grilled beef, tomato-scented rice, beans, and both a tomatillo-lime salsa verde and smoky red chile salsa, which elevate the taste to something extraordinary. The *horchata* is well-spiced and soups of the day vary by season. Large portion sizes mean leftovers for lunch *mañana*.

Rosebud

D1

1500 W. Taylor St. (at Laflin St.)

Phone: 312-942-1117
Web: www.rosebudrestaurants.com
Prices: $$

Lunch & dinner daily
Polk

It's the original, baby. This is where the Rosebud empire started in the late 1970s. Named for the flower of Sicily, it's the kind of place where wise guys and regular Joes loosen up over heaping plates of pasta. Sinatra is on the stereo and autographed photos of celebrities line the walls. It's a bit cliché, but Rosebud revels in it.

Add a vowel to your last name and leave your carb-hating friends at home. The fresh bread arrives right away, but save plenty of room because this place pours it on. Portions are enormous—even the sausage and peppers appetizer arrives oversized. Tasty and well-priced entrées include classics, like rigatoni alla vodka, veal *braciola*, and chicken Vesuvio. Sweet tooths should save room for tiramisu or spumoni.

Sweet Maple Cafe

E1

1339 W. Taylor St. (bet. Loomis St. & Racine Ave.)

Phone: 312-243-8908
Web: www.sweetmaplecafe.com
Prices: ⊖⊖

Lunch daily
Racine

You know that neighborhood breakfast spot where locals grab a cup of coffee *en route* to tide them over while they stand in line outside waiting for a table? In Little Italy, southern-style Sweet Maple Cafe is definitely that place, with a smidge of Southern charm and hospitality mixed in.

Regulars love the large, fluffy pancakes (with honey, applesauce, butter, and syrup); scrambled eggs served with flavorful country-style pork sausage patties; and, requisite at any place that calls itself "southern," those flaky biscuits and buttery grits. Sweet Maple Cafe also serves lunch, but breakfast is served through the lunch hour, and with the omelets, home fries, plus the rest of the breakfast treats, why would you even order lunch?

Tuscany on Taylor

Italian 𝕏𝕏

E1

1011 W. Taylor St. (bet. Miller & Morgan Sts.)

Phone: 312-829-1990
Web: www.tuscanychicago.com
Prices: $$

Lunch Mon – Fri
Dinner nightly

It's easy to fall in love with Tuscany on Taylor. This cushy jewel in the heart of Chicago's Little Italy shares its Italian spirit and warmth with all who enter.

The dining room has an inviting, mood-lifting appeal with cheerful blue-and-white checkered tablecloths, wood floors, and an expansive kitchen. Formally dressed servers anticipate your every need, but after a few bites of Tuscany's homemade pastas, gourmet wood fired pizzas, and tender veal, you won't be wanting for much. Pastas can be light (topped with fresh tomatoes) or hearty (topped with Bolognese sauce); while entrées like grilled NY strip steak, roasted chicken, veal medallions with Gorgonzola sauce, and sausage and peppers are guaranteed to leave you feeling stuffed and comforted.

Remember, stars
(❀❀❀...❀) are awarded
for cuisine only! Elements
such as service and décor
are not a factor.

Gold Coast

GLITZ AND GLAMOUR

What's in a name? When it comes to the Gold Coast, the name says it all. After all, this posh neighborhood is Chicago's wealthiest and most affluent. From the swanky high-rises dotting Lake Shore Drive, to the glittering boutiques of Michigan Avenue, the Gold Coast is luxury defined.

Whoever said money can't buy happiness certainly hadn't strolled through The Magnificent Mile, because this strip presents a serious challenge to that adage. This stretch of shopping where millionaires mingle over Manolos and heiresses hunt for handbags, is one of the world's best and most well-known.

Oak Street, with boutiques from Barneys to Yves Saint Laurent, runs a close second. If in the market for new wheels, take your pick from billionaire boy toys like Bentleys and Bugattis, which both have dealerships here.

HISTORICAL HOMES

It's not just about the glitz and glamour, though. This neighborhood, listed on the National Register of Historic Places, is the perfect paradise for architecture buffs. The mansions and buildings crafted in regal Queen Anne, Georgian Revival, and Richardsonian Romanesque styles are breathtaking.

They're all glorious to simply see, even if you're not in the market for a new home.

APPLAUDING THE ARTS

The glorious Gold Coast takes its history quite seriously, and following this philosophy, area residents host a series of annual events, including the block party extraordinaire, Evening on Astor. This immense event also helps raise money and awareness for preservation. It is home to the Museum of Contemporary Art and the Newberry Library, one of the world's leading research libraries, so it should be no surprise that the neighborhood celebrates the arts in a big way.

The annual Gold Coast River North Art Fair is a must-see celebration of art, music, culture, and food. Whether you're an artist or have constantly dreamed of being one, this is a don't-miss celebration of the visual arts. Culture vultures should rest assured as they are bound to find something edgy and unique at A Red Orchid Theater. Here, an ensemble of artists perform a variety of stunning shows throughout the year.

BOISTEROUS NIGHTS ABOUT TOWN

Just because the Gold Coast is sophisticated doesn't mean this area doesn't know how to party.

Visit any of the pubs, clubs, and restaurants along Rush and Division streets to get a sense of how the other half lives it up. Cold winter winds got you down? Pull up a stool at the kitschy-chic tiki bar at **Trader Vic's**. Enjoy a culinary tour of American classics touched with Asian accents. Your tongue will tingle with such whimsical dishes as barbecue spareribs; Malaysian chicken skewers; and Hawaiian ahi *poke*. Locals and patrons flock here for Trader Vic's juicy medley of cocktails, making this a perfect spot for a rockin' night out.

For a rootin'-tootin' good time, stop by the **Underground Wonder Bar**, where live jazz tunes have been played nightly until the wee hours for over two decades.

FRESH AND FINE FAST FOOD

This stylish neighborhood is a capital of white-glove restaurants, but don't think that means there isn't good junk food available here as well. **Mr. Kite's Candies & Nuts** will have you flying on a sugar high with its tempting array of goodies such as chocolate-covered smores, chocolate-dipped strawberries, ice cream, and delicious caramel apples.

Get your fill of gefilte while keeping kosher at no-frills **Ashkenaz Deli**. Other delicacies include belly lox, smoked sable, and smoked white fish. It's been here since the 1970s and certainly isn't fancy, but it's just the spot for bagels with lox.

DOG DELIGHTS

Up for a double dog dare or merely a hot dog fanatic? Stop by **Gold Coast Dogs** for one or several of its char dogs. These are made even better and more decadent when topped with gooey cheddar cheese. Speaking of crowning hot dogs, famed **Downtown Dogs** carries an equally savory spectrum of traditional treats. Regulars, tourists, et al gather here for char-grilled dogs, scrumptious street eats, and hamburgers galore.

Need to calm and come down from the hot dog high? Duck into **TeaGschwender**, a lovely boutique where you can lose yourself in the world of exotic teas. Don't feel like steeping it on your own? Snag a seat at **Argo Tea**. From hot tea drinks topped with whipped cream, to iced drinks full of flavor, it's like Starbucks without the coffee.

FIND HEAVEN ON EARTH

It is said that God is in the details, and this is most definitely apparent at the famed **Goddess & Grocer**, a neighborhood gourmet store where you can stock up on foods like soups, salads, chillis, gourmet cupcakes, and other delightful desserts just like Mom would make. Homemade in a haute kind of way, it's cupcakes, cheeses, and chocolates galore. To add to the glory, they also cater, so you can pretend like you made those divine and delicate hors d'oevres at the baby's christening all on your own.

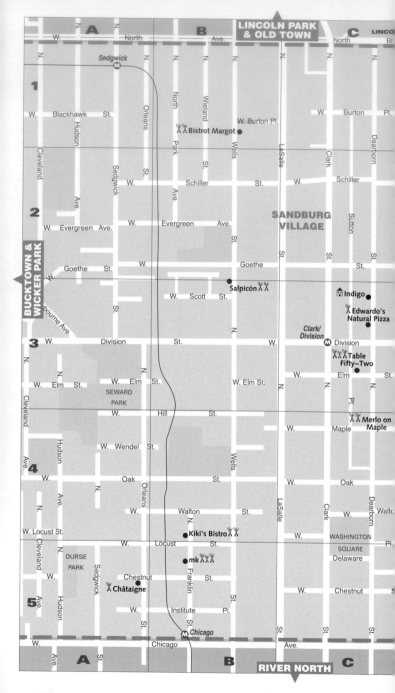

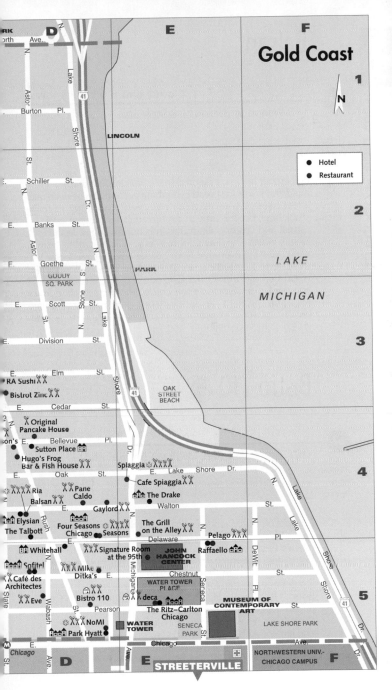

Gold Coast

N

● Hotel
● Restaurant

LAKE

MICHIGAN

orth Ave.

Lake Shore Dr.

41

Astor St.

Burton Pl.

LINCOLN

Schiller St.

Banks St.

Goethe St.

GOUDY SQ. PARK

E. Scott St.

Stone St.

Lake Shore Dr.

E. Division St.

E. Elm St.

RA Sushi

Bistrot Zinc

E. Cedar St.

41

OAK STREET BEACH

Original Pancake House

Bellevue Pl.

son's E.

Sutton Place

Hugo's Frog Bar & Fish House

Spiaggia

E. Oak St.

Cafe Spiaggia

E. Lake Shore Dr.

Ria

Pane Caldo

The Drake

Balsan

E. Gaylord

Walton St.

N. Lake Shore Dr.

Elysian

The Talbott

Four Seasons Chicago

Seasons

The Grill on the Alley

Pelago

Whitehall

Signature Room at the 95th

JOHN HANCOCK CENTER

Raffaello

Delaware Pl.

DeWitt Pl.

Sofitel

Mike Ditka's

Chestnut St.

WATER TOWER PLACE

Café des Architectes

Eve

Bistro 110

deca

MUSEUM OF CONTEMPORARY ART

LAKE SHORE PARK

Pearson

The Ritz–Carlton Chicago

Wabash Ave.

NoMI

WATER TOWER

SENECA PARK

State St.

Park Hyatt

E. Chicago

Chicago Ave.

NORTHWESTERN UNIV.– CHICAGO CAMPUS

STREETERVILLE

D   E   F

Balsan

D4

Contemporary ❌❌

11 E. Walton St. (bet. Rush & State Sts.)

Phone: 312-646-1400
Web: www.balsanrestaurant.com
Prices: $$

Lunch & dinner daily
🚇 Chicago (Red)

Remember how you savored snack time in kindergarten? How much fun it was to spread everything out and maybe even take a few bites of your neighbor's crackers? Get ready to relive snack time, but this time in a more adult and elegant way.

Casual and cosmopolitan Balsan is burrowed inside the chic Elysian Hotel. The dining room is as sexy as its sizzling crowd, encompassing everyone from hotel guests to gazetteers. The menu pivots around small plates, raw bar selections, and wood-fired dishes. It's the kind of place where you may find one person noshing on tuna *crudo*, another sampling frog's legs, and the third devouring ricotta *gnudi*. Prefer a square meal? Opt for a wood-fired pizza, roast chicken, or even grilled salmon or halibut.

Bistro 110

D5

French ❌❌

110 E. Pearson St. (bet. Michigan Ave. & Rush St.)

Phone: 312-266-3110
Web: www.bistro110restaurant.com
Prices: $$

Lunch & dinner daily
🚇 Chicago (Red)

It's right off the Magnificent Mile, but there's nothing touristy about Bistro 110. This cozy restaurant is no flash in the pan; they've been at it for two decades. The look is pure French bistro, with colorful paintings and a long bar, but the attentive service is far from the icy cliché. The warm, inviting ambience is a perfect antidote for a blustery Chicago day.

Bistro 110's menu highlights unfussy, authentic, and well-priced French country classics such as quiche Lorraine, steak frites, roast chicken, and lunchtime prix-fixe menus. The kitchen knows what works, so don't expect trendy. The signature appetizer, a whole artichoke stuffed with melted Brie and served with a rich *pommery* mustard sauce, has been on the menu since 1987 for good reason.

Bistrot Margot

French ✗✗

B1

1437 N. Wells St. (at Burton Pl.)

Phone: 312-587-3660
Web: www.bistrotmargot.com
Prices: $$

Lunch & dinner daily
🚇 Sedgwick

Maybe it's the exposed brick walls and the intimate bistro tables spilling onto the sidewalk, or the feeling that comes from a place named after the Chef/owner's daughter, but there's something particularly charming about Bistrot Margot.

This group-friendly, Old Town spot simply offers amiable service and reasonable prices for quality food. Special promotions are abundant, from half-price wines to $10 lunch and dinner specials. While the menu focuses on French standards like duck confit and steak frites, it caters to the Chicago palate with tasty interpretations. Highlights may include the silky fennel and carrot soup or *pomme de terre farci,* a potato shell stuffed with scrambled eggs, cheese, and bacon topped with horseradish crème fraîche.

Bistrot Zinc

French ✗✗

D3

1131 N. State St. (bet. Elm & Cedar Sts.)

Phone: 312-337-1131
Web: www.bistrotzinc.com
Prices: $$

Lunch & dinner daily
🚇 Clark/Division

Tin ceilings, mosaic tiled floors, peppy yellow walls with framed French posters—it's a whiff of Paris in the heart of the Gold Coast. Bistrot Zinc, named for its handcrafted zinc bar, has that lovable neighborhood restaurant thing down pat. From its décor to its delicacies, it's all very classic French bistro. Even the top-shelf staff (sporting bow ties and rolled up sleeves) smell of charm. Just subtract the fussy accents and frosty demeanors and you're smack dab in the middle of Paris. Flavorful French comfort food is the house specialty: *croque monsieur,* steak frites, French onion soup, and omelets. The compositions are unfussy, but it's exactly what you wanted. Plus, you can still save some pennies for your piggy bank after a meal here.

Café des Architectes

D5

20 E. Chestnut St. (at Wabash St.)

Phone: 312-324-4063
Web: www.cafedesarchitectes.com
Prices: $$$

Lunch & dinner daily
🚇 Chicago (Red)

Nestled into the lobby of the sleek Sofitel Chicago Water Tower, Café des Architectes is a mod brasserie with a stunning interior showing eye-popping Crayola brights, black-and-white photos, zebra-striped vases, and chairs wrapped in midnight blue velvet.

Chef Martial Nougier spins Mediterranean, Asian, and Latin influences into a classic French menu that may kick off with melt-in-your-mouth suckling pig with sautéed broccolini and a lemon-honey reduction; before moving on to a well-charred walleye pike matched with Manila clams, *flageolet* beans, and a pitch-perfect basil purée. An international wine list displays a French bent (*naturellement*), but cocktail hounds would do well to visit the sexy Le Bar, only steps away from the restaurant's entrance.

Cafe Spiaggia

E4

980 N. Michigan Ave. (at Oak St.)

Phone: 312-280-2750
Web: www.cafespiaggia.com
Prices: $$

Lunch & dinner daily
🚇 Chicago (Red)

Located just across the hall from upscale sister Spiaggia, Cafe Spiaggia is the less formal youngling, and like many offspring, oft-overlooked. It makes little sense given the regular-heavy suit crowd spread amidst the bar and dining areas.

The menu here isn't exactly that of a cafe, filled with elegant *cicchetti, formaggi, insalati, paste, classici,* and *al forno* all made with quality ingredients, trained technique, and an appreciation of Italian cuisine. Dishes aren't particularly memorable but seafood sausage stuffed calamari with cherry tomatoes, basil, and breadcrumbs; and red currant panna cotta have diners smitten.

A recent renovation brought a pleasant update to the décor of Cafe Spiaggia's rooms.

Châtaigne

Contemporary ✗

A5

361 W. Chestnut St. (at Orleans St.)

Phone: 312-873-2032
Web: www.chefs.edu/Chicago/Restaurant
Prices: ⊜⊜

Lunch & dinner Mon – Fri
🚇 Chicago (Brown)

 ♿ Named for the majestic tree standing at the entrance of its school, Châtaigne (French for chestnut) is the student-run dining room for Chicago's outpost of Le Cordon Bleu. From the hostess stand to the large kitchen, visible through louvered windows and fully staffed by students and instructors, this pleasant, light-filled classroom is also a restaurant where good food can be had for a great price.

The contemporary menu is divided into categories that begin with "snacks" like house-made pickles or *migas*—a tasty bowlful of bread cubes, lardoons, pork belly, and dates all slicked with *romesco* sauce. Plates and portions go on to range from small–pheasant sausages and daily fritters–to larger entrées of house-cured double pork chops.

deca

Contemporary ✗✗

E5

160 E. Pearson St. (at Water Tower Place)

Phone: 312 573 5160
Web: www.decarestaurant.com
Prices: $$

Lunch & dinner daily
🚇 Chicago (Red)

 ♿ This is surely not what you'd expect of the sole dining option in the Ritz-Carlton. With an open layout on the 12th floor, deca intentionally feels more like a lobby bar than a dining room. The new concept was designed to attract a younger crowd that might typically hang at the Ritz.

The menu offers surprisingly good value with a smaller choice at lunch and more expansive menu at dinner. Food can be a bit inconsistent but the kitchen offers some seriously solid options. Try classic, creamy quiche Lorraine, with a perfectly browned top; or a chicken breast with juicy interior and crispy exterior, paired with rich corn and pristine artichoke hearts. Michigan cherry clafouti (seasonal) is a lovely blend of local product and classic French technique.

Edwardo's Natural Pizza

C3

Pizza

1212 N. Dearborn St. (bet. Division & Goethe Sts.)

Phone: 312-337-4490
Web: www.edwardos.com
Prices: $$

Lunch & dinner daily
Clark/Division

This small Gold Coast outpost is just one of many popular pizza chains that reside in the city and suburbs. A classic kid-friendly pizza joint, Edwardo's does a brisk to-go business, and ships nationwide, should you develop a Chicago-style pizza addiction while in town.

Side dishes such as Buffalo chicken wings are moist and tasty served with the requisite blue cheese and celery. But the real reason to head to Edwardo's is the pizza, and smart diners save room for the hefty stuffed pies, with a flaky pastry crust, gooey cheese, and ample servings of tomato sauce. The spinach soufflé pizza is a healthy favorite ; and deep-dishes take at least 45 minutes to bake, so plan accordingly. Lunch combos are friendly on the wallet, but not the waistline.

Eve

D5

Contemporary

840 N. Wabash Ave. (bet. Chestnut & Pearson Sts.)

Phone: 312-266-3383
Web: www.evechicago.com
Prices: $$

Lunch Tue – Sun
Dinner nightly
Chicago (Red)

This sleek, contemporary getaway (think: white leather tablecloths) near Michigan Avenue offers a modern, minimalist experience. The quiet, unassuming staff is professional, but the kitchen speed assures your meal will have a leisurely pace. The kitchen spices up a traditional menu with offbeat, global ingredient combinations, such as steamed mussels with kimchi broth and the steak and eggs with kimchi, and lobster bisque with vanilla. Portions, like the roasted walleye entrée are large, and served with hearty garnishes like fingerling potatoes. Even the whole grain baguette is a slight twist. Pastry shells are cooked to just the right shade of brown.

Local favorite brew Goose Island and the brunch-time bottomless mimosas pack people in on the weekends.

Gaylord

D4

I n d i a n ✕✕

100 E. Walton St. (bet. Michigan Ave. & Rush St.)

Phone: 312-664-1700
Web: www.gaylordil.com
Prices: $$

Lunch & dinner daily
🔲 Chicago (Red)

Offering both Northern and Southern Indian cuisine, Gaylord draws a loyal following for its popular, budget-friendly lunchtime buffet, conveniently located in a spacious subterranean dining room beneath the primo shopping lining Walton Street.

The enormous menu is also vegetarian-friendly, with plenty of *dosas*, *shorbas*, biriyani; as well as other classic options like the peppery chicken *vindaloo* with creamy *raita*, and freshly baked *roti*. The service staff is warm and efficient, but the kitchen can (at times) be inconsistent, so be forewarned. Some dishes are terrific while others a bit off. Complementary *papadams*, chutneys, carrots, and cucumber sticks kick start appetites, and a mango *lassi* nicely cools any burns from the spicy curries.

Gibson's

D4

S t e a k h o u s e ✕✕

1028 N. Rush St. (at Bellevue Pl.)

Phone: 312-266-8999
Web: www.gibsonssteakhouse.com
Prices: $$$

Lunch & dinner daily
🔲 Clark/Division

There is no better paean to old-school masculinity than Gibson's. Located in the heart of what some call "the Viagra Triangle," this is where new bodies and old money, often in the form of expense accounts, get together to schmooze, eat, and drink amid dark tables and large portions.

Evoking a sense of the Old World, autographed photos of celebs who have dined here line the walls; and servers in white jackets deliver what is expected: robust faithfuls like giant steaks (from filets to Porterhouse) cooked to order, with classic sides like sautéed spinach, broccoli, and French fries. Also sating appetites are iceberg wedges cradling creamy lobster and ample desserts. Don't feel like excess? A medley of half-order sizes will keep you light and lilting.

The Grill on the Alley

E4

American ✗✗

909 N. Michigan Ave. (at Delaware Pl.)

Phone: 312-255-9009
Web: www.thegrill.com
Prices: $$$

Lunch & dinner daily
Chicago (Red)

Don't dismiss The Grill on the Alley simply because it's part of a multi-state chain. This Chicago outpost brings the best of classic American food in a classic American setting of framed sketches, wood-paneled walls, leather booths, bar, and dining room with a flair for nostalgia. However, its professional service, elegant style, and consistent food are what brings it all to life.

Tucked inside the Westin Hotel in the heart of the Gold Coast, The Grill functions as a high-end cafeteria for the area's power brokers. Here, deals are done over generous portions of familiar American cuisine, such as cobb salad; Manhattan clam chowder; or even chicken Parmigiana, tender and moist, served over a bed of angel hair pasta in a garlicky marinara sauce.

Hugo's Frog Bar & Fish House

D4

American ✗✗

1024 N. Rush St. (bet. Bellevue Pl. & Oak St.)

Phone: 312-640-0999
Web: www.hugosfrogbar.com
Prices: $$

Lunch Sat – Sun
Dinner nightly
Clark/Division

Housed in a sprawling setting adjacent to big brother Gibson's, Hugo's always seems packed. The vast dining room sets white linen-topped tables amidst dark polished wood and pale walls decorated with mounted swordfish, fish prints, and model ships: Hugo's bar draws its own crowds with abundant counter seating.

The menu focuses on a selection of fish preparations as well as steaks and chops. These are supplemented by stone crab claws, oysters, crab cakes, chowders, and sautéed frog's legs. Speaking of frog's legs, the restaurant takes its name from the nickname of owner Hugo Ralli's grandfather, General Bruce Hay of Her Majesty's Imperial Forces.

Bring a football team to share a slice of the Muddy Bottom Pie, a decadent (and enormous) ice cream cake.

Kiki's Bistro

French ✗✗

B4

900 N. Franklin St. (at Locust St.)

Phone: 312-335-5454
Web: www.kikisbistro.com
Prices: $$

Lunch Mon – Fri
Dinner Mon – Sat
Chicago (Brown)

This French cuisine mainstay has been attracting locals and tourists long before the new condos and other construction cropped up. Regulars and newcomers are warmly greeted into the dining room, decorated with candles, fresh flowers, natural light, and rustic wood beams.
The kitchen turns out solid, classic French fare. The French onion soup uses good-quality Gruyère cheese, which is glistening and charred on top. Showing off the chef's skill is the texture of the duck confit with Puy lentils—the meat just falls off the bone and is accompanied by a generous serving of the rustic lentils. Also rich and silky is a lime mousse cake with crème anglaise. Owner Kiki himself was once the sommelier at Maxim's of Chicago, so wines are well-paired, although not particularly unusual.

Merlo on Maple

Italian ✗✗

C4

16 W. Maple St. (bet. Dearborn & State Sts.)

Phone: 312-335-8200
Web: www.merlochicago.com
Prices: $$$

Dinner nightly
Clark/Division

This ristorante houses myriad floors, but no matter where you sit, this multi-level beauty boasts Victorian touches (hand-carved banisters and leather banquettes), and an informed waitstaff, who deliver the tastes of Emilia Romagna. Of course, if here on a date, land at the lower level, which–albeit a few feet below–is *the* most romantic space.
Red sauce isn't exactly their signature, but the amiable kitchen is happy to please a lady. So if you crave the typical tomato sauce, order away. The homemade pastas are lovely, but dishes like *stricchetti verdi* tossed with rabbit ragù; or the *imprigionata alla Petroniana* use top-notch ingredients from Italy's culinary epicenter and are definitely their more unique items.

Mike Ditka's

D5

American 🍴🍴🍴

100 E. Chestnut St. (at Rush St.)

Phone: 312-587-8989
Web: www.mikeditkaschicago.com
Prices: $$

Lunch & dinner daily
🚇 Chicago (Red)

Chicago sports legends have a way of becoming restaurateurs at some point, and former Bears coach Mike Ditka is no exception.

However, what is an exception is that locals come here not just because of his 1985 Super Bowl win, but because the food is actually quite good (though lighter appetites might be encouraged to man up). Come very hungry and start with plump Cajun fried shrimp laced with hot sauce. Then, move on to the insurmountable meatloaf stack—layered with jalapeño corn bread, meatloaf, mashed potatoes, and fried onion straws. Doggy bags are de rigueur here, but do try to save room for some banana cream pie.

The space is masculine, comfortable, and lined with sports memorabilia—souvenirs are available for purchase on your way out.

mk

B5

Contemporary 🍴🍴🍴

868 N. Franklin St. (bet. Chestnut & Locust Sts.)

Phone: 312-482-9179
Web: www.mkchicago.com
Prices: $$$

Dinner nightly
🚇 Chicago (Brown)

Chef/owner Michael Kornick delivers a solid performance at mk. After all, those are his initials on the door. Housed in an erstwhile paint factory, mk lead the gastronomic gentrification of the previously gritty, industrial North Side.

From the high ceilinged, three-level space to the raw wood beams and exposed brick walls dripping in contemporary art, mk has perfected the warehouse revival demeanor. Further, it makes a big splash with its creative and updated American menu. Grilled octopus, roast venison, slow-cooked rabbit, and homemade pasta dishes are what hook the hipster scene, split between singles and couples fleeing their kids for the night. Blithely named desserts (two bananas walk into a bar, a pumpkin named Pierre) are simply delicious.

NoMI ✿

Contemporary XXX

D5

800 N. Michigan Ave. (entrance on Chicago Ave.)

Phone: 312 239-4030
Web: www.nomirestaurant.com
Prices: $$$$

Lunch & dinner daily
🚇 Chicago (Red)

♿
🛏
🔥
🍷
🍸
🗝

Park Hyatt Chicago

On the seventh floor of the posh Park Hyatt, NoMI is as chic as they come. The look is as modern and stylish as one of the showstoppers in much-feted designer Tony Chi's portfolio. The flirty dining room wows diners at every turn, and feels rather like the private home of a fashionable art collector.

In fact, there are a number of pieces prominently displayed in this stunning arena, but it is the Dale Chihuly blown glass creation, that demands particular attention. Other knockouts include NoMI's jaw-dropping views of the Water Tower, area skyscrapers, and Lake Michigan.

If people-watching and daydreaming aren't enough, the contemporary French cuisine provides a delightful diversion. The seafood-heavy menu features Maine lobster with Madras curry; salmon with chorizo; and caramelized Diver scallops with split pea purée. And if that doesn't do it, resort to baby *poussin* arranged on a plate and draped with a creamy, dark brown crawfish sauce. No matter the selection, you can take pride in knowing that NoMI is committed to delivering the freshest and best ingredients. From Illinois' small-town farms to Italy's tiny hamlets, NoMI travels the world for its globally influenced fare.

Original Pancake House

American

 D4

22 E. Bellevue Pl. (bet. Michigan Ave. & Rush St.)

Phone: 312-642-7917
Web: www.originalpancakehouse.com
Prices:

Lunch daily
Clark/Division

Disputes run rampant about whether or not this little house is the original location of the Original Pancake House. Maybe not, but it is something to think about while you wait in the inevitable weekend lines.

This is an all-day breakfast joint and people flock here for the warm service, easy setting, and, of course, the pancakes. The Dutch baby is a decadent oven-based treat, with whipped butter, lemon, and powdered sugar that will have you rolling out in a short-term sugar high. The skillets are big enough to serve a hungry Viking, and egg plates come with pancakes instead of toast, if you prefer (go for it). In addition to classic staples, the menu includes more sides like turkey sausage or chicken hash…to go with, of course, more pancakes.

Pane Caldo

D4

Italian

72 E. Walton St. (bet. Michigan Ave. & Rush St.)

Phone: 312-649-0055
Web: www.pane-caldo.com
Prices: $$

Lunch & dinner daily
Chicago (Red)

Shop until you almost drop and then head straight for Pane Caldo. This intimate Northern Italian restaurant is just across the street from Bloomingdale's, but it feels light years away from the flurry and hubbub of nearby Michigan Avenue. The wood floors, mustard yellow walls, and tables dressed in crisp linens are the very essence of smart casual, as is the good looking crowd that frequents this spot.

The staff, dressed in white aprons and black bow ties, is old-school Italian and you might even elicit a groan or two when placing an order. But don't let the gruff waiters detract from what's ahead: simple and straightforward principles guide the kitchen, turning out pizzas (at lunch), homemade pastas, osso buco, and risotto.

Pelago

E5

Italian

201 E. Delaware Pl. (at Seneca St.)

Phone: 312-280-0700
Web: www.pelagorestaurant.com
Prices: $$$

Lunch & dinner daily
🚇 Chicago (Red)

You don't need to be a guest at the Raffaello Hotel to dine at its signature restaurant, Pelago. But, after a hearty Italian meal at this über-chic respite, you just might crave a quick ride to a comfy bed. This is definitely not your grandfather's Italian haunt, so come shod in your best Ferragamos to see-and-be-seen. The striking white and aqua interior is offset by contemporary artwork, but it's the diamonds and duds sported by the fashionable crowd that really sparkle.

Like the scene, the food is upscale and of the moment. Northern and Southern Italian favorites are trumped up with extra oomph (think monkfish osso buco), while *amanti di pasta* will find plenty to twist and tangle with on the á la carte or four- and six-course prix-fixe menus.

RA Sushi

D3

Japanese

1139 N. State St. (at Elm St.)

Phone: 312-274-0011
Web: www.rasushi.com
Prices: $$

Lunch & dinner daily
🚇 Clark/Division

From the same people that brought you the razzle-dazzle knife throwing, food flipping chefs of Benihana, comes RA Sushi. This location–one of three in Chicago–belongs to a nationwide chain of fun, upbeat, and neoteric sushi joints that are part nightclub, part restaurant.

The chefs behind the sushi bar may not be Japanese, but rest assured because the stuff here is really quite good. It's whimsical and casual food—you'll even find funky versions of chips and salsa (spicy tuna tartare alongside wonton chips); and delicate creations like RA-ckin' shrimp served with creamy ginger teriyaki sauce. The rice crispy treats served here are certainly no Kellogg's invention; instead, they are soy paper hand rolls filled with crunchy rice balls and fiery tuna.

Ria ✿✿

Contemporary ✕✕✕✕

D4

11 E. Walton St. (bet. Rush & State Sts.)

Phone: 312-880-4400
Web: www.riarestaurantchicago.com
Prices: $$$

Dinner Tue – Sat
Chicago (Red)

Elysian Hotel

It shouldn't be surprising really that Ria is one of Chicago's most sophisticated dining rooms. After all, it's camouflaged inside the impossibly chic, sexy, and striking Elysian Hotel. What's so shocking about that you ask? The food. This seductive restaurant is anything but a flash in the pan—Ria delivers substance behind all of its sleek style.

The dining room channels an extravagant European feel with shimmering fabrics, leather armchairs, silk-covered pillows, and vivid modern art displays. It is at once refined and restful; and the service is polished and professional without being starched.

From start (a rolling cart of sparkling wines) to finish (rich, flavorful desserts), the experience is ridiculously first rate. There must be some serious OCD behind the scenes—the dishes are meticulously prepared and presented. Plated as if they jumped out from the cover of a food magazine, the selections are elegant and satisfying. Expect explosive flavors from mussel velouté; king salmon with pickled radishes and rye-caraway chips; and king crab-filled leek rolls. Baffled between the guinea hen and *daurade*? Take the plunge and go all out with the six-course chef's tasting menu.

Salpicón

Mexican ✗✗

1252 N. Wells St. (bet. Division & Goethe Sts.)

Phone: 312-988-7811
Web: www.salpicon.com
Prices: $$

Lunch Sun
Dinner nightly
Clark/Division

Sure Bayless may get all the play these days but Priscila Satkoff is the unsung hero of contemporary Mexican cuisine in this town. A native of Mexico City, Priscila and her husband Vincent opened Salpicón in 1995. The colorful décor and lively Mexican soundtrack lend a warm yet elegant vibe to the dining room; and though dinner is always popular, brunch is a worthy affair.

Dishes like the *chiles rellenos* are prepared perfectly, just as you'd find them in Mexico. *Tostaditas de tinga* are a flavorful starter and her chicken mole and *tinga poblana* just outstanding.

It's hard to look away from the 100-plus tequilas on offer but husband and co-owner Vincent Satkoff runs an impressive wine program which pairs an award-winning list perfectly with the menu.

Signature Room at the 95th

Contemporary ✗✗✗

875 N. Michigan Ave. (bet. Chestnut St. & Delaware Ave.)

Phone: 312-787-9596
Web: www.signatureroom.com
Prices: $$$

Lunch & dinner daily
Chicago (Red)

Riding the elevator up to the 95th floor of the iconic John Hancock Center your ears might pop. This should be your first clue that the "location, location, location" mantra applies to restaurants as well as real estate. While there is both a restaurant and a lounge (on the 96th floor) here, people really come for the views first, the food second. The floor-to-ceiling windows show off 360-degree views of the city skyline and, of course, magnificent Lake Michigan.

The menu is continental in style taking influences from around the world and toning them down. A good selection of seasonal monthly specials adds to the sizeable choice. Desserts are a strong point here, though stick to the classics like a slice of cheese cake or a crème brûlée.

Seasons

D4

Contemporary

120 E. Delaware Pl. (bet. Michigan Ave. & Rush St.)

Phone: 312-649-2349
Web: www.fourseasons.com/chicagofs
Prices: $$$$

Lunch Sun
Dinner Wed – Sat
🚇 Chicago (Red)

Lara Kastner

When you've overdosed on nouvelle cuisine, head straight to Seasons. This classic beauty is traditional to a tee. From its customary wood paneling, artwork displayed in gilded frames, sparkling chandeliers, and leather cushioned-wood armchairs, everything seems straight out of your pedigreed grandfather's study. But surely he didn't have views like these? Large windows look upon a busy city from this seventh-floor roost; and with servers fussing over well-dressed diners, you're bound to feel like a master, or mistress, of the universe.

From glammed up, down-home food (spoonbread made with truffled corn and served with Maine lobster and pork belly confit; Maryland crab hushpuppies) and Asian-accented duck with *moo shu* foie gras, to brioche-crusted halibut, the menu is delightfully schizophrenic.

The manic theme extends through dessert, where a candy bar is not just any candy bar and is certainly not your ordinary Snickers bar. This decadent treat pairs Valrhona dark chocolate ganache with green tea mousse and biscuits for a bittersweet and rich finish. The smattering of selections covers all of the bases, though you can never go wrong with the nightly chef's tasting menu.

Spiaggia ✿

Italian 💥XXXX

E4

980 N. Michigan Ave. (at Oak St.)

Phone: 312-280-2750
Web: www.spiaggiarestaurant.com
Prices: $$$$

Dinner nightly
🔲 Chicago (Red)

Jeff Kauck

Guests entering the legendary Spiaggia–tucked into the second floor of a high-rise straddling the corner of Michigan and Oak should look for their stairway to *paradiso Italiano* via an escalator inside the Oak Street entrance. Once inside, the décor harkens back to a Gordon Gekko à la Wall Street 1980s era, with soaring ceilings, marble columns, wire chandeliers, and jumbo windows offering sweeping views.

Spiaggia means beach in Italian, but the menu at this critically acclaimed restaurant takes a more regional approach, with Chef Sarah Gruenberg (who took over for Missy Robbins after she left to preside over New York's two A Voce locations) offering rustic, creative touches to a solidly Italian menu.

Dinner might include a pristine *crudo* plate of Nantucket Bay scallop, yellowtail and tuna belly paired with orange and caviar and laced with an exquisite olive oil; a soft tangle of squid ink *spaghetti alla chitarra* studded with fresh lobster; or an ethereally creamy Meyer lemon mousse with fresh basil and citrus. Grapehounds will have a field day combing through the standout Italian wine selection; and an even better time talking to the staff, who knows the list inside and out.

Table Fifty-Two

American 𝄞𝄞𝄞

C3

52 W. Elm St. (bet. Clark & Dearborn Sts.)

Phone:	312-573-4000	Dinner nightly
Web:	www.tablefifty-two.com	Clark/Division
Prices:	$$	

Table Fifty-Two somehow manages to be both casually elegant and fingerlicking good. Set in a charming white brick house on an otherwise nondescript street, this place has a chic, countrified look that is the very definition of warm and welcoming.

Headlined by Chef Art Smith and his friendly kitchen staff, visible beyond the marble bar, the menu is down-home Dixie with a gourmet bent, as if your mama went to culinary and finishing schools. Fried green tomatoes topped with orange crème fraîche; goat cheese buttermilk biscuits; peppercorn-crusted pork chops set atop potato-chive waffles; and sweet potato custard are just some of the mouthwatering creations. Sundays and Mondays showcase everybody's southern favorite: unbeatable fried chicken.

Look out for **red** symbols, indicating a particularly pleasant ambiance.

Lincoln Park & Old Town

Lincoln Park

History, commerce, and nature come together in these iconic Chicago districts. The eponymous park, running along the Lake Michigan shore, offers winter-weary Chicagoans an excuse to get outside. And to add to the outdoor fun, famed Lincoln Park keeps its patrons happy and frolicking with a splendid spectrum of outdoor cafés, restaurants (ranging from quick bites to the city's most exclusive reservations), and take-out spots perfect for assembling a picnic. Populated by post-college roommates, young families, and affluent yuppies, Lincoln Park is a favorite of locals and visitors, no matter the time of the year. It includes more than a handful of designated historic districts, pre-Great Chicago Fire buildings, museums, shopping, music venues, and the famous (and free) Lincoln Park Zoo.

Delicious Dining

Well-heeled foodies make reservations to come here for some of the most exclusive restaurants in the city (**Charlie Trotter's**, **Alinea**, and **L20**, to name a few).

Weekend nights, the area is hopping, thanks to a combination of the theater, bar scene, and many apartment buildings that cater to the under-30 crowd. On Wednesdays and Saturdays in summer, the south end of the park is transformed into hipster-chef-foodie central during the **Green City Market**. (In winter it is held inside the Peggy Notebaert Nature Museum.) In addition to locally-grown produce, the market draws long lines thanks to its meats, cheeses, and crêpes.

Best of Bakeries

Fans of the sweets made from local ingredients by **Floriole Café & Bakery** have reason to rejoice. Floriole now has a Lincoln Park storefront with a limited lunch menu. Also luring a pack of visitors are their perfect pastries, breakfast delights, sandwiches, salads, cookies, and sweet treats. Those with an affinity (addiction?) for all things baked, can now get them even when Green City is closed.

For other stomach-filling options outside of the market, try **The Meatloaf Bakery**, where meat loaf and mashed potatoes are crafted into all manner of dishes, such as a cupcake-shaped "loaf" (with mashed potato icing).

Other thrilling treats may include the *mother loaf, a wing and a prayer loaf, loaf-a-roma,* and the *no buns about it burger loaf*. Don't let the quirky titles fool you, because this may just be some of the best and most gratifying food in town.

GREASY AND TASTY

Lincoln Park is a great place to satisfy that Chicago hot dog craving. Like many foods (Juicy Fruit, Cracker Jack, and Shredded Wheat, for example), the Chicago-style dog may have originated at the Chicago World's Fair and Columbian Exhibition (in 1893), although that provenance is not definitive. Others credit the Great Depression for its birth.

One newcomer is the chef-driven **Franks 'n' Dawgs**. Bustling at most hours, this Lincoln Park gem employs fresh and locally-sourced ingredients featured in their fun and fine food. Look forward to delectable gourmet sausages, hand-crafted hot dogs, and artisan breads. **The Wieners Circle** is as known for its late hours (as late as 5:00 A.M.) and purposefully rude service, as for its tasty repertoire of dogs and fries. Lincoln Park is one of the dog-friendliest areas around; but then what else would you expect from a neighborhood named after a park?. Satisfy Fido's appetite as well as your own, with a stop at **Three Dog Bakery**, where the chef caters to canine customers.

A PERFECT QUENCH

Wash down all that tasty grease at **Goose Island Brewery**, makers of the city's favorite local beers. Loop the Goose Canoe Tours (offered during the summer) give you a view of the Chicago River island for which the brew is named. If you're still parched, visit the friendly and relaxed **Webster's Wine Bar**. Nab a seat on their streetfront patio, where you can enjoy a glass from their winning and vast wine selection.

HEALTHY AND HEAVENLY

It is a whole different ballgame at **Karyn's Fresh Corner and Raw Café**, a restaurant with a full vegan and raw menu. The adjacent **Fresh Corner market** sells meals to go, plus fresh juices and supplements. "Meatballs" are made from lentils, and "sloppy Joes" from soy protein, and the raw food experience is unlike anything else.

OLD TOWN

The Old Town quarter sports a few quaint cobblestoned streets: the Second City comedy scene (now with a Zanies, too, for even more laughs); June's annual must-see (and must-shop) Old Town Art Fair; Wells Street Art Fair; and places to rest with beers and a good jukebox, like the **Old Town Ale House**. Wells Street is the neighborhood's main drag, and is where browsing should begin. Any epicurean shopping trip should include the **Old Town Oil** for infused oils, aged vinegars, and excellent hostess gifts. Finally, **The House of Glunz**, opened in 1888, is one of Chicago's oldest wine merchants.

Prefer a sweeter vice? **The Fudge Pot** tempts passersby with windows full of toffee, fudge, and other house-made chocolaty goodness. Whether you smoke or not, the **Up Down Cigar** is worth a peek for its real cigar store Indian carving.

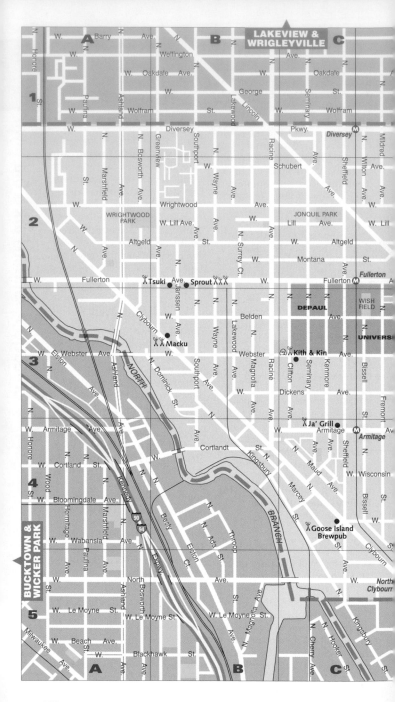

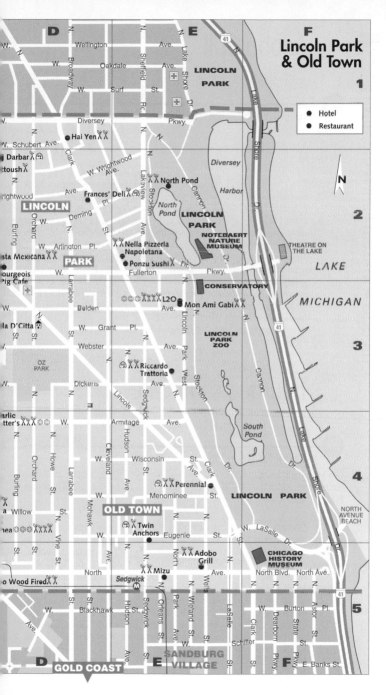

Adobo Grill

E5

1610 N. Wells St. (bet. Eugenie St. & North Ave.)

Phone: 312-266-7999
Web: www.adobogrill.com
Prices: $$

Lunch Sat – Sun
Dinner nightly
 Sedgwick

Fun, festive, and flavorful, Adobo Grill is celebrated as a longtime Old Town favorite for good reason. Housed within a small building, it is at once cozy and lively. Everyone from local denizens to kids with their parents comes to this jamming place. No wonder they have branched out with locations in Wicker Park and Lombard.

First, order a lip-smacking margarita with fresh lime and just a touch of Triple Sec. After a few sips, flag down one of the guacamole carts trolling the dining room. This house classic is made tableside and prepared with just the right amount of heat to suit your mild or wild taste buds. Terrific entrées are made even better alongside rich and smoky *frijoles puercos* and homemade tortillas for sopping up the extra sauce.

Bourgeois Pig Cafe

D2

738 W. Fullerton Pkwy. (at Burling St.)

Phone: 773-883-5282
Web: www.bpigcafe.com
Prices: ⬤⬤

Lunch & dinner daily
 Fullerton

Literary allusions are behind the clever dish names at this character-driven deli in the heart of Lincoln Park. Close to DePaul University and Children's Memorial Hospital, "the Pig," as locals call it, attracts students, doctors, and neighborhood moms to its funky two-story space with a lived-in feel and bookish theme.

Stick to the menu of sandwiches written on oversized chalkboards, choosing from one of their new takes on old classics. Order at the cash register and your "Great Gatsby" will be delivered to your table upstairs. This twist on a club sandwich features focaccia filled with turkey, pesto, mayo, bacon, tomatoes, Swiss, and avocado grilled in a panini press to marry the flavors.

Their eco-friendly to-go containers are made from corn.

Alinea ✿ ✿ ✿

Contemporary ✕✕✕✕

D4

1723 N. Halsted St. (bet. North Ave. & Willow St.)

Phone: 312-867-0110
Web: www.alinea-restaurant.com
Prices: $$$$

Dinner Wed – Sun
North/Clybourn

Tara Kastner

East Coast, West Coast, take a knee: we know you think the Midwest is nothing but hot dogs and conventions, so it's time to ante up. Make your way through the rousing menu at celebrated Chicago restaurant, Alinea, and here's betting a sense-jogging trip through the unconventional recesses of Grant Achatz's mind will turn your notions of progressive cooking on their head.

The succession of Achatz's resolute creativity instantly embraces the diner with a parade of courses including steelhead roe wrapped in a delicate shell of nutmeg glass, paired with plantain purée, ginger foam, and diced papaya. The journey continues with lobster pudding crowned by herbed bread crumbs, toasted pistachio ice cream, white poppy seed foam, and pink grapefruit; and velvety seared duck breast and caramelized foie gras decked with first-of-season morels, sweet peas, Ohio honey gelée, chamomile foam, and candied orange. The term wine pairing doesn't do justice to a perfectly playful array of libations.

This temple of creativity–tucked into an unmarked brownstone in Lincoln Park–is a comfortable setting with creamy walls, pillowed banquettes, sleek mahogany tables, and meticulous service.

Boka ✿

D4

1729 N. Halsted St. (bet. North Ave. & Willow St.)

Phone: 312-337-6070
Web: www.bokachicago.com
Prices: $$$

Dinner nightly
North/Clybourn

Jeff Kauck

Cleverly located down the street from the Steppenwolf Theater, this dark, sultry hideaway is a pretention-free oasis. Boka's dining rooms, bar and lounge, and alluring outdoors draws 'em in droves; and thoughtful touches like a cell phone booth (for the call that can't wait), keep diners focused on contemporary American cuisine showing Mediterranean influences, and dusted with an emphasis on ingredient sourcing.

With Charlie Trotter alum, Giuseppe Tentori steering the ship, Boka's carte displays avant-garde culinary choices. Sensational twists include ruby red tuna from the raw bar, and an appetizer of squid stuffed with minced shrimp and scallops. Entrées may highlight veal sweetbreads in a tangy Moroccan barbecue sauce; roasted duck breast, fanned over a golden barley cake; and velvety foie gras with dark licorice vinaigrette. Equaling the exquisite dishes, are composition and presentation.

The bar offers a deadly "Dealer's Choice," where guests pick a liquor (vodka, gin, tequila, or whiskey) and flavor (sweet, sour, or bitter), and the bartender creates a personalized concoction. Order from the six- and nine-course degustation menus to snag a discount on the reserve wine list.

Charlie Trotter's ╎ ╎

Contemporary 🍴🍴🍴

D4

816 W. Armitage Ave. (bet. Dayton & Halsted Sts.)

Phone: 773-248-6228
Web: www.charlietrotters.com
Prices: $$$$

Dinner Tue – Sat
🚉 Armitage

♿

╎

🍸

☞🔑

Klaing Svehla

With over two decades under its belt, you'd think the shine might have worn off this critically acclaimed Chicago mainstay, but no—like the popular actress who stays in vogue because she really does have *it*, so it goes with Charlie Trotter's self-titled temple of fine American cooking.

Settled inside a gorgeous brownstone in Lincoln Park, those looking for a bit of action can reserve the kitchen table; but others will have to make do with a relatively conservative interior featuring cushioned banquettes, floral arrangements, and pale rose wallpaper. So be it: you don't come to Trotter's for the staid interior, you come for the food.

Trotter is a legend with the pristine ingredients he procures (think farm-raised meats and organic produce), and two rotating nightly menus (there is no à la carte, but there is a vegetarian menu) may unveil a plate of fresh blue prawns served with smooth lemon cream, razor clams, and crunchy salsify; a gorgeous jumble of freshly roasted porcini mushrooms, served whole with caramelized *cipollini* onions in a light rosemary-porcini broth; or an ethereally light, milk chocolate semifreddo with pistachio cream and chocolate praline baton.

137

Fattoush

D2

L e b a n e s e

2652 N. Halsted St. (bet. Diversey Pkwy. & Wrightwood Ave.)

Phone: 773-327-2652
Lunch & dinner Wed – Mon

Web: www.fattoushrestaurant.com
Fullerton

Prices: ⊜⊜

 Blocks from DePaul University—amidst mega stores and bars—emerges this rare find of a place, where fresh, fragrant fare draws chowhounds craving an authentic Lebanese meal. In the main dining room, colorful walls display quaint depictions of pastoral life; while plain white paper covers a dozen plus tables. Prefer to park it on the floor? Take a seat downstairs in the sultry "souk," where lush carpets, pillows, and cushions surround a large table.

From tender vegetarian grape leaves (rice, basil, parsley, tomatoes, and chickpeas in a creamy dressing), to tasty gluten-free spinach pie (that's right, gluten-free!) offerings here are made to order, and with plenty of TLC. The lovely chef makes regular rounds and can be seen smiling and socializing.

Fiesta Mexicana

D2

M e x i c a n XX

2423 N. Lincoln Ave. (bet. Fullerton Ave. & Halsted St.)

Phone: 773-348-4144
Lunch & dinner daily

Web: www.fiestamexicanachicago.com
Fullerton

Prices: ⊜⊜

A long-time hangout for the twenty-somethings and young families living in Lincoln Park, Fiesta Mexicana lives up to the party-style atmosphere its moniker promises. The recently renovated space features a bar and a number of dining rooms with a large mural of a Mexican mountain scene done in bright colors welcoming diners.

Guests are greeted with tasty chips and salsa and an expansive menu offering a cross-section of Tex-Mex, traditional Mexican, and Mexican-inspired fare. The combination platters are a solid way to sample the Tex-Mex choices; while chile poblano-spinach and artichoke *fundido* shows off the kitchens creative juices. Opt for a starter rather than a dessert, as these are the weakest link.

Good value specials are offered at lunch.

Frances' Deli

D2

D e l i 🍴

2552 N. Clark St. (bet. Deming Pl. & Wrightwood Ave.)

Phone: 773-248-4580
Web: www.francesdeli.com
Prices: 🍜

Lunch daily
Dinner Wed – Sun

 Frances' is the kind of place you wish was your neighborhood haunt for casual, everyday dining. Then you'd have a chance to round all the bases of this breakfast-lunch-dinner grand slam. Everything here is a home run from the eggy challe French toast to the gooey turtle brownie sundae.

The sandwiches are especially amazing and all are Hancock tower massive. The turkey Reuben is a go-to with roast turkey, Swiss cheese, Thousand Island dressing, and slaw grilled between slices of challe; but the Lincoln Park with turkey, Muenster, and Honeycup mustard is a local fave. All come with a side of slaw plus fries, potato salad, or a potato pancake. Milkshakes, malts, fountain drinks plus adult beverages quench the thirst built up from all this salty goodness

Goose Island Brewpub

C4

G a s t r o p u b 🍴

1800 N. Clybourn Ave. (at Willow St.)

Phone: 312-915-0071
Web: www.gooseisland.com
Prices: 🍜

Lunch & dinner daily
🚇 North/Clybourn

 Microbreweries aren't a rarity these days, but for over 20 years, Goose Island has had both the brewing and the cooking down. Amid large kettles and brewmasters in boots fielding questions from novice beer makers, the focus here is obvious. Locals come for more than 20 beers on tap, but stay for serious snacks like spicy *sriracha* chicken wings or house-made duck andouille sausage.

The pork sausage sandwich is prepared with a fun twist, served with German Dusseldorf mustard and caramelized onions on a pretzel roll. That chocolate bark, too, has a surprise: it is made with dark Belgian chocolate, sea salt, bacon, and spent grain from the brewing process.

Responsible drinkers may want to grab a Green Line Growler of their favorite brew to-go.

Hai Yen

Vietnamese ✗✗

D1

2723 N. Clark St. (bet. Diversey Pkwy. & Schubert Ave.)

Phone:	773-868-4888	Lunch Fri – Sun
Web:	www.haiyenrestaurant.com	Dinner nightly
Prices:	☕	🚇 Diversey

This friendly, attractive Vietnamese restaurant has all the traditional musts on its large menu. But the most fun dish that distinguishes Hai Yen from others is their signature, *bo la lot*. Listed under the "wraps" section of the menu, flavorful sausage-like rolls of ground beef and pork are enveloped in an aromatic leaf and then grilled. They arrive on a platter of fresh herbs, rice paper, and a bowl of hot water. Wet the rice paper to soften it, wrap up herbs and meat together, dunk in *nuoc cham*, and eat. Tasty, delicious, and fun!

There are plenty of other goodies to follow, such as the *cua rang muoi*—Vietnamese-style Dungeness crabs stir-fried simply with caramelized onions, salt, pepper, and garlic.

A second location resides on West Argyle.

Ja' Grill

Jamaican ✗

C4

1008 W. Armitage Ave. (bet. Kenmore & Sheffield Aves.)

Phone:	773-929-5375	Lunch & dinner daily
Web:	www.jagrill.com	🚇 Armitage
Prices:	☕	

It is more than 1,700 miles from Chicago to Jamaica, but paradise feels right next door at Ja'Grill. Tucked into the upscale shopping mecca of Armitage Avenue, Ja'Grill welcomes visitors with Bob Marley belting from the speakers, a colorful décor with painted murals, and an orange-lit large bar proffering hair-raising drinks. The Jamaican flag shows this is the right place to make everything "cook and curry."

Jerk pork, served juicy, sweet, and tender with coconut-cooked "rice and peas" (peas equal kidney beans in Jamaica), cabbage, carrots, and plantains, is a standout. To spice it up, request the wonderfully hot pepper sauce. Watch your tongue on the beef patties which may burn you up, as they are delivered straight from the microwave.

Kith & Kin

Gastropub ✗

C3

1119 W. Webster Ave. (bet. Clifton & Seminary Aves.)

Phone: 773-472-7070
Web: www.knkchicago.com
Prices: $$

Lunch & dinner daily
🚇 Armitage

Chef David Carrier has some good credentials under his toque, including stints in the kitchens at Trio and The French Laundry. Despite his pedigree, he's ditched tweezered food and bypassed the lab coat to present a refined take on satisfying comfort food. Signatures include a light and flavorful chicken pâté with homemade mustard and cornichons. Or shrimp and grits, with nicely poached shrimp tossed with braised greens over a bed of creamy Anson Mills grits. Tasty banana pudding is crowned by a fluffy cloud of crème chantilly. And of course in the gastropub vein, there's an ample spirit and beer list.

Dining with the wee ones? No worries, the bounteous kids menu features "ants on a log," "fluff-a-nutters," and spaghetti and meatballs.

Macku

Japanese ✗✗

B3

2239 N. Clybourn Ave. (bet. Greenview & Webster Aves.)

Phone: 773-880-8012
Web: www.mackusushi.com
Prices: $$

Dinner nightly

Sushi fans fall into two camps: east and west. There are those who love their westernized maki (spicy tuna anyone?) and those who go the traditional nigiri route. Whether you're a newbie or an aficionado, Macku has you covered.

This contemporary Japanese restaurant literally lays out every option; its neat display of fresh fish at the sushi bar is an enticing sign of what's to come. Start with the straightforward sushi favorites, like salmon, tuna, and yellowtail; or choose from the nice selection of specialty rolls, like the spicy spider roll with soft shell crab, *kanikami*, chili oil, avocado, and cucumber.

The menu may have it all, but this modern and stylish restaurant is small with just a sprinkling of tables and seats at the sushi bar.

L2O ✿ ✿ ✿

Seafood 🍴🍴🍴🍴

E3

2300 N. Lincoln Park West (bet. Belden Ave. & Fullerton Pkwy.)

Phone: 773-868-0002   Dinner Wed – Mon
Web: www.l2orestaurant.com
Prices: $$$$

Katherine Bryant

First, a bit of trivia: the curious name is a riff on the chemical formula for water and über-talented chef and partner, Laurent Gras—who manned the kitchens of celebrated restaurants in France, New York, and San Francisco before helming this elegant and agreeable seafood restaurant in Chicago.

Now, the important detail: eat here now. You won't regret a moment of it. Housed in the landmark Belden-Stratford, intimate L2O is tucked behind a discreet set of doors where you'll find a pretty gold palette dotted with ebony tables, sleek white leather, and blonde Sen wood walls.

Gras' superb seafood menu is broken down into categories like raw, warm, and main; and dinner may unveil innovative spreads like tender octopus with a wickedly good coconut cream, a drizzle of fine olive oil, and a dusting of *shichimi togarashi*; moist, impeccably fresh kampachi glazed with a smoky-sweet teriyaki, and paired with a scrumptious salsa verde, crunchy tempura-battered vegetables, and a chiffonade of ginger; or a killer Tai snapper served with a deconstructed green curry that, when eaten in concert, is nothing short of mind-blowing.

Mizu

E5

J a p a n e s e ✗✗

315 W. North Ave. (at Orleans St.)

Phone: 312-951-8880
Web: www.mizurestaurant.com
Prices: $$

Dinner nightly
🔲 Sedgwick

This Lincoln Park Japanese restaurant is a real find. Chocolate brown banquettes line the walls, while white orb chandeliers cast a soft glow over the beige tiled floors of this contempo-chic gem. For the ultimate Japanese experience, visit the tatami room, located behind sliding wooden doors—it's the real McCoy, complete with the shoes-off sensibility, and mats for sitting on the floor.

The extensive menu lures all by offering a little bit of this (yakitori, their specialty) and a little bit of that (traditional and westernized sushi and sashimi). Oyster shooters, grilled squid, *gyoza*, soba—you name it, and they have it. Maki like the New Mexico with tuna, yellowtail, *tobiko*, avocado, and jalapeño, show the sushi chefs' creative touch.

Mon Ami Gabi

F3

F r e n c h ✗✗

2300 N. Lincoln Park West (at Belden Ave.)

Phone: 773-348-8886
Web: www.monamigabi.com
Prices: $$

Dinner nightly

Inside the historic Belden-Stratford (also home to L2O), Mon Ami Gabi is Lettuce Entertain You Enterprises' take on the classic French bistro. It is in fact the very picture of Paris–with a cozy, dark room displaying closely packed tables, vintage mirrors, and tiled floors–and recalls those quaint salons sitting across the Atlantic.

Up to five diners can choose to eat at the bar and might opt for the trout *Grenobloise*, a golden fillet topped with capers, lemon supremes, and crusty cubed croutons. The menu is chock-full of well-executed classics and may unveil macaroni and cheese married with béchamel and topped with a heavy cap of Gruyère; and a peach parfait decked with raspberry syrup and crunchy pink meringue.

Nella Pizzeria Napoletana

Pizza ✕✕

E2

2423 N. Clark St. (bet. Arlington Pl. & Fullerton Pkwy.)

Phone: 773-327-3400
Web: www.pizzerianella.com
Prices: ⊜⊜

Lunch Sat – Sun
Dinner nightly

Imagine sepia-toned photographs of pizza dough adorning the walls, a pizza oven built with bricks imported from near Mt. Vesuvius, and placemats decorated with wine barrels and Chianti bottles. All that iconography contributes to the reality of this neighborhood pizzeria. There's a sense of humor at work here, too—the waitstaff are dressed in soccer jerseys, that beloved Italian attire.

Get ready for impressive pizza, and not the deep-dish kind. The Neapolitan-style crust is smoke-infused, with crisp charred spots, boasting a pleasantly salted taste and chewy texture. Many are topped with San Marzano tomatoes and fresh mozzarella in the thirteen different versions on offer: from the basic marinara to the calzone, plus pizza combos like the Vesuvio.

North Pond

Contemporary ✕✕

E2

2610 N. Cannon Dr.

Phone: 773-477-5845
Web: www.northpondrestaurant.com
Prices: $$$

Lunch Sun
Dinner Tue – Sun

Built in 1912, as an ice skating warming house, this craftsman-style cottage affords diners a view of Lincoln Park's North Pond, complete with city skyline reflections. The best seats in the house are those at the window tables with the prime views of the pond. Chef Bruce Sherman's menu has a slight bent toward seasonal and local, although not at the expense of all else. Slow-roasted salmon, prawns à la plancha, and Alaskan halibut are typical menu highlights. Desserts are particularly inventive yet reserved, such as a chocolate peanut butter cake, served with a spicy ancho caramel sauce.

A five-course prix-fixe menu is a fairly priced option for those who want to try a little of everything, and brunch is a lovely choice given the setting.

Perennial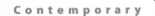

Chicago ▶ Lincoln Park & Old Town

Contemporary ✕✕

E4

1800 N. Lincoln Ave. (bet. Clark & Wells Sts.)

Phone: 312-981-7070
Web: www.perennialchicago.com
Prices: $$

Lunch Sat – Sun
Dinner nightly
🚇 Sedgwick

With views of Lincoln Park, a contemporary feel, and the talented young Chef Ryan Poli at the helm, Perennial hosts a hip crowd of twenty- and thirty-somethings clamoring to get in. Even the plating of dishes here has a modern look.

Chef Poli offers an impressive global resume that includes The French Laundry, and succeeds in creating a cuisine that is as forward-thinking as it is American. Sophisticated dishes may include scallops with short-rib cannelloni or pan-roasted sea bass finished with caramelized onion consommé. Yet the best may be saved for last, with innovative desserts such as the brownies served on a bed of chocolate cookie crumbs with dollops of Bailey's flavored butter cream.

Be sure to look for regular wine list specials.

Ponzu Sushi

Japanese ✕

E2

2407 N. Clark St. (bet. Arlington Pl. & Fullerton Pkwy.)

Phone: 773-549-8890
Web: www.ponzuchicago.com
Prices: 😊😊

Lunch & dinner daily
🚇 Fullerton

Tiny Ponzu Sushi seats just 36 people in its dining room, with room for just five more at the sushi counter. Yet, it is free of any complexes about being small. Colored walls, tablecloths, and napkins exude big personality and brighten the room.

What Ponzu lacks in size, it makes up for in selection. The menu is built around a foundation of sushi and rolls—including classic maki and many signature and specialty rolls. Custom maki are available (except on Friday and Saturday) as well as what they call *tsumiki*, their version of block-style sushi. Try the dragon roll; an inside out roll with shrimp tempura, avocado, and *tobiko* topped with slices of freshwater eel.

Non-sushi eaters dine on dishes from the kitchen like *gyoza*, tempura, *donburi*, or ramen.

Raj Darbar

Indian ✗

D2

2660 N. Halsted St. (bet. Schubert & Wrightwood Aves.)

Phone: 773-348-1010
Web: www.rajdarbar.com
Prices: $$

Lunch Sun
Dinner nightly
🚇 Diversey

This stretch of Halsted has seen its share of change, from college-kid hangouts to upscale boutiques to what was the world's first two-story Home Depot. Amidst this odd mix of retail you will find Raj Darbar, with its somewhat drab décor but seriously talented kitchen.

Alu tikki are a wonderful way to start: smooth and creamy (yet textured) seasoned potatoes create a casing for a chili-rubbed pea filling all dipped in chickpea batter and crisply fried. Tender *jheenga tandoori* is incredible; the shrimp is marinated in a mixture of yogurt, garlic, and ginger with the addition of spices then perfectly roasted in the tandoor. *Biryani*, *pudina paratha*, and *dum ki gobhi* are solid choices while *ras malai* makes for a competent, creamy ending to a fragrant feast.

Riccardo Trattoria

Italian ✗✗

E3

2119 N. Clark St. (bet. Dickens & Webster Aves.)

Phone: 773-549-0038
Web: www.riccardotrattoria.com
Prices: $$

Dinner nightly

Chef/owner Riccardo Michi's family is best-known for its swanky Bice restaurants. When Michi opened his own spot he brought the family know-how, but put his name on the door. The result is a casual, Italian-style trattoria, perfect for either date night or a group dinner.

Friendly, flirty, Italian waiters feed the charming vibe, offering a menu of authentic and reasonably priced Italian dishes. Daily and seasonal specials vary, but dishes might include a tender grilled octopus "Genovese" with crushed potatoes and pesto; or perfectly made gnocchi "bava" in a creamy tomato sauce oozing with fontina and shaved speck. Other nights might offer a smooth porcini mushroom risotto, briny spaghetti with Manila clams, rich osso buco, or a warm fig pie.

Sono Wood Fired

D5

Pizza XX

1582 N. Clybourn Ave. (bet. Halsted St. & North Ave.)

Phone: 312-255-1122
Web: www.sonowoodfired.com
Prices: $$

Dinner nightly
 North/Clybourn

Check out the curvaceous, Italian import attracting all that attention over there: she's quite a stunner. Of course, we're talking about the restaurant's eponymous centerpiece—that colorfully tiled, wood fired oven is the reason for all the buzz. Sono's space is styled in bare wood, latte colored walls, and exposed brick, with a lively, full service bar.

But the best spot in the house is at the six-seat wooden counter near the fiery gal herself. Bubbling hot, thin crust pizzas are the name of the game—whether topped with spinach, garlic, goat cheese; or spicy *soppressata*, *mozzarella di bufala*, and charred onions.

Bookend this pizza indulgence with tender, fried artichoke hearts aside crispy sage, to start; and a creamy tiramisu, to finish.

Sprout

B2

Contemporary XXX

1417 W. Fullerton Ave. (bet. Janssen & Southport Aves.)

Phone: 773-348-0706
Web: www.sproutrestaurant.com
Prices: $$$

Dinner Tue – Sat
 Fullerton

Intimate and sophisticated Sprout flaunts a dash of au naturel (twig tangles) and a zing of richness with brûléed wall tiles. A cozy cubby in the back carries a tiny table, while the main dining room wears a banquette lined with cushy chairs.

You may think it, but the techno tunes and chatter don't wreck the harmony, so bring your best dress and foodie friend. The staff knows the menu best, so heed their council and relish a lightly breaded soft shell crab over avocado purée pocked with pistachios. Other uncommon pairings find harmony in dishes like a tender cod fillet joined by a potato salad, cucumber, and radish ribbons; "grilled cheese" sandwich made sinful with sweet apples and onions; and syrupy fennel sided with a roulade of figs and almonds.

Tsuki

B2

Japanese 🍴

1441 W. Fullerton Ave. (at Janssen Ave.)

Phone: 773-883-8722
Web: www.tsuki.us
Prices: $$

Dinner Wed – Sun
🚇 Fullerton

Tsuki is hipper than most sushi-yas, thanks to a sleek glass bar, mosaic tiles, private booths, and the adjacent lounge that attracts young crowds. Beyond the décor, this is a great spot to enjoy hot and cold dishes, traditional sushi, and delicious contemporary rolls.

Start with miso soup brimming with deep-fried tofu, scallions, and kelp; or perhaps steamed *gyoza*, a tender dumpling encasing ground pork heavily infused with ginger and garlic. Nightly specials vary, but focus on interesting interpretations of the tried-and-true, like the *kari kani maki*, with shrimp tempura, creamy avocado, and sweet mango inside the roll, and spicy caramelized crab aïoli topped with toasted walnuts on the outside. For a surprise, try the nigiri with smoked duck.

Twin Anchors 😊

E4

Barbecue 🍴

1655 N. Sedgwick St. (at Eugenie St.)

Phone: 312-266-1616
Web: www.twinanchorsribs.com
Prices: $$

Lunch Sat – Sun
Dinner nightly
🚇 Sedgwick

Chicago may have been Frank Sinatra's kind of town, but Twin Anchors was his kind of restaurant. This Sinatra sweetheart is a local institution, and has been dishing out barbecued ribs since 1932. It is definitely the kind of place where everybody knows your name—when you visit, ogle the list of regulars who frequent this easygoing establishment. Regulars and regular Joes line up (there are no reservations) for a taste of the tender and smoke-flavored barbecued ribs, chicken, and pulled pork. It's a go big or go home kind of place; so pass by the burgers, steaks, and sandwiches and go for the ribs with a side of fries and zesty baked beans.

Come dressed for a mess since the vibe is unfussy; and if you can't stomach the long wait, opt for take-out.

Bucktown & Wicker Park

Ukranian Village · West Town

FINESSE AND FLAIR

Like many of the Windy City's neighborhoods, Bucktown and Wicker Park have seen its fair share of transition. Ranging from Polish immigrants to wealthy businessmen (who have built stately mansions on Hoyne and Pierce avenues), it has been home to people from all walks of life. But, don't let the hushed residential streets and bewitching brownstones fool you—this neighborhood still knows how to mix it up. While you're more likely to run into bankers than Basquiats these days, Bucktown and Wicker Park remains an international hotbed of creative energy and trendsetting style.

SHOPPING SANCTUM

Shake out the remains of your piggy bank before arriving. After all, this neighborhood has some of the most stylish shopping in the Midwest. It is worlds away from the international chains of the Magnificent Mile. Instead, think über-cool indie shops. Don't have time to travel the world for funky home accessories? Fake the well-traveled look and visit **Fenway Gallery**, where you can pick up an exotic home accessory or two. Love the flea market look but don't want to get out of bed on the weekends? **Embelezar** indulges all by stocking many of those cute one-of-a-kind

pieces that will definitely get your house guests talking.

To experience a taste of Wicker Park's vast and vivid music scene, be sure you make the time to stop by Reckless Records and get schooled on the latest underground band. You can even get creative and design your own t-shirt at the appropriately named T-Shirt Deli—and rest assured as this is only the beginning of a wonderful journey.

GATHERING OF THE ARTS

The neighborhood shows off its artistic roots by hosting two of the city's largest festivals. Wicker Park Fest is an annual two-day music festival held each July that features no less than 28 bands. The Around the Coyote festival held each fall shines a spotlight on local artists practicing creative and visual arts. Wicker Park is also home to a number of art galleries, including the unique 4Art Inc., where artists create their works during the opening night show.

Even starving artists can find something to eat in foodie-friendly Bucktown and Wicker Park. Hot dog fanatics simply must take a tour of the famed **Vienna Beef Factory**; visitors are bound to be blown away by the production lines of products made here. After a view of the manufacturing line, return to your appetite and dine in the employee cafeteria.

Parched after all the meat-eating? Quench your thirst, and head straight for **Black Dog Gelato**, where you can savor outstanding whisky gelato bars dipped in milk chocolate and candied bacon; or taste unusual flavors like goat cheese cashew caramel.

FASCINATING FOOD SCENE

The name sounds a little sketchy, but vegetarians love the **Farwax Café** for its over-the-top funky décor, which is kind of Grateful Dead-meets-India. This inexpensive and idyllic eatery presents tasty, multinational all-veggie meals, including a breakfast menu that is served all day. So if you're craving eggs Benedict for dinner, you know where to head. Other food faves include the seitan ruben overflowing with sauerkraut, swiss cheese, and creamy dressing; as well as the sweet potato and black bean quesadilla spread with cilantro pesto.

Go whole hog and bone up on your cooking skills at **Cooking Fools**, and you won't ever be teased about your tiramisu again. If you're planning to entertain friends with a delicious meal at home, be sure to swing by the **Wicker Park & Bucktown Farmer's Market** for fresh produce, glorious cheeses, and other specialty goods. And while

basking in cheese paradise, don't forget to grab a pie at either **Piece** or **Crust**. Both are widely known and considered Chicago's most favored pizza places. However, Crust has garnered a gaggle of locals who come by not only for their crunchy pizzas, but also for a delicious spectrum of appetizers, salads, and sandwiches.

A SWEET DEAL

Sweet tooths worth their salt certainly know all about **Red Hen Bread**. Atkins would turn over in his grave if he ever got a taste of the bread and pastries from this terrific bake shop. French pastries are all the rage at **Sweet Thang**. Think your mama makes good pie? Grab a fork and taste a lip-smacking piece from **Hoosier Mama Pie Company**. Run by Paula Haney, the former pastry chef at Trio, it's a little slice of heaven. No bake shop is complete without cake, and **Alliance Bakery**'s window display of cakes is quite stupendous.

CROWNING COCKTAILS

Speaking of stupendous, lull on the late night at **Violet Hour**, the speakeasy that serves some of the most heavenly cocktails in town. Slurp up these concoctions while chowing on toasty treats like spiced nuts, deviled eggs with smoked paprika and goat cheese, and smoky chili cheese mini-dogs topped with mustard and onion. **Marie's Rip-Tide Lounge** is a bit of retro fun. With soulful beats emanating from a jukebox and an incredibly energetic vibe, the hopping

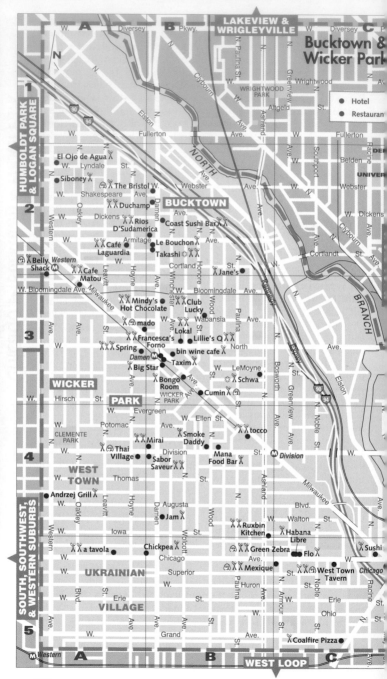

WRIGHTWOOD
PARK

● Hotel
● Restaurant

HUMBOLDT PARK
& LOGAN SQUARE

El Ojo de Agua

Siboney

The Bristol

Duchamp

BUCKTOWN

Rios
D'Sudamerica

Coast Sushi Bar

Café
Laguardia

Le Bouchon

Takashi

Belly
Shack

Cafe
Matou

Jane's

W. Bloomingdale Ave.

Mindy's
Hot Chocolate

Club
Lucky

mado

Wabansia

Lokal

Francesca's
Forno

Spring

Lillie's Q

bin wine cafe

WICKER

Taxim

Big Star

Bongo
Room

Schwa

WICKER
PARK

Cumin

PARK

Hirsch St.

Evergreen

CLEMENTE
PARK

Potomac

Mirai

Ellen St.

Smoke
Daddy

tocco

Thai
Village

Division

WEST
TOWN

Sabor
Saveur

Mana
Food Bar

Division

Thomas

Andrzej Grill

Jam

Ruxbin
Kitchen

Habana
Libre

a tavola

Chickpea

Green Zebra

Flo

Sushi

UKRAINIAN

Superior

Mexique

West Town
Tavern

Chicago

VILLAGE

Huron

Coalfire Pizza

Western

A   B

WEST LOOP   C

SOUTH, SOUTHWEST,
& WESTERN SUBURBS

lounge draws a regular group of late night revelers. Marie, now in her 70s, lives upstairs and decorates this frozen-in-time space for all of the holidays. The perenially-packed **Moonshine Brewing Company** shows a solid and serious beer collection, with packs brewed on-site; while **Silver Cloud** is foolproof for sidewalk boozing.

LATE NIGHT REVELRY

Definitely defining the 'tude of the 'hood is the **Cellar Rat Wine Shop**. If you thought exceptional wines at excellent value was never a possiblility, think again, as this place will prove you wrong. Displaying a splendid array, this neigborhood delight never fails to satisfy, no matter the day or time.

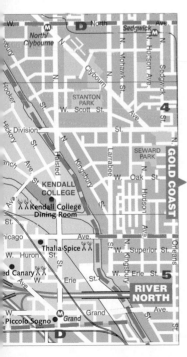

Carry on your Saturday night fever at **Salud Tequila Lounge**. Alongside a sinfully splendid selection of tequilas, Salud also salutes foodies with south-of-the border spreads from gooey guacamole, nachos, and quesadillas, to tortas, tacos, and other specialties. Straight from the horse's mouth, eat well but drink better at **Angels and Mariachis**. This bar may be rustic-looking, but it reverberates nightly with a raucous set. Watch them groove to the beats of rock and country, whilst sipping and savoring a menu of eats 'n treats. From martinis, margaritas, tequila, and cerveza, to a range of Mexican faithfuls, this cantina struts it all.

WHOLESOME WAYS

Local Folks Food is a family-run enterprise whose chief charge is to develop delicious, natural, and gourmet condiments (mustard and hot sauce anyone?) perfect for slathering upon burgers. Find these tangy, tantalizing treats at the **Green Grocer** and elevate your burger to ethereal.

And finally, much to every foodie's delight, Bucktown and Lincoln Park now share a fabulous and fantastically unique **Whole Foods**. Lauded as the third largest store nationwide, this particular paragon is complete (and replete) with food stations (like mini restaurants), an International Cookie Club, and a delightful wine (**Da'Vine**) and beer bar. Pick your food, then your beverage (wine and beer either by the bottle or glass), and while away an evening at this wholesome haven. No time to linger? Push a cart around, sipping as you shop!

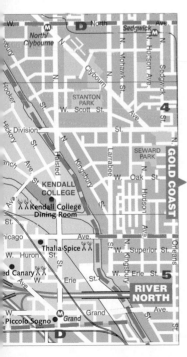

Andrzej Grill

A4

Polish 🍴

1022 N. Western Ave. (bet. Augusta Blvd. & Cortez St.)

Phone: 773-489-3566   Lunch & dinner Mon – Sat
Web: N/A
Prices: 💍

No trip to Chicago would be complete without a super filling, inexpensive, and authentic Polish feast. If you're not invited into someone's home for such a satisfying meal, the homey Andrzej Grill is as good a choice. The diminutive, no-frills stop is as popular for take-out as dining in.

Service is efficient and straightforward, which can be said of the food, too. For less than $10, diners can fill up on the Polish platter, which includes a crisp potato pancake; stuffed cabbage roll (tender leaves of cabbage surrounding a steamed filling of herb-scented rice); a smoky, well-seasoned, grilled kielbasa; and that star of the Polish culinary world: plump *pierogi*. And on top of all this comes a side of tasty sauerkraut, made with cabbage and carrot.

a tavola

A5

Italian 🍴🍴

2148 W. Chicago Ave. (bet. Hoyne Ave. & Leavitt St.)

Phone: 773-276-7567   Dinner Mon – Sat
Web: www.atavolachicago.com
Prices: $$

This long-time mainstay is housed in a small brick townhouse, and inside both the dining room and menu continue this petite trend. The dining area is simply decorated with striking black-and-white photographs (a combo of nudes and landscapes) and white linen tablecloths. But that old saw, "good things come in small packages," applies here.

The regular menu is selective, with a few specials, which the server will read to you. For years, the don't-miss dish has been the brown butter gnocchi, topped with fried sage leaves. Order it as a starter, leaving room for a seasonal entrée special, such as the pork shank braised with white wine, cloves, and juniper berries, and served aside cannellini beans. The waiter will also pair wines with the meal on request.

Belly Shack

A2·3

1912 N. Western Ave. (at Milwaukee Ave.)

Phone: 773-252-1414
Web: www.bellyshack.com
Prices:

Lunch & dinner Tue – Sun
Western (Blue)

 Chef/owner Bill Kim is worlds away from his ex-luxury lair, Le Lan, at this Asian-Latin snack shop. A hip crowd fills this minimalist-urban spot, burrowed beneath the El. Order at the counter and wait for the flava' to arrive.

Sandwiches like the tasty pocket with savory meatballs, dressed noodles, and an ample squirt of *sriracha*; or the hot and sour soup with hominy and cilantro, show the chef's terrific melody of Mexican and Asian tones. A sometime special of *bulgogi*, thinly shaved cheesesteak-style beef doused with spicy mayo and cilantro, wedged between crisp, salty plantains is a work of Korean-Latino fusion genius.

Belly Shack's soft serve swirls in playful scoops of mint brownie, with a guest chef appearance by Mindy Segal, on the brownie topping.

Big Star

Mexican

D3

1531 N. Damen Ave. (bet. Milwaukee & Wicker Park Aves.)

Phone: 773-235-4039
Web: www.bigstarchicago.com
Prices:

Lunch & dinner daily
Damen (Blue)

   Fun, tasty, and super-cheap, Big Star is worthy of its cultish following for good Mexican street food, courtesy of Paul Kahan. The taco *al pastor* has been the talk of the town for the past year for good reason. The marinated, spit-roasted pork piled into a tender handmade tortilla, topped with grilled pineapple, onion, and cilantro, is one of the best two dollar treats Chicago has to offer.

It's standing room only most nights, where hipsters and foodies jockey for stools with a *michelada* (beer, lime juice, chili sauce, and spices) in one hand and a taco in the other. Whiskey cocktails and tequila lists are enough to impress even the edgiest rocker. Can't snag a stool? Head to the patio or grab a taco to-go from the cash-only, walk-up window.

155

bin wine cafe

American 🍴

 1559 N. Milwaukee Ave. (bet. Damen Ave. & Honore Sts.)

Phone: 773-486-2233
Web: www.binwinecafe.com
Prices: $$

Lunch Sat – Sun
Dinner nightly
🚆 Damen (Blue)

♿
⛱

Just south of the Bucktown/Wicker Park epicenter intersection, this American café attracts young families, older gaggles, eclectic locals, and others, for its spot-on eats.

 A particularly satisfying treat is the frittata, moistened with sweet crab and crunchy artichokes. This perfect opener is served hot, with just the right amount of tang. The kitchen's take on the BLT is made with smoked bacon and whole grain bread that is kissed with the right amount of basil pesto; the crispy french fries are a pefect match for this sandwich. As ought to be the case at a place known for its brunches, Bin's mugs of coffee are served hot and strong. The wine list is interesting, and all of the wines served here are available to take home, too.

Bongo Room

American 🍴

 1470 N. Milwaukee Ave. (bet. Evergreen Ave. & Honore St.)

Phone: 773-489-0690
Web: www.thebongoroom.com
Prices: 🍪🍪

Lunch daily
🚆 Damen (Blue)

♿

This cheerful spot with a jaunty name offers Wicker Park residents a hearty start to the day. Fuel up on eggs any style, a heaping breakfast burrito, and sides such as candied bacon; but when gifted a puckish collection of pancakes, grab 'em! Be warned though that the lemon ricotta-blueberry pancakes, a decadent stack crested with a scoop–not a pat–of butter laced with brown sugar and gingersnap crumbs, may send you back home for a nap. For lunch, an array of sandwiches and salads will perfectly pacify you until sun down.

The sunny room, offset by an upbeat staff, is outfitted with yellow painted furnishings and a dining counter that doubles as an excellent roost for those kooks who are best left alone until after that all-important first cuppa'.

The Bristol

American

B2

2152 N. Damen Ave. (bet. Shakespeare & Webster Aves.)

Phone: 773-862-5555
Web: www.thebristolchicago.com
Prices: $$

Lunch Sun
Dinner nightly

This is why you live in the city—to have this kind of place as your neighborhood haunt. Maybe it's the communal butcher-block tables or maybe it's the sharable buzz-worthy food, but this spot brings the cool crowd together. It's warm and lively (read: loud) and the sort of place where friendships are formed elbow-to-elbow over duck fat fries and monkey bread slathered with dill butter and sea salt.

The seasonally driven and locally sourced American food is flat out fab. Chef Chris Pandel makes the simple sophisticated with dishes like braised morels, shrimp toast, and butter-roasted klingklip. It may be a riff on the classic nutter butter, but these peanut butter-filled dark chocolate cookies, perhaps paired with chili-infused mead, are seriously good.

Café Laguardia

Cuban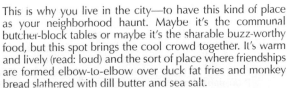

A2

2111 W. Armitage Ave. (bet. Hoyne Ave. & Leavitt St.)

Phone: 773-862-5996
Web: www.cafelaguardia.com
Prices: 🪙

Lunch & dinner daily
🚇 Western (Blue)

A portrait of one of history's most fervent Cuba-lovers, Ernest Hemingway, hangs on the wall in this second generation Cuban haunt. Red-topped tables are paired with chairs upholstered in a riot of animal prints, lending the place a marked south-of-the-border expat feel.

The menu renders an armchair trip to Cuba, with an affordable sampling of filling sides and entrées. A particular bargain is the Taste of Cuba platter, which shows off the kitchen's specialties: *picadillo criollo*, a ground beef dish with raisins and olives, is hot and flavorful; the fried pork medallions are crunchy, caramelized, and tender; and the ham croquette sports an appealing (and golden) exterior. Black beans, white rice, and grease-free fried plantains complement the meaty menu.

157

Cafe Matou

A3

French XX

1846 N. Milwaukee Ave. (bet. Leavitt St. & Oakley Ave.)

Phone: 773-384-8911
Web: www.cafematou.com
Prices: $$

Dinner Tue – Sun
Western (Blue)

Since 1997, Cafe Matou has been providing Bucktown residents with a taste of Paris that captures its romance without seeming pretentious. Neat and upscale with glossy wood floors, green leather chairs, exposed brick, and an eye-catching assortment of artwork, this café lures Francophiles and well-dressed sophisticates seeking that inimitable Proustian experience.

The dishes are classically French, perhaps including the tempting, crisp-skinned duck confit with merlot-prune reduction. Other items that may emerge from the kitchen, sometimes carried by Chef/owner Charlie Socher, range from rabbit meatballs atop linguine in a pool of tomato broth, or a vegetable plate comprised of freshly baked Swiss chard tart, stuffed peppers, and grilled eggplant.

Chickpea

A-B5

Middle Eastern X

2018 W. Chicago Ave. (bet. Damen & Hoyne Aves.)

Phone: 773-384-9930
Web: www.chickpeaonthego.com
Prices: ⊜⊜

Lunch & dinner daily

Jerry Suqi has brought some of the most scene-y spots to Chicago nightlife over the last decade. There was Sugar: A Dessert Bar, La Pomme Rouge, Narcisse, and then Jam. His newest spot looks like an unassuming campus sandwich shop, but it is no less ambitious than his other previous efforts.

With his mom (Amni Suqi) as executive chef, Suqi is trying to bring the vibe and the food of his native Palestine to the city. Posters and signage in Arabic set the scene, but the scene-stealer is the affordable, get-it-and-go food. The star is the *kufta* pita, made with lamb, grilled green peppers, and a remarkable tahini sauce. Mama's lentil soup should not be missed either as it's unbelievably creamy and delicious touched with favas and a swirl of olive oil.

Club Lucky

B3

Italian ✗✗

1824 W. Wabansia Ave. (at Honore St.)

Phone: 773-227-2300
Web: www.clubluckychicago.com
Prices: $$

Lunch & dinner daily
Damen (Blue)

Quiet by day but boisterous by night, this family-friendly favorite brings to life a bygone era of classic Italian-American dining from its commanding location on the corner of Wabansia and Honore. The nostalgic ambience also includes cordial service and a generous sidewalk for al fresco dining in fair weather.

Inside, the dusky room highlights red vinyl booths, painted brick walls, and crowds indulging in this idyllic Italian-American experience. The black Formica tables display a quintessential spread of vegetable antipasti starring portobellos, carrots, beets, and beans in balsamic; as well as pastas like rigatoni with veal meatballs, creamy mozzarella, and tomato sauce. Desserts showcase crispy *cannoli* and a sweetened martini slate.

Coalfire Pizza

C5

Pizza ✗

1321 W. Grand Ave. (bet. Ada & Elizabeth Sts.)

Phone: 312-226-2625
Web: www.coalfirechicago.com
Prices: ⊜⊜

Lunch Sat – Sun
Dinner Tue – Sun
Chicago (Blue)

Few restaurants are as aptly named as Coalfire. The pizzas from this local favorite are cooked in an oven fueled by a coal fire. That 800-degree fire sets the stage for the kitchen and the menu.

The menu does include a few other Italian favorites, such as salads and calzones, but really there's no reason to consider them, because you (and everyone else in town) are here for the pizza, and that in itself says a great deal. These are not Chicago-style pies. Rather, 14-inch, Neapolitan-style pies. Pick from one of nine combos or create your own. Options include fresh or regular mozzarella cheese, thin sliced hot salami and red bell pepper, and pesto. A decent beer and wine list round out the offerings (the restaurant is no longer BYOB).

Coast Sushi Bar

Japanese ✕✕

2045 N. Damen Ave. (bet. Dickens & McLean Aves.)

Phone: 773-235-5775   Dinner nightly
Web: www.coastsushibar.com
Prices: $$

Animated chatter and softly thumping music give Coast Sushi Bar a definitive vibe and immediate sense of vitality. Choose to sit at the counter staffed by personable sushi chefs for a first-row seat as the broad, crowd-pleasing menu of sushi, maki, and a range of cooked dishes and daily specials are prepared and artfully arranged.

The fish here is fresh and appealing, as in the starter of warm shrimp salad with sweet-tasting garlic-wasabi dressing and corn tempura. Sushi selections are highlighted on a blackboard of fresh specials, all thinly sliced and beautifully draped over small balls of rice; they may include ivory-white hamachi, fatty salmon, or pristine cuts of ruby-red tuna. Upgrade to the freshly grated wasabi for a nominal charge.

Cumin

Indian ✕

1414 N. Milwaukee Ave. (bet. Evergreen & Wolcott Aves.)

Phone: 773-342-1414   Lunch Tue – Sun
Web: www.cumin-chicago.com   Dinner nightly
Prices: $$ 🚇 Damen (Blue)

Every seat will be filled and everyone will be smiling, but brave these crowds and try not to fill up on the near-addictive papadam and chutneys placed on the table. As delicious as the first taste may be, it is all uphill from here.

While this Nepalese-Indian restaurant is a newcomer, its friendly, unrushed service, tasteful décor, and instantly acclaimed food prove that there is nary a misstep in sight.

While the lunchtime Indian buffet focuses on the standards, the time to explore the cuisine here is at dinner, when the authentic and unique Nepalese specialties grace the tables. Explore the likes of tender goat *chhoela* marinated in Nepalese spices and herbs, or *aalu ra simi*, with cubed potatoes and green beans in a wonderfully heady tomato sauce.

Duchamp

American

B2

2118 N. Damen Ave. (at Charleston St.)

Phone: 773-235-6434
Web: www.duchamp-chicago.com
Prices: $$

Lunch Sun
Dinner Tue – Sun

Folks from the West Loop nightclub Lumen gave birth to Duchamp—a global baby whose comfort food beats what's being served at most taverns across town. The interior feels a trifle dark and swanky and emanates a modern, sleek sense. The inspired menu demonstrates east-meets-west twists. Watch those unfold in small plates like hot wings, lamb meatballs, and Scottish salmon gravlax; or larger portions including lobster-topped flatbread pizza, fish and chips (made with crispy skate wing), chicken *paillard*, and braised pork shoulder. Locals rave about the signature burger, made from flavor-rich, juicy ground beef, served on a toasted brioche spread with tomato remoulade, and topped with creamy Havarti cheese.

El Ojo de Agua

Mexican

A2

2235 N. Western Ave. (at Lyndale St.)

Phone: 773-235-8807
Web: N/A
Prices:

Lunch & dinner daily
🚇 Western (Blue)

Hankering for a taco? Get over to this no-frills Bucktown taqueria, where they come fresh and piled high on delicious homemade corn tortillas, for just a handful of change. Though burritos, quesadillas, and other standard goodies are offered, the tacos are a critical fave. Munch on the *al pastor* taco—smoky spit-roasted pork marinated with dried chiles, onion, and pineapple; or the mouthwatering *carne asada*, splashed with spicy red salsa.

All are adorned with sliced radishes and charred jalapeños, and topping choices come in "regular" (cilantro and chopped white onions); or "super" (sour cream, cheese, and guacamole), which are generously heaped onto whichever tasty taco you fancy. Wash it all down with a creamy cinnamon *horchata* or a cool *agua fresca*.

Flo

Mexican ✗

1434 W. Chicago Ave. (bet. Bishop St. & Greenview Ave.)

Phone: 312-243-0477
Web: www.eatatflo.com
Prices: 〇〇

Lunch Tue – Sun
Dinner Tue – Sat
Chicago (Blue)

A cornerstone of this rapidly gentrifying neighborhood, Flo's packs 'em in. The joint is open for three squares a day, but it is the breakfast and brunch menus that draw lines out the door. The pretty exterior sets the tone, with a plant-filled window and an array of mirrors down one inside wall.

Quality ingredients and a playful menu mimic the décor with a funky yet wholesome vibe. The vibrant spice of the southwest is evident in the vast offerings starting with signature breakfast dishes, such as *huevos rancheros*, breakfast tacos, and *chilaquiles*, all made with fresh salsa, warm tortillas, and savory black beans. Lunch and dinner playfully continue with a vamped-up Frito pie, hearty pork tamale bowl, or the spicy and saucy sloppy Flo.

Francesca's Forno

Italian ✗✗

1576 N. Milwaukee Ave. (at Damen Ave.)

Phone: 773-770-0184
Web: www.miafrancesca.com
Prices: $$

Lunch Sat – Sun
Dinner nightly
Damen (Blue)

Perhaps the crown of the well-respected, local chainlet, Francesca's is a great big place for tasty Italian food that is meant for sharing. Its bright corner location offers plentiful windows, wood furnishings, and an open kitchen with a wood-burning oven to create a genuinely relaxed, trattoria ambience.

The menu features a range of pasta, pizzas, and Northern Italian entrées in portions that often echo *abbondanza*. *Pollo alla Valdostana* is as massive as it is delicious, with moist, juicy chicken, rich, earthy mushroom sauce, prosciutto, and melting Fontina cheese. Nonetheless, large servings do not compromise quality here, as in the luscious tiramisu, alternating thick layers of mascarpone cheese and espresso-soaked cake.

Green Zebra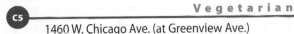

C5

Vegetarian ✗✗

1460 W. Chicago Ave. (at Greenview Ave.)

Phone: 312-243-7100
Web: www.greenzebrachicago.com
Prices: $$

Lunch Sun
Dinner nightly
🚇 Chicago (Blue)

Named for the heirloom tomato, Green Zebra, this is a sleek, serene arena with a Zen-like attitude and accommodating vegetarian menu that even carnivores can abide.

Chef/owner Shawn McClain (who also owns Spring) has created an offering of small plates and shared entrées designed for grazing—with many vegan options and even a meat dish or two toward the bottom of the list. The minimalist décor complements the subtle flavors and seasonings, as in the ricotta gnocchi, crisped golden brown, tossed with chunks of roasted squash, rapini, and preserved lemon. Playful desserts, like the milk chocolate dome with rice crispies, malted milk, and orange soda, are not to be missed.

The wine list features organic and bio-dynamic selections.

Habana Libre

C5

Cuban ✗

1440 W. Chicago Ave. (bet. Bishop & Noble Sts.)

Phone: 312-243-3303
Web: N/A
Prices: 🍤🍤

Lunch & dinner Mon – Sat
🚇 Chicago (Blue)

Habana Libre reveals its Cuban heritage with antique furnishings and décor. In keeping with local culture, the music is colorful and lively, the hospitality and service is warm and attentive, and the food is flavorful and ample. Naturally, this combination attracts many regulars.

The menu is loaded with a dozen appetizers, daily specials, eight Cuban sandwiches, some entrées, and a few desserts. Order smartly and you are guaranteed to leave with enough for lunch the next day, without breaking the bank. "Twilight" fans beware: the dishes here are loaded with garlic. While this may not bode well for vampires, the waitstaff will ask you how garlicky you like your dishes, so you can dial it back. Sandwiches are served with filling black beans and white rice.

Jam

B4

Contemporary

937 N. Damen Ave. (bet. Augusta Blvd. & Walton St.)

Phone: 773-489-0302   Lunch Wed – Mon
Web: www.jamrestaurant.com   Dinner Wed – Sat
Prices:

As small as its name is short, Jam has been flanked with big buzz since its launch in 2010. The owners had intended for it to be brunch-only, but latched on dinner service after much clamoring by the locals. The raves are owed to Chef Jeffrey Mauro, formerly of Charlie Trotter's and North Pond, and restaurateur-about-town, Jerry Sugi, for his mod aesthetic.

Even with a dinner menu, breakfasts are the big draw here. Whether seated inside under the flicker of ceiling fans or in the outdoor garden, relish basics like fresh, creamy, comforting oatmeal. Also sinful are specialties that may include buckwheat pancakes; or an egg sandwich heaped with pork, apple, ricotta, and chutney, served on ciabatta. The *panino cristo* is served with mustard jam, of course.

Jane's

B2

Contemporary

1655 W. Cortland St. (bet. Marshfield Ave. & Paulina St.)

Phone: 773-862-5263   Lunch & dinner daily
Web: www.janesrestaurant.com
Prices:

A neighborhood charmer in an 1890's house typical of the area, Jane's can hardly be called hip, yet it is regularly packed with hipsters (and their offspring) who live in the neighborhood.

The menu has not evolved much since Jane's opened in 1994, and some of the dishes, such as the Asian chicken salad and the goat cheese-stuffed chicken, may seem dated. But Jane's does well what it does well. Portions, such as the fettucine with roasted poblano, are ample and well-prepared. The potato leek soup–available during winter months–is creamy, but not so rich that it fills you up before your entrée arrives. The menu is exceedingly vegetarian-friendly, and breakfast is available until 3:00 P.M. on weekdays. Expect a wait for a table during the popular weekend brunch.

Kendall College Dining Room

International 🍴

D4

900 North Branch St. (at Halsted St.)

Phone: 312-752-2328
Web: www.kendall.edu/diningroom.com
Prices: $$

Lunch Mon – Fri
Dinner Tue – Sat
🚇 Grand (Blue)

Imagine that dining out could be a sneak peek at a future Michelin-starred chef. That's a real possibility in this dining room and kitchen, which doubles as a test space for culinary arts students. Forgive the jitters as servers-in-training deliver your meal, which you can watch being prepared through floor-to-ceiling windows onto the kitchen.

The lunch prix-fixe menu includes three courses for under $20, with dishes such as a green gazpacho and a buttermilk panna cotta that rivals what may be served in nearby fine restaurants. Additionally, enjoy many other fine dining indulgences, such as an amuse-bouche, intermezzos, and very good bread.

It is not just the chefs who come from the school: many of the herbs and vegetables are grown in campus gardens.

Le Bouchon

French 🍴

B2

1958 N. Damen Ave. (at Armitage Ave.)

Phone: 773-862-6600
Web: www.lebouchonofchicago.com
Prices: $$

Lunch & dinner Mon – Sat
🚇 Damen (Blue)

In lieu of intercontinental travel, head straight for Le Bouchon. One step inside this endearing restaurant and you'll think you've died and gone to bistro heaven. Pressed-tin ceilings, red walls, tile floors, framed pictures of Paris, and cramped tables only enhance its authenticity.

Still, Le Bouchon embodies more than the classic bistro look. Wholesome and fuss-free preparations of French comfort food headline the menu, as Chef/owner Jean-Claude Poilevey flits about from table to table. This kitchen knows how to soothe the soul with its cooking, as in salad Lyonnaise with a perfectly poached egg and crisp bacon lardons; warming crocks of cassoulet with white beans, chunks of ham, duck confit, and sausage; or the smooth, lovely chocolate marquis.

Lillie's Q

B3

Barbecue ✗✗

1856 W. North Ave. (at Wolcott Ave.)

Phone: 773-772-5500
Web: www.lilliesq.com
Prices: $$

Lunch & dinner daily
Damen (Blue)

A note to traditionalists: the goods here are referred to as urban barbecue, so expect a few tasty tweaks on some cherished favorites. Meats are massaged with "Carolina Dirt"—the house dry rub—and then may be given a glaze; or finished with one of five flavorful sauces, all of which can be found neatly lined on the tables. Feast on tangy apple glazed baby back ribs, tender tri-tip, smoky baked beans, sweet potato fries, and fried pickles.

The popular spot rocks a rustic chic style, with exposed ducts and brick walls; metal chairs beneath wooden tables; and filament bulbs in iron fixtures. Service pieces follows the theme—steamy sides roll out in cast iron dishes, meats on paper lined metal trays, and cold bevs in old-fashioned Mason Ball jars.

Lokal

B3

American ✗✗

1904 W. North Ave. (bet. Winchester & Wolcott Aves.)

Phone: 773-904-8113
Web: www.lokalchicago.com
Prices: $$

Lunch & dinner daily
Damen (Blue)

This European-flecked American café gets the urban vibe going with its stylish interior dressed in square tables, white molded chairs, and large canvases of modern art. The lounge area hosts guest DJs who pump up the volume when the lights go down, augmenting the retro feel.

At Lokal, lunch and dinner are different experiences, but each is worthy on its own. Lunches are a simpler affair (see: sandwiches and salads); while the dinner menu is more complex (the likes of grilled pork tenderloin with gnocchi, roasted striped bass with wilted spinach, and duck breast with cheddar grits). Lokal is lauded for its fresh, first-rate ingredients that may present itself, for example, in a spinach salad joining cherry tomatoes, shaved fennel, and halved kumquats.

mado

Contemporary ✗

A3

1647 N. Milwaukee Ave. (bet. Damen & Wabansia Aves.)

Phone: 773-242-2340
Web: www.madorestaurantchicago.com
Prices: $$

Dinner Tue – Sun
🚇 Damen (Blue)

The rather unassuming exterior and low-key interior of wood floors and exposed brick walls may give the impression of mado being lesser than it is. What it lacks in appearances it more than makes up in food, especially the quality of products sourced. A clear commitment to best quality Midwestern produce is exceptional at this local favorite and a list of supply farms can be read on the blackboard. The menu is small and changes daily depending on the deliveries *du jour* but might include unfussy dishes like a silky-soft chicken liver parfait with crunchy *croutes*, or a perfectly charred hangar steak with creamy Gorgonzola polenta.

You will find terrific value here so break into your wine vault and bring a serious red as mado is BYO.

Mana Food Bar

Vegetarian ✗

B4

1742 W. Division St. (bet. Paulina & Wood Sts.)

Phone: 773-342-1742
Web: www.manafoodbar.com
Prices:

Lunch Sat
Dinner nightly
🚇 Division

Located in a neighborhood that is partly grungy, partly chic, and completely trendy, this compact vegetarian spot satisfies every appetite with big, fresh flavors. The space is suitably industrial-chic: one wall is exposed white-washed brick and the other is smooth and gray, set off by a wood bar, hand-hewn chairs, tables, and booths.

The menu is small but very tasty, with just a few soups, salads, and plates that can be ordered as appetizer or entrée portions. Inspiration may range from the refreshingly tangy Thai pineapple salad with mint and spicy green chilies, to the pumpkin-filled tomato pasta ravioli, to Mana Sliders–mini brown rice burgers made meaty with mushrooms.

Mana is only open for lunch on certain days, so call ahead for daytime eats.

Mexique 😀

Mexican ✗✗

C5

1529 W. Chicago Ave. (bet. Armour St. & Ashland Ave.)

Phone: 312-850-0288
Web: www.mexiquechicago.com
Prices: $$

Lunch & dinner Tue – Sun
🚇 Chicago (Blue)

Bold, surprising, and sophisticated, Mexican food with French flourish is the signature here. The contemporary art, décor, and white walls that showcase rough bricks peeking through are an apt backdrop for this creative cuisine.

This spot is loved by locals, who arrive for a quick taco at lunch or more elaborate meal at dinner, when both complexity and prices of dishes escalate. Takes on classic tacos may include the *barbacoa* with tender, coffee-braised lamb between corn tortillas with pickled jalapeños cutting the richness. Other highlights may include the *cochinita pibil* taco, with annatto-tequila marinated pork, braised and shredded, topped with tangy slices of pickled onion and drizzles of sweet and impressively spicy mango-habañero coulis.

Mindy's Hot Chocolate

Contemporary ✗✗

B3

1747 N. Damen Ave. (bet. St. Paul Ave. and Willow St.)

Phone: 773-489-1747
Web: www.hotchocolatechicago.com
Prices: $$

Lunch Wed – Sun
Dinner Tue – Sun
🚇 Damen (Blue)

The name, the cocoa-colored interior, and Chef/owner Mindy Segal's reputation may tempt you into this oft-crowded, industrial-chic restaurant and straight to dessert.

Dessert can't–and shouldn't–be skipped here, but neither should the savory contemporary items. Daily soups may change, but the macaroni and cheese made with Wisconsin Gruyère and cheddar is a year-round sensation. Recommending just a handful of desserts is like being asked to select your favorite child. When pressed, though, the warm brioche doughnuts with hot fudge sauce have been a bestseller since the restaurant opened. There are also six variations of hot chocolate on the menu. The wine list is impressive and, unsurprisingly, offers a nice selection of dessert wines.

Mirai

Japanese 🍴🍴

B4

2020 W. Division St. (bet. Damen & Hoyne Aves.)

Phone: 773-862-8500
Web: www.miraisusi.com
Prices: $$

Dinner nightly
🚇 Damen (Blue)

Mirai is a bit like Disney World. You know it's not real, but who cares? The Japanese food is westernized and by no means traditional, but unless you're dining out with Mr. Miyagi, rest assured that nobody will cry foul.

Bold and appetizing flavors beg to take center stage. It's really all about the sushi at this spot—just look around and you'll find most devotees feasting on sashimi, *unagi*, and maki. If raw fish doesn't float your boat, take a shot at one of the house specialties like *kani nigiri*, a baked king crab concoction. There is also a surfeit of hot dishes, think chicken *togarashi* with spicy, sweet, and tangy flavors. Affable and alert service and a relaxed atmosphere, especially on the front patio, make this a hit with area residents.

Piccolo Sogno

Italian 🍴🍴

D5

464 N. Halsted St. (at Milwaukee Ave.)

Phone: 312-421-0077
Web: www.piccolosognorestaurant.com
Prices: $$

Lunch Mon – Fri
Dinner nightly
🚇 Grand (Blue)

In an area better known for its nightclubs than its restaurants, Piccolo Sogno (which means "little dream") is a quaint bistro, with options for dining in or out. In fact, the outdoor area nearly doubles the seating capacity. Think of this as a neighborhood joint without the neighborhood vibe.

Helmed by a former Coco Pazzo executive chef, Piccolo Sogno has a straightforward Italian menu with a selection of Neapolitan-style pizzas at lunch, plus pastas, a few daily specials, and an expanded offering for dinner. Dishes are cooked consistently well with fresh ingredients, like a grilled sea bass with asparagus and roasted potatoes. A thin crust, prociutto-strewn pizza hits the mark. End the meal with a yummy panna cotta topped with fruit and caramel.

169

Red Canary

D5

695 N. Milwaukee Ave. (bet. Morgan & Sangamon Sts.)

Phone: 312-846-1475
Web: www.theredcanarychicago.com
Prices: $$

Lunch Sat – Sun
Dinner nightly
 Chicago (Blue)

  Billed as a "gastrolounge," the Red Canary is a 1920s-style speakeasy meets the 21st century. Here, diners luxuriate in cushy red booths in the main area or perched in balconies. The Victorian, art deco space is crowned by a giant crystal chandelier.

Sultry ambience and a desirable cocktail menu make this nest a natural choice for post-work drinks and apps. Pair drinks like the "Muckraker Mojito" with some Vienna beef pigs in a blanket or fried green tomatoes; or just hit the comfort food carte with fried chicken aside red-skinned mashed potatoes, luscious seafood pot pie, or spring strawberry shortcake made with flaky biscuits.

Locals love the expansive ivy-lined large beer garden in back, which often hosts live jazz among its olive trees and flowers.

Rios D'Sudamerica

B2

2010 W. Armitage Ave. (bet. Damen and Hoyne Sts.)

Phone: 773-276-0170
Web: www.riosdesudamerica.com
Prices: $$

Lunch & dinner daily
 Damen (Blue)

 This sophisticated Peruvian restaurant goes to great lengths to distinguish itself from the many Latin eateries in the neighborhood and in the city. It starts with the ambience: choose between the front area for plush seating, drinks, and small bites; main dining room, with banquettes and murals; or a more romantic second-floor mezzanine.

While the heart of the restaurant is Peruvian, there are also choices of traditional Central and South American dishes to sample. Their excellent *tamal verde* features smooth Andean corn dough with cilantro wrapped around tender cubes of chicken, egg, and chile peppers, steamed in husks. Desserts include a passion fruit cheesecake, a mousse-like twist on the common finale, with an intensely sweet-tart punch.

Ruxbin Kitchen

851 N. Ashland Ave. (at Pearson St.)

Phone: 312-624-8509
Web: www.ruxbinchicago.com
Prices: $$

Dinner Tue – Sun
 Division

Eclectic, fun, and maybe a tad bizarre, this über-popular Noble Square favorite is as successful as it is freewheeling (note the no-reservations policy). The funky setting is comprised of all things refurbished, reclaimed, and repurposed to fashion a timeless interior that may never grow boring (see the cookbook pages decoupaged on the ceiling).

On the menu, find a comparably eclectic offering of American bistro fare made with talent and globetrotting flair. The limited, seasonal offerings may include humble empanadas with a headspinning range of fillings, from traditional Oaxaca cheese to the unexpected kimchi. Flaky, fresh, and perfectly pan-seared trout demonstrates the kitchen's skill, creatively set atop young asparagus and sticky sweet dates.

Sabor Saveur

2013 W. Division St. (bet. Damen & Hoyne Aves.)

Phone: 773-235-7310
Web: www.saborsaveur.com
Prices: $$

Lunch Sat – Sun
Dinner Tue – Sun
 Damen (Blue)

While many have heard of the creative dishes on the menu at this BYO, few have tasted anything like them before. Here, enchiladas are reinvented with unfamiliar fillings like Maine lobster, shrimp, hazelnuts, and coconut-guava slaw. Chile poblano is stuffed with walnuts, ricotta, and a flavorful tomatillo sauce; while beef, pork, and fruit tamales eschew the familiar husk and are wrapped in delicate phyllo.

Forget the classics when dining here. Instead, find modern Mexican kissed by French flavors and techniques. Inside, modern minimalism takes center stage with a black-and-white palette, simple furnishings, and dramatic candelabra. The open kitchen showcases the action and dedicated staff behind these cross-cultural culinary creations.

Schwa ✿

Contemporary

B3

1466 N. Ashland Ave. (at Le Moyne St.)

Phone: 773-252-1466
Web: www.schwarestaurant.com
Prices: $$$

Dinner Tue – Sat
Division

nickb@hystk

This cutting-edge, BYOB restaurant definitely has the goods to back up its hype, but you'll have to jump through a few hoops first—namely, a frustrating reservations system and a sketchy hump out to the fringes of Wicker Park. Wear your glasses: tucked behind an unassuming façade along a seedy stretch of Ashland, it's easy to cruise past the three-story standalone brick structure that houses Schwa.

But let none of that dissuade you, for one bite of Schwa's fare—compliments of the talented Michael Carlson and his small army of brilliant chefs—and you'll quickly forget all that. In this small, intimate dining room dressed in warm walls, find one of the country's most novel restaurants, where the chefs are your servers and the food is out of this world.

Carlson, who worked with Heston Blumenthal and Grant Achatz before going solo, offers two prix-fixe menus nightly; and though the menu changes often, yours may unveil baby biscuits (using the chef's grandmother's recipe) with fried sweetbreads and braised mustard greens, laced in an irresistible red-eye gravy; or pristine Wagyu beef with shad roe, a creamy sauce made from a coddled hen egg, sautéed Brussels sprouts, and parsley purée.

Siboney

Cuban ✗

A2

2165 N. Western Ave. (at Palmer Ave.)

Phone: 773-904-7210
Web: www.siboneychicago.com
Prices: 💰

Lunch & dinner daily
🚇 Western (Blue)

In many ways, Cuba's kitchens are an amalgam of the best Spanish, African, and Caribbean traditions. The neighborhood that houses Siboney (named for a city in Cuba) is likewise an amalgam and celebration of its culture. This is a lovely, bright, and tidy corner location graced with many windows for people watching and a front lounge that hosts occasional music performances.

Siboney captures Cuba's vibrant cuisine by focusing on the country's staples (chicken, pork, lobster, and fish) and preparing them with authenticity, whether raw or stewed. The Cuban-style pork ribs are incredibly tender and sweet, the tantalizing bread pudding is spiked with lots of cognac, and the dark, rich, coffee blended with milk and sugar will have you feeling truly *cubano*.

Smoke Daddy

Barbecue ✗

B4

1804 W. Division St. (at Wood St.)

Phone: 773-772-6656
Web: www.thesmokedaddy.com
Prices: 💰

Lunch & dinner daily
🚇 Division

Sometimes you just need to slow down: southern drawls, slow-cooked barbecue, and blues usually do the trick. Such relaxing influences can be found at this neighborhood joint, with nightly live music and a mouthwatering menu of wood-smoked goods. A corrugated aluminum bar, low lighting, and 1950s-era photographs give "The Daddy" its laid-back, retro vibe.

Whether your tastes run to Memphis, Kansas City, or Carolina barbecue, the trifecta of tabletop sauces gives everyone a taste to crow about. Douse your pulled pork, brisket, or ribs then buy a bottle of your fav for the home grillmaster. Ribs are smoky and tender, but the chicken a bit dry and not worth the calories. Save those for the pork-studded, smoky baked beans or the gooey macaroni and cheese.

173

Spring

 A3

2039 W. North Ave. (bet. Damen & Hoyne Aves.)

Phone: 773-395-7100
Web: www.springrestaurant.net
Prices: $$$

Dinner Wed – Sun
Damen (Blue)

You can leave your rubber ducky behind when visiting Spring. Once the historic Luxor Bathhouse, built in 1923 and styled after the Russian and Turkish baths, this retreat now lures visitors with mostly seafood, not suds. The sunken dining room recalls its former incarnation, while the minimalist décor creates a Zen-like mood.

The New American cuisine puts a spring in your step. Let your tongue tingle with teasers like farm egg ravioli served over a brown butter sauce and spiked with white truffle oil. Seafood pops up all over the menu, which reads like a world traveler's itinerary (Australian barramundi, Maine sea scallops, Pacific sea bass). Sides like Korean pancakes with peekytoe crab and Thai-dressed Brussels sprouts show off an Asian influence.

Sushi X

C5

1136 W. Chicago Ave. (bet. May St. & Racine Ave.)

Phone: 312-491-9232
Web: www.sushi-x.net
Prices: $$

Lunch Mon – Fri
Dinner nightly
 Chicago (Blue)

The *animé* projected on a side wall is your first clue that this is not your average sushi joint. Add in the techno music, small stone tables, low-lighting, and 20- and 30-something crowd from the neighborhood, and you'll have your gut feeling confirmed.

The menu further confirms that this is not a place to come for traditional sushi. The crowds flock in for contemporary rolls loaded up with long lists of ingredients. Among the don't-miss dishes are the Red Dragon Roll, a spicy roll with tempura shrimp, chili sauce, jalapeño, and *tobiko* that is topped with piquant tuna, sliced scallions, and smoky-sweet eel sauce. The spicy tuna roll is truly spicy. Those who are not into raw fish should try the smoky, hot asparagus beef roll.

Takashi ✿

Contemporary ✗✗

B2

1952 N. Damen Ave. (at Armitage Ave.)

Phone: 773-772-6170
Web: www.takashichicago.com
Prices: $$$

Lunch Sun
Dinner Tue – Sun
🚇 Damen (Blue)

Tyllie Barbosa Photography

Unlike the rest on this busy Bucktown block, Takashi successfully manages to straddle the terrain between a great neighborhood niche and that nearby dining destination ideal for every celebration. Chef/owner Takashi Yagihashi routed and ran Okada at the Wynn in Las Vegas, before setting his sights on Chicago. With his Windy City transition, he also brought to town devoted service, wise wine masters, a polished staff, and an alluring French-American-Japanese carte.

In this bungalow, the ambience is serene and the décor cutting edge, further accentuated by naked tables and a semi-open kitchen where Takashi himself can be seen manning the fire. His menu is divided between small plates (hot and cold) and large; so come prepped and don't deny yourself a touch. It may be prudent to pick from each category though—veal sweetbreads and Maine skate wing cooked to perfection make for a lovely start.

Dishes that show off Takashi's skill and technique include the winter roll, a cylinder of prosciutto, briny shrimp, peppery arugula, pine nuts, and a sweet and tart mustard-caper-golden raisin vinaigrette. Providing a remarkable contrast in textures is a crouton, tucked inside the roll.

175

Taxim

Greek

1558 N. Milwaukee Ave. (bet. Damen & North Aves.)

Phone: 773-252-1558
Web: www.taximchicago.com
Prices: $$

Lunch Sat – Sun
Dinner Wed – Mon
 Damen (Blue)

Sharing a tasty spread of hot and cold dishes is the best way to go at Taxim. So grab a group of gastronomes and head over to the Wicker Park newcomer, where cuisine takes a pan-Hellenic adventure, traversing the islands, villages, and cities of Greece. From *Xoriatiti salada*—heirloom tomatoes tossed in tangy red wine vinaigrette, Greek oregano, cucumbers, and feta; *loukaniko kaisareias*—spicy lamb sausage served with pickled spring onion and *kasseri* cheese; to sumptuous green lentils fused with fermented sheep's feta, dishes are exquisitely authentic and fresh.

Inside, arched entry ways, exposed brick walls, and richly colored throw pillows on wooden banquettes create an old-world vibe. A lovely list of regional Greek wines adds to the experience.

Thai Village

A4

Thai

2053 W. Division St. (at Hoyne St.)

Phone: 773-384-5352
Web: N/A
Prices: 🍪🍪

Lunch & dinner daily
 Damen (Blue)

The carved wood door and decorative woodwork indicate that you're at the right place when you walk up to this corner storefront. Inside, exposed brick walls, high wooden booths, pressed-tin ceilings painted blue, and Thai-style artwork set the mood.

The menu here is served hot and made to order, with sizzling sounds enticing diners from behind a brick wall. Start with the likes of golden brown fish cakes served warm, with a salad of cucumbers, red chilies, and fresh cilantro, then move on to a delicious curry. The single dessert option is a homemade carrot cake—moist and tender beneath its bright orange glaze. Those with a sweet tooth can also enjoy the traditional Thai iced coffee, strong and dark with a sweet kick from the condensed milk.

Thalia Spice

D5

Asian

833 W. Chicago Ave. (at Green St.)

Phone: 312-226-6020
Web: www.thaliaspice.com
Prices: $$

Lunch Sun – Fri
Dinner nightly
 Chicago (Blue)

Cruise into this sexy spot and find an exotic-meets-urban landscape, where locals and free spirits pack a space rocking rustic brick walls, exposed duct work, and neon colored light installations. Around the corner from Chicago Avenue, the massive carved wooden doors make an impressive greeting, though the actual entrance is a few feet over on Green Street. Now, if you've come here seeking sushi, we'd suggest skipping it.

Focus instead on the delectable South Asian specialties—there's even the option to customize a meal according to your country of choice. Savor the Laotian *nomtok* salad—tender chicken tossed with onions, roasted peanuts, ginger, lime, and cilantro; yummy *yaya* noodles; warm Malaysian *roti canai*; or one of five versions of fried rice.

tocco

B4

Italian

1266 N. Milwaukee Ave. (bet. Ashland Ave. & Paulina St.)

Phone: 773-687-8895
Web: www.toccochicago.com
Prices: $$

Dinner nightly
 Division

In a space that is as much a homage to haute couture as it is a trendy Italian restaurant, the only thing thinner that the crust is the clientele. Even the bronzed sunglass-wearing host looks like he'd be more at home on Valentino's yacht in the Riviera. Still hotter than the crowd, the black-and-white dining room dons pink faux-ostrich leather walls, shiny white resin chairs, and hip Italian furniture. Wood-burning ovens churn out cracker-crisp artisanal pizzas (the way to go) in addition to pastas and heartier entrées, like *involtini di pollo*, with prosciutto and rosemary rolled around thinly sliced chicken breasts.

If talk of the latest fashion leaves you feeling empty, enjoy free Sunday yoga lessons in the courtyard during the summer months.

West Town Tavern

American ❌❌

C5

1329 W. Chicago Ave. (at Throop St.)

Phone: 312-666-6175
Web: www.westtowntavern.com
Prices: $$

Dinner Mon – Sat
 Chicago (Blue)

If comfort food is what you need, consider letting Chef/owner Susan Goss do the cooking. She and her husband Drew (who brings genuine hospitality to the front of house) are active in the community; and, as a result, their warm tavern has become a neighborhood gathering place and local leader in home-style fare.

The bulk of their business comes from regulars who clamor for nightly specials, like fried chicken and biscuits or the Wagyu beef burger with curried sweet potato chips. The velvety-tender zinfandel-braised pot roast with tangy Pennsylvania Dutch black vinegar sauce and hearty garlic mashed potatoes is one of their long-time favorites. No comfort food fest would be complete without dessert: try the bourbon pecan pie or the apple turnover.

Your opinions are important to us. Please write to us at: michelin.guides@ us.michelin.com

Humboldt Park & Logan Square

Albany Park • Irving Park

This collection of vibrant north side neighborhoods is the heart and soul of where locals live and eat. While the area may lie a few blocks off the beaten path, it is great for anyone seeking that perfect dessert, ethnic grocer, hidden bodega, or quick falafel. Plus, any trip through these up-and-coming neighborhoods is sure to be heavenly with tree-lined streets, quaint architecture, and affordable, trendy stops. Begin your adventure in Chicago's Koreatown, a commercial thoroughfare spanning miles along Lawrence Avenue, from Cicero to California Avenue.

HUMBOLDT PARK

The core of the city's Puerto Rican community is found here. If there's any confusion as to exactly where it begins, just look for the Paseo Boricua, the flag-shaped steel gateway demarcating the district along Division Street. These storefronts are as much a celebration of the diaspora as the homeland, with their impressive and delicious array of traditional foods, hard-to-find ingredients, and authentic taquerias.

LOGAN SQUARE

An eclectic mix of cuisines (from Cuban and Mexican, to Italian) combined with historic buildings and boulevards, attract a crowd of hipsters,

working-class locals, artists, and students to this quarter. Within this community, locally-minded at-home cooks and foodies flock to the **Dill Pickle Food Co-op** for bulk groceries. Visitors opt for Sunday's **Logan Square Farmer's Market** on Logan Blvd., with stalls hawking everything from artisanal soaps and raw honey to organic zucchini. Adults and kids have been saving their allowances for a trip to **Margie's Candies**, for its homemade chocolates, toffees, and hot fudge sundaes.

A melting pot of global foods, Albany Park offers every gastronomic delight at budget-friendly prices. Highlights include **Al Khayyam Bakery**, a Middle Eastern grocery with cheeses, olive oils, and flatbreads. For dessert, lull at **Nazareth Sweets** for brittles and pastries like walnut or baklava. **Charcoal Delights** is a time-tested, unique burger favorite with its array of chicken, cheesesteak, and hot dogs with "the works" rounding out the menu.

You will be in good hands at **The Fishguy Market**, which supplies restaurants and home-cooks with quality seafood and service. The nearby **Independence Park Farmer's Market** is also worth a trip. This fast-growing market will satisfy with its array of produce, plants, and baked goods.

Accanto

C4

2172 N. Milwaukee Ave. (at Francis Pl.)

Phone: 773-227-2727
Web: www.accanto-chicago.com
Prices: $$

Lunch & dinner Wed – Mon
🚇 California (Blue)

This slick space, located below the Lucky Vito's pizza sign, feels as much like a lounge as a restaurant. Upbeat music, mod light fixtures, and large antique mirrors fuse Old and New worlds.

Italian-born, Chef Domenico Acampora hails from Milan, but cooked in the Philippines and Saudi Arabia, and brings that global experience to his Italian menu with light modern touches. For example, the classic antipasto of prosciutto and melon comes instead with tissue-thin slices of Serrano ham and a creamy cantaloupe gelato. The bone-in, pan-roasted veal chop, topped with a slice of Parma ham and melted Emmenthal cheese, is a playful take on *saltimbocca*, while a molten dark chocolate cake is paired with mango ice cream.

Arun's

B1

4156 N. Kedzie Ave. (at Berteau Ave.)

Phone: 773-539-1909
Web: www.arunsthai.com
Prices: $$$$

Dinner Tue – Sun
🚇 Kedzie (Brown)

Chef/owner Arun Sampanthavivat oversees every detail at this culinary mainstay. Even the music on the restaurant's website is his creation, and the stunning mural in the back of the restaurant was painted by his brother.

The idea behind this upscale Thai is that there is only one menu option available, a 12-course prix-fixe of six appetizers, four entrées , and two desserts, all served family-style. When booking reservations, you'll be asked if you have any allergies, and that information will be taken into account. The dishes change regularly, but expect creations like the spicy tomato soup, served with tempura-fried chrysanthemum leaf.

The meal is nicely paced, and the wine list does justice to the menu. Arun's is an experience as much as a meal.

Azucar

B3

Spanish

2647 N. Kedzie Ave. (bet. Milwaukee & Schubert Aves.)

Phone: 773-486-6464
Web: www.azucartapasrestaurant.com
Prices: $$

Dinner Wed   Sun
Logan Square

There is no dearth of small plate spots in the city, yet this dinner-only tapas and cocktail bar across from the Logan Square El is worth seeking out. The narrow room is outfitted with dark wood, exposed brick, mosaic tiles, and glass ceiling pendants. Ingredients are all-important here, where the kitchen makes its own chorizo, and offers a good selection of imported cheeses with honey, fig jam, and almonds to accompany those glasses of wines from Spain. On the menu, find the likes of roasted red peppers and cheese garnished with lemony chickpea purée; tempting paella with plump whole clams; or slices of spice-rubbed pork tenderloin with a sweet and sour pomegranate gastrique and farro studded with dried blueberries and pistachios.

Brand BBQ Market

B4

Barbecue

2824 W. Armitage Ave. (at Mozart St.)

Phone: 773-687-8148
Web: www.brandbbqmarket.com
Prices: ⊜

Lunch Mon   Fri
Dinner nightly
Western (Blue)

Tender pulled duck sandwich with a side of bourbon creamed corn? Check. Venison sausage stuffed with Gorgonzola and wrapped in bacon atop fried onions and brandy cherry sauce? Check. Old-fashioned barbecue getting a mouthwatering makeover? Double check. Amp up those 'cue cravings and step into this wooden oasis where wood banquettes and thick varnished tables adorn the space; while aromatic woods like apple and hickory, smoke those juicy meats. A retail area selling chunks of wood, entices the ambitious to recreate the experience at home.

Sample the selection of savory sauces on the table, from smoky chipotle to tangy-sweet brown sugar-cayenne. Vegetarians, you won't feel left out with meaty smoked tofu and portobello mushrooms, but don't forget to BYOB.

Bonsoirée 🏶

Contemporary ✗✗

2728 W. Armitage Ave. (bet. California Ave. & North Point St.)

Phone: 773-486-7511
Web: www.bon-soiree.com
Prices: $$$

Dinner Tue – Sat
California (Blue)

Bonsoirée

Don't have a chef in your inner circle? Don't fret. Bonsoirée will come through for you—it bleeds that dinner-with-friends feel. There is no sign outside as the chef likes to keep things on the down-low (he scored his stripes cooking underground dinner parties), but once inside this intimate space, you'll know you've arrived. It's mod minimalism with a bit of Japanese know-how—envisage wood floors, leather chairs, and shoots and stalks decorating the odd corner.

A word to the wise: don't come armed with a laundry list of requests. Bonsoirée is strictly prix-fixe, so choose a four- or seven-course menu (13 courses are available with advance notice), sit back, and await a cavalcade of photogenic and flavorful dishes. From scallop and peekytoe crab *motoyaki* presented inside a shell over a salt bed, to a wooden box filled with applewood-smoked pork cheek bacon with quail egg and star anise marshmallow, dinners are a feast for all of the senses.

The staff will educate you. Perhaps just a tiny sprinkling, but they revere the chef and wax poetic about the ingredients and preparations. There is no wine cellar, so tote your own or stop by a nearby store (some deliver with notice).

Chilapan

C4

Mexican ✗

2459 W. Armitage Ave. (at Campbell Ave.)

Phone: 773-697-4374
Web: N/A
Prices: $$

Dinner Mon – Sat
 Western (Blue)

It's a rip-roaring scene in Chilapan's kitchen, where blaring beats keep a lively team of young cooks (and one revered elder) on their toes, as they spin out plate after plate of soulful scrumptiousness. This sure ain't your average taco stand; and though the space is snug and the El may be raging directly above, the flavor-packed menu will grab every ounce of your attention.

Savor the orange-*guajillo* glazed wild salmon, an ample fillet grilled to perfection, served atop sweet potato purée and mango salsa; tender skirt steak stuffed with spinach and *arbol* tomato salsa; or empanda *potosina*, loaded with *chihuaha*, *panela*, and chiles, and served with tomatillo salsa. Close with warm chocolate cake, oozing with cinnamon cream, and never look back.

Flying Saucer

C5

American ✗

1123 N. California Ave. (at Haddon Ave.)

Phone: 773-342-9076
Web: N/A
Prices:

Lunch daily

The Flying Saucer may look retro, like a 1950s-esque diner complete with a Formica counter, but there's nothing "Leave It To Beaver" about this anti-establishment gathering place. A well-pierced and tattooed crowd enjoys breakfast all day in this spot where the walls are lined with local artists work.

The kitchen created a homey diner menu with a twist, popular with vegetarians and locavores. Try the *huevos volando*, two eggs (organic for a few cents more) cooked your way and smothered in a homemade, spicy and smoky salsa, *guajillo* sauce, tangy pepperjack, and ripe avocado over warm corn tortillas. A side of organic black beans accompanies, and bright cilantro and sweet chopped onion finish the dish. Wash it all down with refreshing lavender lemonade.

Chicago ▲ Humboldt Park & Logan Square

Kuma's Corner

American ✗

B3

2900 W. Belmont Ave. (at Francisco Ave.)

Phone: 773-604-8769   Lunch & dinner daily
Web: www.kumascorner.com
Prices: 🍴

Dig out your old Metallica t-shirt and you'll fit right in at this heavy metal-themed burger joint and dive bar serving locally made beers. It's racy and raucous with head-banging music, so leave Grandma and the kids behind. Forget about any conversation since Iron Maiden will be pounding in your ears, but in a place with burgers this good, your mouth will be otherwise engaged.

Keeping with the unconventional theme, each burger is named for a heavy metal band from Megadeth to Black Sabbath. Juicy and delicious, these heavenly burgers are the clear draw, as in the Lair of the Minotaur, served on a pretzel roll piled high with caramelized onions, pancetta, creamy Brie, and bourbon-soaked pears.

Lula Café 🍴

American ✗

B3

2537 N. Kedzie Ave. (off Logan Blvd.)

Phone: 773-489-9554   Lunch & dinner Wed – Mon
Web: www.lulacafe.com   🚇 Logan Square
Prices: $$

Husband-and-wife owners Jason Hammel and Amalea Tshilds (also of Nightwood) turned this funky, offbeat eatery into one of the city's leading organic and sustainable restaurants. While they are serious about the locavore movement, they don't take themselves too seriously. The staff here is young, hip, and relaxed; the diners are regulars.

Over the years their loyal following and inventive menu have expanded, but favorites keep locals returning to this fun, quirky dining room decorated with Busy Beaver buttons, an upright piano, and picture window. Entrées may include a perfect nest of spaghetti in a sweet and spicy chili sauce with bacon, and fresh cheese. Soups and desserts, like the moist carrot cake, sustain the pleasure from start to finish.

Longman & Eagle

Gastropub 🍴

2657 N. Kedzie Ave. (at Schubert Ave.)

Phone:	773-276-7110	Lunch & dinner daily
Web:	www.longmananddeagle.com	🚇 Logan Square
Prices:	**$$**	

Dig out the old Buddy Holly glasses, squeeze into your skinny jeans, and groom that goatee for a night out at Longman & Eagle. This Logan Square hipster has that studied laid-back aspect: on the surface, the uncut diamond seems a dash dank, but don't let that scare you away, it's all part of a plan.

Inside is boho chic at its best with well-worn tables and chairs arranged in that miscellany casual gastropub sort of way. The trendy staff has cornered the market on nerd chic, but hang around the expert bartenders and you'll feel like one of 'em. This place really sings brown—they've got whiskey flights, a mighty list of bourbons, and other fascinating boozey things.

Pub fare gone gastro is what this kitchen doles out, and it is drop-dead creative. Got a hankering for wings? Go for frog's legs prepped Buffalo wing-style, paired with aerated blue cheese dip. It may sound weird, but it is mmm mmm good. Feeling less reckless? Elect the masterful English pea *agnolotti* fluffed with porcinis, pea tendrils, Parmesan, and truffled butter. The decadent desserts (gooey chocolate banana bread pudding with bourbon anglaise) are oh-so-seductive and will leave you forever infatuated.

Maiz

Mexican

 C5

1041 N. California Ave. (bet. Cortez & Thomas Sts.)

Phone: 773-276-3149   Dinner Tue – Sun
Web: N/A
Prices: ⊜⊜

An authentic Mexican restaurant in the heart of Humboldt Park isn't a surprise. Faithful Mexican-American life is what this area is all about. But even here, Maiz Antojitos Y Bebidas is a standout.

The menu is a celebration of corn and its common variations found as Mexican snacks, as the name suggests. Try anything corn-heavy like the *elote*, served street-style slathered with butter, mayo, cheese and chile powder; or the *tamal de elote*, two uniquely corn-flavored tamales served simply with lettuce and tomato. The *corundas*, a heavenly street food from Michoacan, are a delightful find here bathed in a dark mole with onions, crumbled cheese, and *crema*. Get a little green mixed in with your yellow by adding the *nopales*, a salad of diced cactus paddles.

Mirabell

German

B2

3454 W. Addison St. (bet. Kimball & St. Louis Aves.)

Phone: 773-463-1962   Lunch & dinner daily
Web: www.mirabellrestaurant.com   Addison (Blue)
Prices: $$

Looking for a taste of the Old Country without leaving your leafy environs? Head straight for Mirabell, where locals have been raising their steins since 1977. From the dirndl-clad waitresses and the accordion and Alpine music, to the pastoral German murals and shaded *biergarten*, this place is Bavarian from head to toe.

Wursts, schnitzels, spaetzle, sauerkraut, and spicy beef goulash—it's enough to bring a tear to the eye of even the steeliest *frau*. Mirabell is meat lover's paradise, so save the date with your veggie friend for another day (though there are some sandwiches and salads, but why bother?). It might not be fancy, but it sure is flavorful; and the traditional food is complemented by an almost exclusively German list of brews.

Noon-O-Kabab

Persian

B1

4661 N. Kedzie Ave. (at Leland Ave.)

Phone: 773-279-9309

Web: www.noonokabab.com

Prices: 💿

Lunch & dinner daily

🚇 Kedzie (Brown)

Noon-O-Kabab is that great little neighborhood spot you hit up for its good food, reasonable prices, and über friendly service. Tucked into arched alcoves, the tile floors and wood furnishings may be simple, but its walls are adorned with beautiful tile murals of dancing figurines.

Delightful Persian specialties are the order of the day. Swing by for a comforting bowl of *ghormeh sabzi*—a stew of lamb, red beans, spinach, fenugreek, and cilantro; or *joujeh kouhideh*—skewers of juicy, saffron-flavored, charbroiled chicken, served with dill-lima bean basmati rice, and the traditional charbroiled whole tomato. Their bustling catering business a few doors down (also the spot for pick-up and delivery), sells the best *bastani* (Persian gelato) in sunnier months.

Pork Shoppe

Barbecue

C3

2755 W. Belmont Ave. (bet. California & Washtenaw Aves.)

Phone: 773-961-7654

Web: www.porkshoppechicago.com

Prices: 💿

Lunch & dinner Tue – Sun

🚇 Belmont (Blue)

Step into this den of macho—boasting boutique barbecue—and thank your stars the men are brilliant behind the smokers, as they certainly make for dull decorators. The stoic dining room (imagine wood floors, a rusted communal bar, tables, and chairs) is barely enriched by framed mirrors and relics of old farming equipment.

But, pork is Prada here and shoppers have perfected the routine: place an order, take a number, a wad of brown towels, and sauce (sweet, tangy, and wicked) up! A sammy with smoked pork belly pastrami may steal the show; but window-shop your way through other items like Texas brisket tacos, crunchy and fragrant with onion and cilantro; and oversized chocolate chip cookies. Best with your barbecue is beer, wine, and…bourbon.

189

Chicago ▲ Humboldt Park & Logan Square

Semiramis

Lebanese ⑂

B1

4639 N. Kedzie Ave. (bet. Eastwood & Leland Aves.)

Phone: 773-279-8900 Lunch & dinner Mon – Sat
Web: www.semiramisrestaurant.com Kedzie (Brown)
Prices: ⑤

This Lebanese café outshines the competition in an ethnically diverse area filled with Middle Eastern eateries, Korean restaurants, and halal meat shops.

Inside the pleasant space, where colorful tapestries brighten the walls as art, Semiramis offers tasty takes on standards, from refreshing salads to golden-brown falafel patties with hints of garlic, sesame oil, and parsley, wrapped in warm and tender flatbread. Have that alongside French fries topped with sumac and garlic for a serious non-burger-and-fries treat.

With its focus on good, simple, fresh Lebanese food made from quality ingredients, Semiramis does it right, while providing an inviting place to sit and eat. Both eat-in and to-go orders are filled quickly by the friendly staff.

Smoque BBQ

Barbecue ⑂

A2

3800 N. Pulaski Rd. (at Grace St.)

Phone: 773-545-7427 Lunch & dinner Tue – Sun
Web: www.smoquebbq.com Irving Park (Blue)
Prices: ⑤

City-dwellers and suburbanites alike flock to this Irving Park spot just off the Kennedy for one good reason: righteous Texas-style barbecue. The counter service is friendly and the ambience energetic, but people really come here for the applewood-smoked meats.

And what dreamy meats: smoky, juicy, sauce-splattered barbecue perfection. Smoked for 12 hours, the result is tender and sweet with those divine bits of crispness. Options include pulled pork, brisket, chicken, Texas sausage and meaty ribs—both baby back and St. Louis-style. Even the slaw and cornbread are done just right—a further testament to the owners dedication to the craft. The peach cobbler is a must add-on to any tray; sure you're full but who doesn't have room for a little more goodness?

Taqueria Moran

Mexican 🍴

2226 N. California Ave. (bet. Lyndale St. & Milwaukee Ave.)

Phone: 773-235-2663
Web: N/A
Prices: 😋😋

Lunch & dinner daily
California (Blue)

Here, in the shiny, wide-open stainless steel kitchen, Guadalupe Moran whips up lip-smacking Mexican eats all day long—yep, that's breakfast, lunch, and dinner. Hop into this beloved neighborhood taqueria–practically hiding under the blue line–and find a spanking clean and colorful room replete with terra-cotta ceilings and a bright mural depicting a bucolic, south of the border scene.

Tuck in a napkin and brush up on your *español* as you tackle the vast, delicious menu (having a decent hold on the language helps; not all the friendly servers are English speaking). Whether it's juicy pork *adobado* tacos; cilantro packed *carne asada*; or sizzling *fajitas mixtas* (chicken, shrimp, or beef with beans, tortillas, and veggies), food here seriously satisfies.

Urban Belly

Asian 🍴

3053 N. California Ave. (bet. Barry Ave. & Nelson St.)

Phone: 773-583-0500
Web: www.urbanbellychicago.com
Prices: 😋😋

Lunch & dinner Tue – Sun
Belmont (Blue)

Chef/owner Bill Kim welcomes diners into a space that is decidedly understated and minimalist, highlighting Chinese elmwood communal tables and chunky stools—great for larger groups as well as socially minded solo diners. Just remember to order at the counter before choosing your perch. The Asian menu shows strong Korean influence, but sates any appetite with its variety of dumplings, as in the excitingly delicious lamb and brandy with sun-dried tomato relish. Pan-Asian seasonings and interesting combinations, such as pork belly fried rice with pineapple *brunoise*, tempt some to abandon the chopsticks and just pick up a fork. Noodle dishes are substantial, like udon with shrimp in a sweet chili-lime broth. Tableside condiments add even more zest.

Lakeview & Wrigleyville
Roscoe Village

"Peanuts! Get your peanuts!" When the Cubs are playing, expect to hear the call of salty ball-game snacks through the north side's best-known neighborhood, though locals may actually be stopping into **Nuts on Clark** for some pre-game caramel corn. Lakeview is the umbrella term for the area north of Lincoln Park, including Wrigleyville (named after its iconic ball field) and Roscoe Village.

ENTER EASTERN EUROPE

Even when the beloved Cubs aren't playing at Wrigley Field (as sadly happens each October), American summertime classics continue to shape the area's cuisine, yet for historic reasons. Thanks to their large Eastern European immigrant population, an abundant variety of sausages and wursts can be found in casual eateries and markets located on a number of blocks.

Showcasing these juicy and tender specialties is the beloved **Paulina Meat Market**, where expected items like corned beef, lamb, veal, and turkey are offered alongside the more novel offerings such as ground venison, loin chops, and "baseball bat summer sausages." The local Swedish population knows to come here for tried and true favorites such as pickled Christmas hams and cardamom-infused sausages.

CLASSIC CHICAGO

Equally important and comparably carnivorous is Chicago's love for the humble hot dog. Here, chefs, foodies, and touristas stand in lines that may wraparound the block at **Hot Doug's**, the lunch-only purveyor of creatively encased meats in combinations named either to celebrate sultry starlets (like the spicy "Keira Knightly"), or maybe immortalize their friends. Fridays and Saturdays are particularly crowded, because that's when Doug (the bespeckled gentleman at the counter) serves duck fat fries.

Byron's Dog Haus isn't as gourmet, but both the hot dogs and burgers are classic Chicago and very tasty. Note that the location near Wrigley only has outdoor picnic tables and no inside seating.

BAKING IN BAVARIA

Even Chicagoans can't live on hot dogs alone. When they crave something else, they have their choice in Lakeview. Bavarian baked goods have been a mainstay of **Dinkel's Bakery** since 1922 (and in its current locale since 1932). Originally opened by a master baker who hailed from Southern Bavaria, the business is still family run and remains famous for its traditional renditions of strudels, butter kuchen, and, stollen (items can be purchased fresh, but are also available frozen for shipping). Also praiseworthy is Dinkel's Burglaur (a big breakfast sandwich), and their delightful donut selection is addictive and all the rage.

NOURISH YOUR SWEET TOOTH

For a different type of sweet, stop in for the globally-influenced, Chicago-based **Mayana Chocolates** in flavors as accessible as cookies n' cream and rasberry-dark chocolate; or the more exotic Turkish coffee and hazelnut and coriander praline. At her **Bittersweet Pastry Shop**, Chef/owner Judy Contino is famous for her wedding cakes, pastries, and other delights like breakfast breads, cheesecakes, brownies, and cupcakes. She's been sculpting these sweet treats for almost two decades now.

Those seeking a more local, sustainable, and punk-rock experience should head to the **Bleeding Heart Organic Bakery** for cakepops, bars, and cupcakes that are listed as either Plain Jane (as in chocolate raspberry), or the Fancy Schmancy (ginger-mint mojito maybe?). They also strut an array of breakfast and dessert items.

Another laudation (even if they come in buttery and sugary packages) to Chicago's neighborhoods, is **City Caramels**. Walk in to this sanctum of sweet to be greeted by simple, lip-smacking treats. Eat your way through Bucktown (think coffee-inspired caramels with chocolate-covered espresso beans); Lincoln Square (toasted hazelnuts anybody?), and Pilsen (fragrant cinnamon, ancho chili, and *pepitas*) with their respective caramel and candy cuts. However, Chicagoans who prefer to end their meals with a bite, should head to **Pastoral**—hailed as one of the country's top spots for cheese. Their selection of classic and farmstead cheeses as well as fresh breads and olives is a local favorite, as are their weekend classes and tastings.

FASCINATING FOOD FINDS

An offbeat, quirky vibe is part of what makes Lakeview thrive. Testament to this is **The Flower Flat**, that cooks up a comforting breakfast and brunch in an actual flower shop. Meanwhile, **Uncommon Ground** is as much a restaurant serving three meals a day, as it is a coffee shop known for its musical acts. From June through September, stop by on Friday evenings to tour America's first certified organic rooftop garden before tasting its bounty on your plate downstairs.

REVEL IN ROSCOE VILLAGE

The Landshark Lager Oyster Festival attracts folks to Roscoe Village each September with Irish and American music, plenty of beer, and a certain mollusk believed to have aphrodisiac qualities. Homesick New Yorkers and transplants take note: this neighborhood is also home to **Apart Pizza**, Chicago's very own homage to the thin-crust pie, though you might be wise to refrain from admitting how much you enjoyed it. Remember, this is a true find and guilty pleasure in deep-dish land.

Lakeview & Wrigleyville

A **B** ANDERSONVILLE, EDGEWATER & UPTOWN **C**

WELLES PARK

Sunnyside Ave.

W. Montrose Ave.

Montrose Ave. Ⓜ Glenn's Diner X

W. Pensacola Ave. 𝖷𝖷 Chalkboard Ⓧ 𝖷 Mixteco **1**

W. Cullom Ave. Cullom

W. Berteau Ave. W. Berteau

Warner Ave.

Ⓐ 𝖷𝖷 Browntrout ●

Plaine W. Belle

𝖷 Sticky Rice ● Belle LAKE SCH PA **2**

W. Irving Park W. Irving Park Rd. Ⓜ

REVERE PARK St. *Irving Park* Ave. N.

𝖷 Always Thai ●

W. Byron St. 𝖷𝖷 Sola W.

W. Grace St. W.

LAKEVIE

W. Waveland Ave.

Addison St. Ⓜ *Addison* **3**

W. Addison W.

W. Cornelia Ave.

𝖷 El Tinajon ● *Paulina* Ⓜ

W. Roscoe St. 𝖷𝖷 Frasca

PARK 457 St. W. School St. 𝖷 Wishbone 𝖷

DEVRY UNIVERSITY

FELLGER PARK W. Belmont Ave.

W. 𝖷 A La Turka ● **4**

Barry HAMLIN PARK

W. Wellington St.

W. George St.

W. Diversey Pkwy. W. Diversey

W. Logan Blvd.

A BUCKTOWN & WICKER PARK **B** LINCOLN PARK & OLD TOWN **C**

HUMBOLDT PARK & LOGAN SQUARE

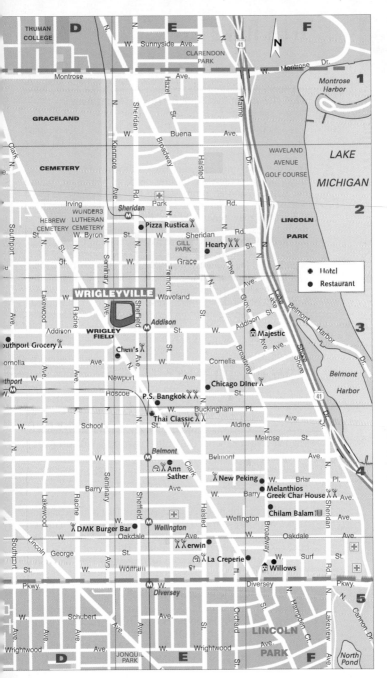

A La Turka

Turkish 🍴

3134 N. Lincoln Ave. (bet. Barry & Belmont Aves.)

Phone: 773-935-6101
Web: www.alaturkachicago.com
Prices: $$

Lunch Thu – Sun
Dinner nightly
🚇 Paulina

Feel like the ruler of your own Ottoman Empire at this beguiling, if somewhat kitschy, Turkish restaurant, where the attentive and accommodating staff treat everyone like a sultan. From the kilim-covered pillows and the Bedouin tent-style curtains to the vivid colors, this lively spot is a true feast for the eyes. There is even a small front area where diners can kick off their heels and sit akimbo among the many silk pillows strewn across the floor.

A La Turka's feast is not just for the eyes, though. The Turkish and Mediterranean cuisine is both authentic and delightful, perhaps including delicious mezes of grape leaves stuffed with currants and pine nuts served alongside fantastic pita bread. Impressive entrées include the tender grilled kebabs.

Always Thai

Thai 🍴

1825 W. Irving Park Rd. (bet. Ravenswood & Wolcott Aves.)

Phone: 773-929-0100
Web: www.alwaysthaichicago.com
Prices: 🍜

Lunch & dinner daily
🚇 Irving Park (Brown)

Nestled under the Brown Line El, Always Thai is more than just Thai. With satay, curries, edamame, tempura, and *shu mai* on the menu, it is a pan-Asian eatery, with a substantial take-out business for neighborhood residents. The room, which seats about 40, isn't fancy, but a colorful mural brightens the scene. *Nam sod* (ginger salad) is served in a fun, footed bowl, with a slightly sweetened lime dressing and is a light, unexpected start to the meal. *Pad kee mao* needs an extra kick from the chili sauce on the table but is a tasty dish of drunken noodles, served with plump shrimp. There isn't a specific regional focus to the menu here, but there aren't many missteps either, making Always Thai a good choice for post-Cubs games or a casual dinner.

Ann Sather 🐾

S c a n d i n a v i a n 🍴

E4

909 W. Belmont Ave. (bet. Clark St. & Wilton Ave.)

Phone: 773-348-2378
Web: www.annsather.com
Prices: 🍪

Lunch daily
🚇 Belmont (Brown/Red)

The cinnamon rolls served at this Swedish bakery and restaurant could rival deep-dish pizza as the iconic Chicago food—that's how strongly locals feel about them.

But those hot, fresh rolls glazed with sugar aren't the only reason breakfast-goers flock here. Despite the large volume of business Ann Sather does, the kitchen still pays attention to every detail. The roast duck comes out greaseless, and topped with the traditional sweet yet tart lingonberry sauce. Meats, pickled herring, Swedish meatballs, homemade sauerkraut with caraway seeds, and excellent spaetzle are all cooked to perfection, so a sampler plate is a good choice for the indecisive. The bottomless cups of coffee are an added bonus, as are a few more of those cinnamon rolls to-go.

Browntrout 🐾

A m e r i c a n 🍴🍴

B2

4111 N. Lincoln Ave. (bet. Belle Plaine & Warner Aves.)

Phone: 773-472-4111
Web: www.browntroutchicago.com
Prices: $$

Lunch Sun
Dinner Wed – Mon
🚇 Irving Park (Brown)

Whilst honeymooning in New Zealand, Chef Sean Sanders serendipitously fell upon a lasting meal, and from there grew Browntrout his most fresh find yet. Elegantly easygoing, this darling is adored by locals who may linger at the bar, nude tables, or central communal console.

Everything about this fishing retreat feels novel, from crimson and espresso walls hung with serene oils, sketched chalkboards listing prix-fixes, and farm finds, to the cordial staff who recite Sanders' verse on sustainable food. Furthermore, a rooftop garden sprouts fresh herbs featured in a beet and arugula salad dressed in shallot vinaigrette; an ample white lake bass fillet frilled with potato *rösti* and mushrooms; and a blackberry parfait finely finished with anise hyssop.

Chalkboard

Contemporary ✕✕

B1

4343 N. Lincoln Ave. (bet. Montrose & Pensacola Aves.)

Phone: 773-477-7144
Web: www.chalkboardrestaurant.com
Prices: $$

Lunch Sun
Dinner Wed – Mon
Montrose (Brown)

The long, framed, namesake chalkboard that displays each night's menu not only anchors this cozy space, but adds to its neighborhood charm. In the kitchen, Chef Gilbert Langlois lovingly prepares an astonishing array of contemporary fare that can include everything from homemade pâté and refreshing watermelon salad to blackened catfish, hanger steak, and Indiana plum duck. If the wonderfully crunchy and juicy fried chicken is available, get it.

The dining room, complete with white framed mirrors, tiled floors, and striped banquettes, calls to mind a European tea room. No surprise, since afternoon tea is served on weekends. Polite and professional service is complemented by Chef Langlois, who often makes the rounds and chats up customers.

Chen's

Asian ✕

E3

3506 N. Clark St. (bet. Cornelia Ave. & Eddy St.)

Phone: 773-549-9100
Web: www.chenschicago.com
Prices: ⊜⊜

Dinner nightly
Addison (Red)

Almost anything that sits in the shadow of the beloved Wrigley Field could draw a crowd. One of the charms of the neighborhood is that there's always someone out and about. But the 20- and 30-somethings who live in the area flock here not just because of its fun, convenient location, but because Chen's serves up solidly satisfying Chinese food.

Best-sellers include sesame plates, like the chicken sesame platter with crispy chicken coated in a sweet and spicy glaze of honey, garlic, and pepper, topped with toasted sesame seeds. The hot and sour soup may not be at all authentic, but has the signature punch, thanks to a splash of vinegar and white pepper. There is also a short list of sushi for those who crave a taste of Japan with their Chinese delights.

Chicago Diner

Vegetarian ✗

E3

3411 N. Halsted St. (at Roscoe St.)

Phone: 773-935-6696
Web: www.veggiediner.com
Prices: 💰💰

Lunch & dinner daily
🚇 Addison (Red)

This small, tightly packed dining room features retro red tables lined with stainless steel, black vinyl chairs, rustic pine booths, and, when weather permits, a large outdoor garden for dining alfresco.

The garden's luscious and the neighborhood is convenient to Wrigley Field and all manner of North Side attractions. But people come here for the ample vegetarian menu. Since 1983, the kitchen has specialized in dishes with faux meats. This is where former carnivores come to satisfy a craving, such as the gyros seasoned like lamb and served with vegan-friendly *tzatziki*. Other favorites include the Fib Rib and Radical Reuben sandwiches. The Chicago Diner's sumptuous baked goods are available around town.

Chilam Balam

Mexican 🍴

F4

3023 N. Broadway (bet. Barry & Wellington Aves.)

Phone: 773-296-6901
Web: www.chilambalamchicago.com
Prices: $$

Dinner Wed – Mon
🚇 Wellington

The name comes from the Mayan prophecy that all will end in 2012. To help assuage that doom, Chef Chuy Valencia invokes a green and local philosophy at his subterranean hot spot. Chilam Balam is tight, so if you spot a seat, nab it! The surrounding exposed brick is enriched by paints and wall sconces and *estrellas* hang above noisy groups; but a tiny bar at back reveals a semi-open kitchen where ladies in colorful bandanas toil away.

The deal is BYO, so bring your mezcal to sip alongside seasonal Mexican plates like cornmeal-crusted veal sweetbreads moistened with poblano ice cream; chicken *flautas* topped with a chipotle-mezcal sauce; tender alligator Milanesa kissed with avocado and tomatillo; and a chocolate mousse creamed with spiced goat cheese.

199

DMK Burger Bar

American 🍴

E4

2954 N. Sheffield Ave. (at Wellington Ave.)

Phone: 773-360-8686
Web: www.dmkburgerbar.com
Prices: ☕☕

Lunch & dinner daily
🚇 Wellington

Want a stellar burger? Hit DMK Burger Bar, brainchild of David Morton (of steakhouse fame) and Michael Kornick (mk). Grab a seat at the lengthy bar or cop a squat on an old church pew and admire concrete floors contrasting chocolaty-purple pressed-tin ceilings. What this place lacks in comfort, it makes up for in comfort food.

Follow the locals, and order by number. Perhaps #11: sheep's milk feta, olive tapenade, and *tzatziki*, atop a grass-fed lamb patty; or go for beef topped with pastrami, Gruyere, sauerkraut, and remoulade. Cross over to the bad side and pair your sammie with hand-cut gourmet fries. And for a fine finale, slurp up a cold brew or maybe a homemade soda.

Feel virtuous about this calorie splurge—a portion of sales goes to local charities.

El Tinajon

Guatemalan 🍴

B3

2054 W. Roscoe St. (bet. Hoyne & Seeley Aves.)

Phone: 773-525-8455
Web: N/A
Prices: ☕☕

Lunch & dinner Mon & Wed – Sat
🚇 Paulina

A mainstay of the residential Roscoe Village neighborhood, El Tinajon offers authentic Guatemalan dishes. The bright, friendly décor includes Mayan handicrafts throughout the storefront. Bring an appetite and focus on the well-made dishes. Perhaps start with the *yucca con ajo*, tender cassava in a rich garlic butter sauce. Do not skip the *jocon cobanero*, a soulful and tart green chicken and potato stew with elegant tomatillo flavor. Each element of the stew is cooked perfectly and sided with colorful rice; it's a positively lovely dish. *Rellenitos* make a unique and enjoyable finish of rich plantains stuffed with cinnamon and chocolate sweetened black beans.

The appealing breakfast menu provides a promising start to any gray, winter day.

erwin

American ✕✕

E5

2925 N. Halsted St. (bet. George St. & Oakdale Ave.)

Phone: 773-528-7200
Web: www.erwincafe.com
Prices: $$

Lunch Sun
Dinner Tue – Sun
🚇 Wellington

Former public school teachers turned restaurateurs, husband-and wife team Erwin and Cathy Drechsler have been earning top marks for their charming American café since 1994. This duo knows how to make everyone feel welcome—even the birds tempted by the eclectic birdhouses in the front window are greeted with smiles.

The gourmet comfort food perfectly complements this cozy restaurant, where a mural of blue skies and Chicago rooftops gives the impression of perpetual summer. Meanwhile, the kitchen offers a scrumptious slice of Americana, in fried green tomatoes topped with smoky bacon and buttermilk dressing; hamburgers with homemade pickles and hand-cut fries; and wedges of Michigan sour cherry pie with a dollop of homemade vanilla ice cream.

Frasca

Italian ✕✕

C3

3358 N. Paulina St. (at Roscoe St.)

Phone: 773-248-5222
Web: www.frascapizzeria.com
Prices: $$

Lunch Sat – Sun
Dinner nightly
🚇 Paulina

Frasca isn't your usual pizza place. There are no red checkered tablecloths, and no guys in white tees hurling dough in the air—this respite wears a refined country-casual look. On warm nights, the patio is packed with patrons, while the comfortable dining room beckons during colder months. With nine varieties and a comprehensive toppings menu, Frasca is at its core a pizzeria and wine bar, but entrées and pastas supplement the typical menu. Diners can tick off their choices on the farmer's table menu, which spotlights cheeses, cured meats, and bruschette. This gem doesn't take itself too seriously, and in fact, offers such capricious takes on the holidays as Guinness crust pizzas on St. Patrick's Day and Mexican-topped pizzas on Cinco de Mayo.

201

Glenn's Diner

American 🍴

C1

1820 W. Montrose Ave. (bet. Ravenswood & Wolcott Aves.)

Phone: 773-506-1720
Web: www.glennsdiner.com
Prices: $$

Lunch & dinner daily
🚉 Montrose (Brown)

Find this oddball diner nestled under the Brown Line El, with its alfresco tables, and interior cereal box décor. Glenn's aims to be an affordable, neighborhood haunt uniting two groups that don't usually mingle in the same circle—fresh seafood and cold cereal anyone? To further illustrate this, blackboards throughout display daily seafood specials.

On most days the menu proffers more than 25 kinds of cereal (Trix to Cheerios), and 16 fish forms from barramundi to crab cakes. Dining on a budget? Come during the week for all-you-can-eat specials; savory eggs and sweet baked goodies (pies perhaps?) help complete the menu on those days when neither cereal nor fruits from the sea will do. The restaurant is BYO, so bring a bottle to pair with the Fruity Pebbles.

Hearty

American 🍴🍴

E2

3819 N. Broadway (bet. Grace St. & Sheridan Rd.)

Phone: 773-868-9866
Web: www.heartyboys.com
Prices: $$

Lunch Sun
Dinner Wed – Sun
🚉 Sheridan

Dan Smith and Steve MacDonagh, affectionately known as the Hearty Boys, aren't out sleuthing and solving mysteries. Instead of chasing crimes, these two are mixing mayhem in the kitchen. Their food revisits American trailer park classics, but these dishes aren't anything you've torn from the pages of *Good Housekeeping*. Rather, they advertise a ramped up and gourmet repertoire. Corndogs are made with rabbit sausage, served with spicy apple slaw and Red's Rye ale syrup; and this tuna casserole really is a surprise—it is a marriage between panko-crusted ahi tuna and sweet saffron cream noodles.

From the repurposed soda cans fashioned into flowers to the black wood floors and aquamarine tiled mahogany bar, Hearty's edgy mien is perfect for the swank crowd.

La Creperie

French ✗

F5

2845 N. Clark St. (bet. Diversey Pkwy. & Surf St.)

Phone: 773-528-9050 Lunch & dinner Tue – Sun
Web: www.lacreperieusa.com   Diversey
Prices: 💰

One of the world's greatest culinary pleasures can be found in the simple crêpe, marrying your favorite sweet or savory ingredients and a paper-thin pancake in perfect, melted bliss. La Creperie knows the value of this French specialty and has been serving them since 1972. Family-run, this place feels comfortably lived-in with its weathered plank flooring and retro French travel posters.

The menu includes a selection of appetizers, sandwiches, and brunch items, but the crêpes are really why everyone is here. There is a dizzying array of choices from the simple chicken and goat cheese in a buckwheat crêpe, to more unusual, like coq au vin or bœuf Bourguignon. Just don't forget dessert, perhaps filled with chocolate, coconut, or crème caramel.

Melanthios Greek Char House

Greek ✗✗

F4

3116 N. Broadway (bet. Barry Ave. & Briar Pl.)

Phone: 773-360-8572 Lunch & dinner daily
Web: www.melanthiosgreekcharhouse.com
Prices: $$

You won't have any trouble finding such an anchor on this stretch of Broadway—just look for the building that appears as if it were were transplanted from Greece. It's an all-around good time at Melanthios, where high spirits reign and the staff makes you feel like *en famille*. Even if you dine outside, or retire indoors—where white-washed walls, ceiling fans, and a brick fireplace exude a rustic air—brace for a gleeful affair. One glance at this menu, and it's enough to bring tears to your *yia yia's* eyes. Oldies but goodies like moussaka, *saganaki*, *taramasalata*, and *spanakopita*; as well as the glistening goodness of the rotisserie-cooked gyros feature among a gamut of traditional Greek dishes. Come on weekends for whole roasted lamb or pig.

Mixteco Grill

Mexican

C1

1601 W. Montrose Ave. (at Ashland Ave.)

Phone: 773-868-1601
Web: N/A
Prices: 😊

Dinner nightly
🚇 Montrose (Brown)

Set on a stretch of Montrose that houses everything from a retro electronics store to a pilates studio, Mixteco lives up to its name, offering a delightful mix of Mexican specialties. This grill isn't about burritos and quesadillas. Instead, Mixteco dishes up fab regional Mexican cooking that hungry diners lap up as if it were going out of fashion.

The easygoing 'tude and warm flavor make this resto a fave of neighborhood denizens and deal seekers. Choose from lentil cakes with Oaxacan cheese and sweet peppers atop wilted fresh spinach, and served with a gorgeous tomato-*guajillo* sauce; *sopes di pollo*, corn masa boats floating with chicken, mole, and sesame seeds; or sinful *crepas de cajeta*—that is if you haven't already gorged on the tortilla chips.

New Peking

Chinese

F4

3132 N. Broadway (bet. Barry Ave. & Briar Pl.)

Phone: 773-528-1362
Web: N/A
Prices: 😊

Lunch & dinner daily
🚇 Belmont (Brown/Red)

 Looking for a low-key evening chowing on cheap Chinese? Swing by this casual Lakeview spot for tasty Beijing specialties, steamy soups, and homemade noodles. The well-kept space is small–with seating for about forty–spotlighting glass-topped tables, and black framed chairs with turquoise cushions atop a grey carpet.

Subtle flavors punctuate a plentiful menu: start off with a sizzling rice soup (listen to the puffed rice crackle when the server pours a flavorful broth into the bowl), swimming with whole pea pods, pounded white chicken, super fresh shrimp, and served with zingy chili sauce. Offerings include your pick of protein in popular dishes such as lobster sauce, plum sauce, *kung pao*, or Hunan black bean sauce. Service is friendly and attentive.

Pizza Rustica

Pizza ✗

E2

3913 N. Sheridan Rd. (bet. Byron & Dakin Sts.)

Phone: 773-404-8955
Web: www.pizzarusticachicago.com
Prices: ⊙⊙

Lunch & dinner
Wed – Mon
🚇 Sheridan

Before hitting a Cub's game, stop at Pizza Rustica just blocks from Wrigley Field. Golden curtains adorn the front windows of this neighborhood spot. Local artistry adorns the walls along with posted chalkboards touting the day's specials. Regulars saddle up to the black tiled bar; follow suit or pull up an aquamarine upholstered chair to your table.

This BYOB serves up rectangular Roman-style pizza. Skip the overdressed salad and head straight for a four-sided pie; orders come by the slice, half, or whole pie. The half is a hefty portion, and the whole is a crowd pleaser. Try the Half Tutta, affectionately called "Garbage Pizza," topped with sausage, pepperoni, mushrooms, onions, black olives, and blue cheese, piled on their signature buttery crust.

P.S. Bangkok

Thai ✗✗

E3

3345 N. Clark St. (bet. Buckingham Pl. & Roscoe St.)

Phone: 773-871-7777
Web: www.psbangkok.com
Prices: ⊙⊙

Lunch & dinner daily
🚇 Belmont (Brown/Red)

In the bustling heart of Lakeview–not far from the Dunkin' Donuts parking lot which is a 24-7 underage hippie magnet–the warm and clean dining room of P.S. Bangkok has been welcoming patrons for more than 25 years. Disciples of this Thai treasure get matching floral upholstery, soft rock music, and enticing aromas.

Fresh ingredients are a hallmark of the kitchen, which churns out a range of Thai-American classics like spring rolls and noodle dishes. But if bodacious, don't turn away as the menu also showcases more unusual items like red corn curry; and lotus blossom curry floating with coconut milk and cabbage petals cradling seafood. The green papaya salad (dressed in lime and green chilis) pops in your mouth with carrot and green bean strips.

Sola

B2

Contemporary ✗✗

3868 N. Lincoln Ave. (at Byron St.)

Phone: 773-327-3868
Web: www.sola-restaurant.com
Prices: $$

Lunch Thu – Sun
Dinner nightly
Irving Park (Brown)

Chef/owner Carol Wallack was known and admired for Deleece, the Irving Park eatery where she cooked before Sola. Here she brings a more Southern California/Hawaiian vibe to the city's north side (note: the address is on Lincoln, but the entrance is on Byron).

Virtual travel to the tropics is possible through the Sola menu. Try the scallops, served with apple-crab risotto, beans, and apple-curry butter. Or the Kahlua potstickers, which are stuffed with slow-cooked pork and served with mango salsa. Even the cocktails are adventurous. The Wicked Whahini, for example, sounds far out with its fruit juices, vodka, star anise, and ground black pepper, but it works. For a deal, try the ingredient-themed prix-fixe menus offered during the week.

Southport Grocery

D3

American ✗

3552 N. Southport Ave. (bet. Addison St. & Cornelia Ave.)

Phone: 773-665-0100
Web: www.southportgrocery.com
Prices: ☜

Lunch daily
Southport

Open for breakfast and lunch, this sleek neighborhood bistro also offers (as the name suggests) enough homey dishes for take-away and extensive top-of-the-line ingredients to keep even the most finicky foodie happy. Locals love this place, which occasionally leads to long lines on weekends and lots of high-energy conversations inside.

The made-from-scratch vibe is apparent in all the dishes, providing a welcome alternative to greasy spoon breakfasts. The chopped salad with herbed buttermilk dressing is a meal unto itself. Sandwiches may include the roast beef melt, with pickled vegetables, smoked Swiss, and crispy shallots. Save room for the grilled coffee cake, stuffed with cream cheese and grilled until gooey—it's as decadent as it sounds.

Sticky Rice

Thai ✗

A2

4018 N. Western Ave. (at Cuyler Ave.)

Phone: 773-588-0133
Web: www.stickyricethai.com
Prices: ⊜⊗

Lunch & dinner daily
🚇 Irving Park (Blue)

Lots of heart went into decorating this hipster hangout, focused on the regional cuisine of Northern Thailand. Bright yellow and orange paint, huge wood carved flowers and screens make it the brightest Thai joint around. The same degree of heart goes into the food, prepared lovingly (and slowly) by the kitchen.

The menu stands out, and as one would hope given the name, the sticky rice is fantastic. A daily special might include super-tender baby cuttlefish with crispy tentacles accented by thai basil, onions, ginger, and lemongrass. Their *larb* is piquant, made here with ground pork instead of the more commonly found chicken. Save room for desserts featuring guess what–more sticky rice–perhaps accompanied by some funkadelic durian.

Thai Classic

Thai ✗✗

E4

3332 N. Clark St. (bet. Buckingham Pl. & Roscoe St.)

Phone: 773-404-2000
Web: www.thaiclassicrestaurant.com
Prices: ⊜⊗

Lunch & dinner daily
🚇 Belmont (Brown/Red)

Spotless and pristine, Thai Classic has remained a staple of this vibrant area of Lakeview for over 20 years now. Large windows anchor the dining room allowing for streams of natural light, and of course, plenty of people-watching opportunities. The menu chronicles not just Thai typicals like spring rolls, *satay*, salads, curries, rice and noodle dishes, but ventures beyond the classics with an array of special entrées. *Gai yaang* is a house specialty made with boneless Thai barbecued chicken, pounded flat and marinated in coconut milk and an enticing reserve of herbs and spices.

Another home hit is the jungle curry, bathing with chicken, crisp vegetables, and spicy chili oil. The weekend offers an afternoon buffet perfect for bodies on a budget.

Wishbone

C4

American

3300 N. Lincoln Ave. (at School St.)

Phone: 773-549-2663
Web: www.wishbonechicago.com
Prices:

Lunch daily
Dinner Tue – Sun
Paulina

From the wraparound counter with glimpses of a bustling kitchen to the booths and ample tables topped with comforting, all-American food, this place is just plain fun. Competence and comfort extend to the lightening-fast service, making it a favorite for larger groups and families.

A quirky yet genuine vibe runs from the walls adorned with chickens, roosters, and murals of farm scenes, to the menu's unique take on American favorites. The counter is filled with regulars on a first-name basis, enjoying a limited all-day breakfast menu. A more extensive dinner offering may include specials like smoky and spicy Cajun salmon served alongside perfect collard greens with smoked turkey and perhaps a side or two of fresh-baked cornbread and house coleslaw.

Taking a pet on your holiday? Look for 🐾 indicating a hotel that will welcome you and your furry friend!

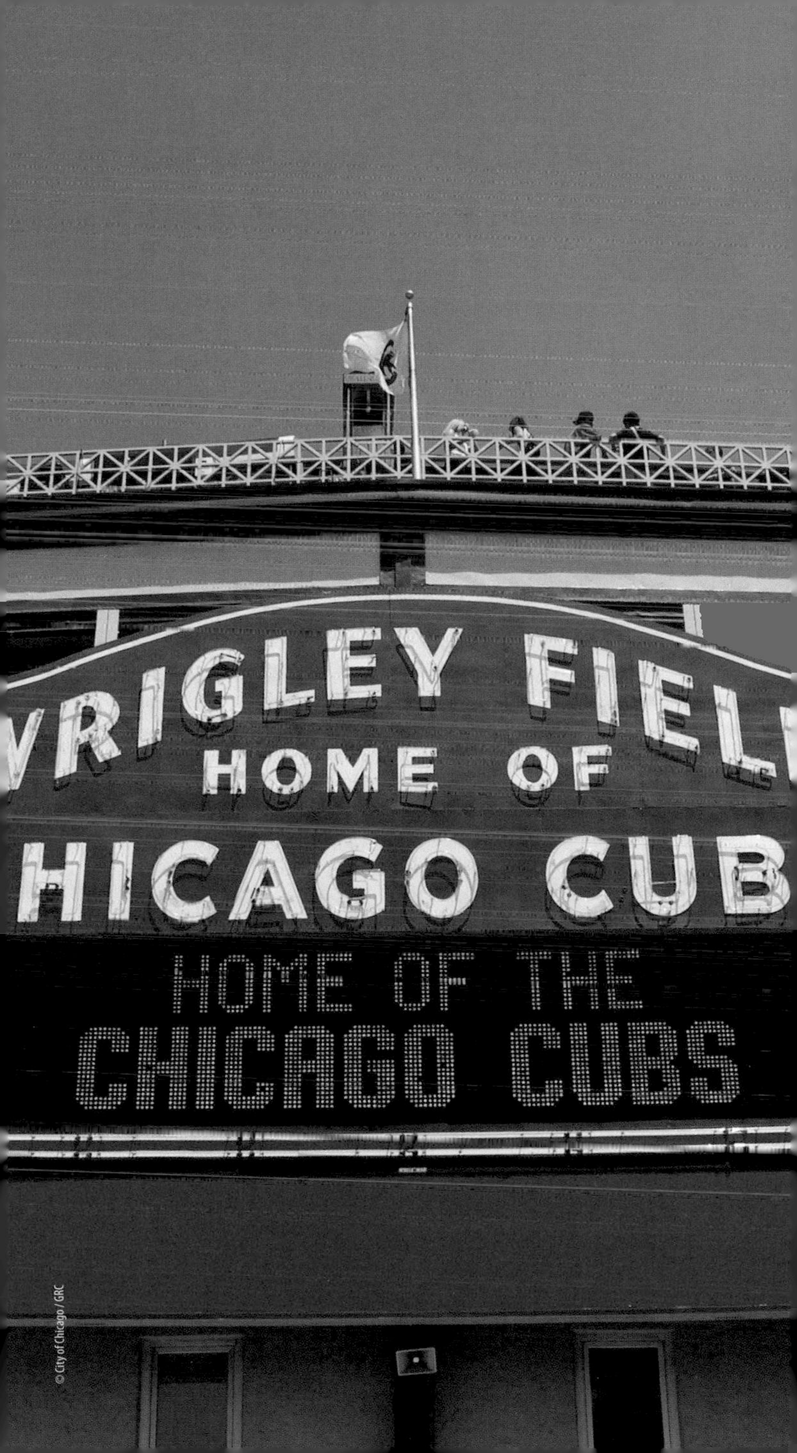

Andersonville, Edgewater & Uptown
Lincoln Square • Ravenswood

This rare and diverse collection of spirited neighborhoods in Chicago's north side is like a real-world Epcot theme park, with visitors easily flitting from one immigrant ethnic tradition to the next, and all the while sampling international cuisines, but without a passport.

ANDERSONVILLE'S SWEDISH SPREADS

From the art on the lamppost banners to the Swedish American Museum Center, you can see the influence of Andersonville's historical roots upon arrival on Clark Street.

Happily, much of that can be explored with your taste buds, starting the day at **Restaurant Svea**. This well-known spot is also home of the hearty Viking breakfast of Swedish-style pancakes, sausage, roasted potatoes, and toasted *limpa* bread (to name a few of the offerings).

Meanwhile, **Wikström's Gourmet Foods** is one of the last standing Swedish emporiums of packaged and prepared favorites, still stocked with everything needed for a traditional smörgåsbord, from Swedish meatballs to herring to lingonberry preserves.

BASK 'N BAKE

Locals yearning for authentic baked goods eagerly take a number and wait in line at the **Swedish Bakery**. Many of its traditional baked goods are available in individual sizes, as well as larger portions perfect for those looking to entertain. For more instant gratification, scout a seat at the counter by the window and enjoy that miniature coconut-custard coffeecake right away, with a complimentary cup of creamy coffee.

Andersonville also caters to its worldly community with **Middle East Bakery & Grocery**. Make a massive meze feast from spreads, breads, olives, and an impressive range of hummus among other goodies available in the deli. Or, stock up on dried fruits, spices, rice, rosewater, nuts, and teas from the grocery section. Either way, you will have ample for a magnificent Middle Eastern menu.

ITALIAN-INSPIRED

On the pizza front, **Great Lake** has won many raves for its pizza, despite the infamously long lines and a lack of interest in expansion that, according to some hungry pizza-lovers, is downright un-American.

Nonetheless, these delicious Chicago-style pies are made with the country's premium ingredients—its menu is a virtual Who's Who of local, organic vegetable farmers and heirloom breeders. After this indulgence, stop by **The Coffee Studio** for a cup of joe prepared by what critics have named one of the country's best boutique coffee shops. Superlatives aside, **Pasticceria Natalina** offers European character and marble-topped counters neatly displaying Sicilian sweets flavored with citrus zest, anise, and lavender. Or, take home a pretty little green box of chocolate-dipped glacée fruits to devour all by yourself.

AN ASIAN AFFAIR

Uptown's Argyle Street is known for being a pocket of intermixed East Asian culture—even the Argyle Red Line El stop is thematically decorative. A terrific concentration of Chinese, Thai, and Vietnamese delis, bakeries, herbalists, noodle shops, and restaurants line these streets; and there is endless tasting to be done along these blocks.

The real draw in Edgewater is its art deco architecture, especially evident along Bryn Mawr Avenue and Lake Michigan's beaches. This neighborhood also boasts a vibrant community who convene at **The Metropolis Café**, an offshoot of Chicago's lauded Metropolis Coffee Company. Watch a plethora of students, professionals, and locals gulp down oodles of their creative coffee quenchers.

HOT DOG HAVEN

This is Chicago, so there's always a good hot dog nearby, and one of the best red-hots uptown is as delicious as it is easy to spot. Just look for the iconic pitchfork piercing a sausage over the name **Wolfy's**, and know that you have arrived. Try the classic dog, but know that by the time the limitless listing of toppings are piled on, the meat will be invisibly buried beneath piccalilli, pickles, peppers, and other impossibly colored yet divine condiments.

LINCOLN SQUARE AND RAVENSWOOD

Evidence of the German immigrants who helped develop Lincoln Square still lingers in this quaint area. Highlights include a century-old apothecary as well as the new, yet Old World-inspired butchers and specialty items that abound at **Gene's Sausage Shop**.

For an impressive array of fresh chops, steaks, free-range poultry, smoked European sausages, as well as bacon in its many glorious forms, plan to sample the many wears of **Lincoln Quality Meat Market**.

The **Lincoln Square Farmer's Market** has long been loved and frequented (on Tuesdays); they now showcase a new Thursday evening market, pumping with live music alongside a medley of fruits, vegetables, and flowers, which remains a draw for locals with day jobs.

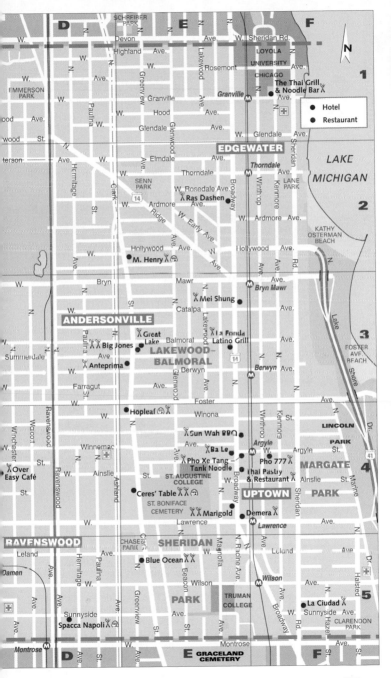

Legend:
- Hotel
- Restaurant

Map labels (selected):

SCHREIBER PARK, W. Devon Ave., W. Highland Ave., Greenview Ave., W. Granville Ave., W. Hood Ave., W. Glendale Ave., LOYOLA UNIVERSITY CHICAGO, Granville, The Thai Grill & Noodle Bar, Rosemont, Lakewood, W. Sheridan Rd.

EMMERSON PARK, Paulina, Hermitage, Clark St., Ridge Ave., Glenwood Ave., EDGEWATER, W. Elmdale Ave., Thorndale, SENN PARK, W. Rosedale Ave., Ras Dashen, W. Ardmore Ave., Broadway, Winthrop, Kenmore, LANE PARK, W. Glendale Ave., Sheridan, LAKE MICHIGAN

W. Early Ave., W. Ardmore Ave., KATHY OSTERMAN BEACH, W. Hollywood Ave., M. Henry, Hollywood Ave.

W. Bryn Mawr Ave., Mei Shung, Bryn Mawr, Lake, FOSTER AVE BEACH

ANDERSONVILLE, W. Catalpa, Great Lake, Balmoral, La Fonda Latino Grill, Big Jones, LAKEWOOD–BALMORAL, Anteprima, W. Berwyn, Berwyn Ave., Summerdale, Paulina, Glenwood Ave.

W. Farragut Ave., Foster Ave., Winona, LINCOLN PARK, Hopleaf, Sun Wah BBQ, Winthrop, Kenmore, St.

Ravenswood, Winchester, Wolcott, Winnemac, Over Easy Café, W. Ainslie St., ST. AUGUSTINE COLLEGE, Ba Le, Pho Xe Tang – Tank Noodle, Argyle, Pho 777, MARGATE PARK, Thai Pastry & Restaurant, Ainslie St., Marine Dr.

Ashland, Ceres' Table, ST. BONIFACE CEMETERY, Marigold, UPTOWN, Demera, Broadway, Sheridan, W. Lawrence Ave.

RAVENSWOOD, CHASE PARK, SHERIDAN, Leland, Hermitage, Paulina, Clark, Blue Ocean, Beacon, Magnolia, N. Racine Ave., Leland, Damen Ave., Wilson Ave., Wilson, PARK, TRUMAN COLLEGE, Halsted, Dr.

Sunnyside, Greenview, Spacca Napoli, Ainslie, La Ciudad, W. Sunnyside Ave., CLARENDON PARK, Hazel, Montrose, GRACELAND CEMETERY

N

213

Anteprima

E3

Italian

5316 N. Clark St. (bet. Berwyn & Summerdale Aves.)

Phone: 773-506-9990

Web: www.anteprimachicago.net

Prices: $$

Dinner nightly

Berwyn

The painted landscapes of the Italian lakes region are among the elements that transform this Andersonville eatery to a little oasis. This small 50-seat restaurant is steeped in all things Italian, including a bustling atmosphere that contributes to the rustic, regional vibe.

The menu changes according to the season and availability of local ingredients, but includes a generous selection of antipasti, as well as pasta available in whole or half portions. The spaghetti *cacio e pepe* is tossed with cracked black pepper, pecorino cheese, and fresh arugula to cut the richness of the cheese. The pork osso buco entrée sits majestically atop of a bed of saffron risotto. Top off an evening with an ice cold cordial of their homemade *limoncello*.

Ba Le

E4

Vietnamese

5014 N. Broadway (at Argyle St.)

Phone: 773-561-4424

Web: www.balesandwich.com

Prices:

Lunch & dinner daily

Argyle

Moving just a few doors down did exactly what the owners hoped it would. This storefront is still the north side's hot spot for authentic French-Vietnamese sandwiches; but now within a more sleek sphere, starring an L-shaped counter overlooking Broadway (also a first-rate perch for people-watching).

The menu is heavy on *banh mi* variations, that tasty ensemble made with crusty French bread and swelled with fixings like grilled pork, cilantro, and house-pickled daikon. The affordable price tags plus large portions make for a sweet pair with leftovers for later. Natives in the know gulp down the quirky Vietnamese FOCO pennywort drink; while salads, pastries, desserts, sodas, and teas round out the menu and sate the more prudent palate.

Big Jones

Southern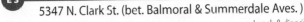

E 3

5347 N. Clark St. (bet. Balmoral & Summerdale Aves.)

Phone: 773-275-5725
Web: www.bigjoneschicago.com
Prices: $$

Lunch & dinner daily
🚇 Berwyn

Y'all will definitely want to come back here. Big Jones brims with big Southern charm and hospitality. Green brocade wallpaper, blown glass-and-iron chandeliers, and cute bistro tables give the place a welcoming look and feel. And it's no surprise it reminds you of your long-lost Aunt Weezie's place, since this spot shines a little southern warmth in chilly Chicago. There wouldn't have been a war between the states if they had food this good. It all starts with fluffy cornbread beside a glass of sweet tea, and continues with Southern specialties like shrimp and grits; Cajun boudin fritters; gumbo; and Carolina barbecue pork. Honey, with fried green tomatoes, red velvet cake, and bourbon bread pudding, it's definitely worth putting off the diet for a day.

Bistro Campagne

French 🍴🍴

C5

4518 N. Lincoln Ave. (bet. Sunnyside & Wilson Aves.)

Phone: 773-271-6100
Web: www.bistrocampagne.com
Prices: $$

Lunch Sun
Dinner nightly
🚇 Western (Brown)

This cozy bungalow in the middle of Lincoln Square's busiest drag may appear unassuming, but behind the gates find a stunning oasis-in-the-city outdoor garden. Whether you eat indoors or out, the spaces offer a warm and inviting French country experience.

The rustic French menu (with floods of French wines, of course) starts off with a crusty mini baguette and Mediterranean white bean spread. After, choose from classic French dishes like a mushroom tart, boeuf Bourguignon with buttery pappardelle, pork shoulder braised in apple cider, or a lamb cassoulet. Even the simple soft-cooked egg laid on melted leek fondue is just right. A cozy spot for romantic dinners, Bistro Campagne also pleases the larger lot by hosting live jazz music on Sunday evenings.

215

Blue Ocean

E5

J a p a n e s e XX

4650 N. Clark St. (at Leland Ave.)

Phone: 773-334-6288
Web: www.blueoceansushi.net
Prices: 🍜

Lunch Mon – Fri
Dinner nightly
🚇 Wilson

One of the neighborhood's newcomers, Blue Ocean is a large, contemporary, and colorful addition Uptown. Its menu, described as "contemporary sushi," brings a modern sensibility to the Asian favorite. The sleek sushi counter does not offer seating, instead enjoy your meal at one of the dark blue-stained wood tables.

In addition to sushi, the menu includes an offering of small plates such as braised short ribs (soy, sake, and ginseng braised short ribs served with short rib maki,) plus appetizers such as a bacon-wrapped scallop cake and yuzu hamachi. Sushi is souped-up. For example, the Blurashi features an oversized rice bowl served on a deep square platter topped with uni, salmon roe, salmon, tuna, snapper, raw shrimp, and cooked octopus.

Ceres' Table

E4

M e d i t e r r a n e a n XX

4882 N. Clark St. (bet. Ainslie St. & Lawrence Ave.)

Phone: 773-878-4882
Web: www.cerestable.com
Prices: $$

Dinner Mon – Sat
🚇 Lawrence

It is most probable that Ceres herself (the Roman goddess of agriculture and harvest) would have been quite pleased to dine here, what with the bountiful, Mediterranean offerings spun out of locally sourced, seasonal products. Chef Giuseppe Scurato and wife Carolyn, are at the helm of this lovely operation—a casual uptown bistro boasting a menu that's every bit as affordable as it is appetizing.

A mosaic-tiled entry leads you into a room designed with tranquil blues, cozy black leather booths, and a full bar. Dig into fresh goat cheese ravioli with plump rock shrimp, favas, and ripe heirloom tomatoes; or luscious lobster *agnolotti* with seared scallops. The Wednesday night prix-fixe is a steal—an appetizer, entrée, dessert, and glass of wine for $35.

Demera

E4

Ethiopian

4801 N. Broadway (at Lawrence St.)

Phone:	773-334-8787	Lunch & dinner daily
Web:	www.demeraethiopianrestaurant.com	Lawrence
Prices:	$$	

A short skip off the red El at Lawrence, this bright corner location is as welcoming for a quick bite or drink and good people watching as it is for an authentic Ethiopian feast. On the weekends Demera also welcomes musicians for live performances, promising that this spot goes beyond other ethnic eateries.

As is tradition, Demera serves *injera*, the spongy, pancake-like bread used as a utensil on a communal plate. Its tangy flavors pair wonderfully with the *yebug-alicha* dish of tender lamb in a rich and creamy aromatic green sauce; as well as the *ye-kwanta firfir*, featuring beef tips stewed in a spicy Berber sauce. Don't skip the Ethiopian tea, which is an oregano tea infused with anise, clover, and cinnamon. Sweeten with honey and savor.

Great Lake

E3

Pizza

1477 W. Balmoral Ave. (bet. Clark St. & Glenwood Ave.)

Phone:	773-334-9270	Dinner Wed – Sat
Web:	N/A	Berwyn
Prices:	$$	

The outside seats at Lydia Esparza and Nick Lessins' pizza parlor, Great Lake, aren't so much for al fresco diners, as they are for the throngs of waiting (BYOB to bide the time) patrons. When the door unlocks, peek in a space simply dressed with wood floors and exposed brick walls, welcoming guests to a tiny, communal room.

Service can be slow (the pizza oven can hold only two at a time), but fresh, beaming salads (heirloom tomatoes joined with basil, *mona* cheese, Tellicherry black pepper, and walnut oil); and a blackboard touting pristine purveyors make Great Lake a culinary cult-hit. Your patience may be rewarded with a perfectly charred thin crust laden with summer sweet corn, garlic, and fresh cream; or the more familiar tomato and mozzarella.

Hopleaf

Gastropub ✗

E4

5148 N. Clark St. (bet. Foster Ave. & Winona St.)

Phone: 773-334-9851
Web: www.hopleaf.com
Prices: $$

Dinner nightly
🚇 Berwyn

Don't be confused when you arrive with a hankering for mussels and see a standing room-only bar. First and foremost, Hopleaf is a tavern—and an excellent one at that—with more than 200 beers, many of them on draught, craft, and from Belgium.

Once you put away that ID, slide back through the bar to find a charming full-service hideaway waiting to exceed your culinary expectations of a bar. Starters may include a roasted rutabaga salad or rabbit saddle roulade stuffed with house-made mortadella. Creative entrées may feature twists on classics, like the CB&J sandwich, made creamy with homemade cashew butter, fig jam, and *Morbier* cheese; or the all-time favorite side dish of macaroni and cheese made with Stilton.

La Ciudad

Mexican ✗

F5

4515 N. Sheridan Rd. (bet. Sunnyside & Windsor Aves.)

Phone: 773-728-2887
Web: N/A
Prices: 🍜🍜

Lunch & dinner daily
🚇 Wilson

From first sight, within a strip mall of pawn shops and iron bar-covered windows, this newcomer is not the most inviting. But walk through the doors, and things sure change. This little BYOC (*cervezas*) is not your typical, grubby taqueria. Fire engine red walls are modestly dotted with black and white prints of D.F.

The food is as pleasant a surprise as the interior; appetizers like plump shrimp with corn salsa and chipotle cream demonstrate the kitchen's ability to think outside the quesadilla box. The Angel's combo plates nicely grilled *carne asada* with an outstanding smoky, charred skin *chile relleno*. One upside of this dicey 'hood is liquor stores are plentiful and reasonable. You bring the tequila, they'll provide the lime.

La Fonda Latino Grill

Latin American ✗

E3

5350 N. Broadway (bet. Balmoral & Berwyn Aves.)

Phone: 773-271-3935
Web: N/A
Prices: $$

Lunch & dinner Tue – Sun
🚇 Berwyn

Quality ingredients and an extensive pan-Latin menu are the hallmarks of this small Edgewater gem. The grill is the centerpiece of the kitchen, with an emphasis on meats–pork, beef, and chicken–that are grilled as ordered.

The menu here may not be ambitious, but what La Fonda does, it does extremely well. Meals may begin with silky tamales stuffed with luscious chicken and green olives, topped with an avocado "hot" sauce. Favorite entrées may include the beef *lengua*, served tender with a tomato sauce and crunchy green peas. Diners are sure to leave feeling full, particularly if they have been wise enough to save room for dessert. Their flan is a wonderfully silky and caramel-laquered custard, served with strawberries and just the right hint of rum.

LM

French ✗✗

C5

4539 N. Lincoln Ave. (bet. Sunnyside & Wilson Aves.)

Phone: 773-942-7585
Web: www.lmrestaurant.com
Prices: $$$

Lunch Sat – Sun
Dinner Tue – Sat
🚇 Western (Brown)

This intimate jewel box of a space within a Lincoln Square townhouse barely seats two dozen patrons (so save the sweet nothings for later), but what it may lack in size it makes up for in culture.

LM, named for the owner's children Luc and Mary, is decidedly French. From the tangerine and chocolate palette to the chrome light fixtures and chic leather chairs, the dining room is at once modern and romantic. Behind the scenes, the kitchen focuses on the classics with dishes like flavorful sweetbreads set atop a ravioli stuffed with caramelized onions, tender and richly flavored boeuf Bourguignon with mushrooms and lardoons, or tarte Tatin with plump apples. Brunch brings together French and American favorites, from *croque monsieurs* to burgers.

Los Nopales

Chicago ▶ Andersonville, Edgewater & Uptown

C5

4544 N. Western Ave. (bet. Sunnyside & Wilson Aves.)

Phone: 773-334-3149
Web: www.losnopalesrestaurant.com
Prices:

Lunch & dinner Tue – Sun
Western (Brown)

As much a feast for the eyes as the belly, "nopales" which literally translates to "cactus," is an efficacious ingredient on the menu and in the design of this bright and enticing Mexican storefront. One of the owners used to helm the stoves at the Palmer House Hilton and Heaven on Seven, and due to that level of professionalism, Los Nopales rises above and beyond the typical taqueria.

Embark on this feast with chips and salsa, made new and exciting with a duo of homemade salsas: one is smoky and spicy with chipotles, the other silky with avocado and tomatillo. Don't miss the tortilla soup, teeming with shredded chicken, avocado chunks, and fried tortilla strips; or an outstanding *tres leches* cake, frosted with hints of maple, caramel, and chocolate.

Marigold

Indian

E4

4832 N. Broadway (bet. Ainslie St. & Lawrence Ave.)

Phone: 773-293-4653
Web: www.marigoldrestaurant.com
Prices:

Dinner Tue – Sun
Lawrence

As popular as it is ambitious, this Indian eatery knows how to please local crowds—right down to sitar music in the background, playing classic rock. Visually, the long dining room is attractive and kitsch-free with vivid colors and polished woods lending a slightly industrial look. Friendly, upbeat service enhances the relaxed, neighborhood vibe.

The menu offers a tasty departure from the expected Indian classics. Here, find a concise listing of dishes that highlight contemporary twists, such as mussels steamed in turmeric-infused coconut broth or duck confit cured in Indian spices. "Naanwiches" and curries in tasting and entrée portions are a hit, as are the signature dishes, like Kalonji chicken, which are as artfully plated as they are delicious.

Mei Shung

Chinese

E3

5511 N. Broadway (bet. Bryn Mawr & Catalpa Aves.)

Phone: 773-728-5778
Web: N/A
Prices: 💰💰

Lunch & dinner Tue – Sun
🚇 Bryn Mawr

No one goes to Mei Shung for the décor. This storefront looks like 1,001 other Chinese joints, and once you open the door and step inside and see the paper tablecloths, your mind will not be changed.

What will make you think differently is the extensive menu, chock-full of authentic Taiwanese and Mandarin dishes (particularly from the Shandong region). The hot and sour soup is just the right degree of spicy, thanks to white pepper and vinegar. Other must-tastes include the flavorful, chewy steamed bean curd roll, Taiwanese sausage, and noodle soups. The Mandarin dishes might include Peking duck, that aforementioned hot and sour soup, and fish with spicy salt. And if you have room, order the Taiwanese-style steak—it is also über popular.

M. Henry

American

E2

5707 N. Clark St. (bet. Edgewater & Hollywood Aves.)

Phone: 773-561-1600
Web: www.mhenry.net
Prices: 💰💰

Lunch Tue – Sun
🚇 Bryn Mawr

Even before the staff warmly welcomes brunch goers to this local favorite, a line out the door is their first greeting. Nonetheless, the food and service here are well worth the wait. Breakfast and brunch are M. Henry's strong suits, and locals flock here for the unusual stacks of pancakes, like the aptly named Mango-Sour Cherry Bliss Hotcakes, served golden brown and fluffy, topped with a crunchy toasted oat crumble beneath fresh and dried fruits.

Salads and sandwiches, like the giant vegetable-stacked Dagwood, are equally creative and filling for non-brunch goers. Both the breakfast and lunch menus are vegetarian-friendly and made from seasonal and organic ingredients when possible. A bakery showcase makes it easy to run in for a sweet to-go.

Opart Thai House

Chicago ▶ Andersonville, Edgewater & Uptown

C5

Thai 🍴

4658 N. Western Ave. (bet. Eastwood & Leland Aves.)

Phone: 773-989-8517
Web: www.opartthai.com
Prices: 💰💰

Lunch & dinner daily
🚇 Western (Brown)

Steps from the El, Opart's is a simple spot serving an extensive selection of Thai dishes that range from enjoyable to excellent. Inside the pleasant dining room warmed with carved woodwork and exposed brick, find ample seating for groups large or small as well as a window for orders to-go.

The large menu features well-prepared curries, soups, and entrées, like the crispy, deep-fried catfish served with a rich red curry that makes the flavorful coconut and spices stand out more than the heat. Another highlight is the classic *tom yum koong* , which arrives piping hot and deliciously tart with meaty straw mushrooms, fresh shrimp, and kaffir lime leaves. Coffee with condensed milk sweetens the meal's end.

Over Easy Café

D4

American 🍴

4943 N. Damen Ave. (bet. Ainslie & Argyle Sts.)

Phone: 773-506-2605
Web: www.overeasycafechicago.com
Prices: 💰💰

Lunch Tue – Sun
🚇 Damen (Brown)

When Over Easy Café shuttered due to a fire in 2007, neighborhood residents bemoaned the loss of their favorite breakfast spot so loudly that the owners had to rebuild it. When it reopened, its local following was even greater with folks lining up for these yolks for breakfast, brunch, and lunch. Complimentary Julius Meinl coffee helps placate those who have to wait for a table.

Many of the dishes have a south-of-the-border zeal such as eggs with chorizo, guacamole, cheddar cheese, and ancho ketchup. For a more Midwestern taste, order the eggs with grilled bologna and spicy maple mustard. Pancakes with cinnamon butter, or banana-spiked French toast satisfy sweet lovers.

The cozy room packs 'em in, so be prepared to rub elbows with your neighbor.

Paprika

B4

2547 W. Lawrence Ave. (bet. Maplewood & Rockwell Sts.)

Phone: 773-338-4906

Web: www.paprikachicago.com

Prices: $$

Dinner nightly

🚇 Rockwell

Chef Shah Kabir and his family know hospitality. Prepare to be swept up in their warmth and care the minute you enter; and even be greeted at the door by the chef himself and likely be welcomed to sit and sip a cool, refreshing *lassi*. After a 13-year run at his former spot, Indian Gourmet, in Rogers Park, Kabir went out in search of smaller digs, re-routing to this delectable destination in Lincoln Park.

From aromatic, homemade curries to tasty twists on *dahls* (*turka dahl ki shabzi* is a revelation), the menu bursts with expert deliciousness. Even your everyday veggie samosa gets a yummy revival—a soft, light shell replaces the standard crunchy exterior, stuffed with spices, potatoes, peas, and cauliflower, served up with a trio of tangy chutneys.

Pho 777

F4

1063-65 W. Argyle St. (bet. Kenmore & Winthrop Aves.)

Phone: 773-561-9909

Web: www.pho777chicago.com

Prices: 💰

Lunch & dinner Wed – Mon

🚇 Argyle

This strip of Argyle Street is destination No. 1 when it comes to Vietnamese food. The décor may not distinguish Pho 777 from the pack, but good quality makes it an easy choice.

Of course, the namesake dish is a must. The broth of the *tai bo vien pho* (beef noodle soup with round steak and meatballs) is scented with cardamom, ginger, and clove. It might be a bit mild but tables are topped with an assortment of chili pastes and oils to spice things up. Start off with some spring rolls, filled with rice noodles, shrimp, mint, carrots, bean sprouts, and basil, served with a punchy peanut sauce. Charbroiled pork rice plates, catfish simmered in a clay pot, and an assortment of flavored bubble teas (think: papaya, taro, plum, and mango) complete the menu.

Pho Xe Tang - Tank Noodle

Vietnamese ✗

E4

4953 N. Broadway (at Argyle St.)

Phone: 773-878-2253
Web: N/A
Prices: 🍜

Lunch & dinner Thu – Tue
🚇 Argyle

Also known as "Tank Noodles," Pho Xe Tang is one of the highlights of Little Saigon. Tables are dotted with caddies containing chopsticks, plastic and steel flatware, *sriracha*, soy sauce, and pickled jalapeños. Unlike other nearby eateries, Pho Xe Tang has a louder vibe, with lots of pulsating bass in its music.

No visit to a Vietnamese restaurant would be complete without slurping up *pho*, traditionally served with a plate of lime wedges and fresh greens (bean sprouts, fresh mint, basil, and sliced jalapeños). The *pho tai nam ve don* is as good a choice as any, its tender skirt steak spiced with star anise and cinnamon. Starters like the papaya salad and steamed rice flour roll provide additional (and authentic) tastes.

Pizza D.O.C.

Italian ✗

C4

2251 W. Lawrence Ave. (at Oakley Ave.)

Phone: 773-784-8777
Web: www.mypizzadoc.com
Prices: $$

Lunch Fri – Sun
Dinner Tue – Sun
 Western (Brown)

In Italy, where purity of products is a matter of national pride, D.O.C. (*denominazione di origine controllata*) is a government-controlled seal of quality. Here in Chicago, self-ordained Pizza D.O.C. assures each diner that it takes its ingredients just as seriously, from the Sicilian olive oil drizzled on the lightly charred crusts to the thinly sliced salami that tops it.

These uncut 12-inch pies are as good for taking out as eating in, whether at the large, popular bar or group-friendly dining room with exposed brick and festive wreaths. Just keep in mind that pizza here is in the Neopolitan style, so the thin crusted, lightly sauced delicacies that emerge after only minutes in the brick oven won't hold up to heftier, Chicago-style toppings.

Ras Dashen

Ethiopian

E2

5846 N. Broadway (bet. Ardmore & Thorndale Aves.)

Phone: 773-506-9601
Web: www.rasdeshenchicago.com
Prices: $$

Lunch & dinner daily
Thorndale

&

Welcoming and all-embracing, Ras Dashen is a good pick for both the neophyte to Ethiopian cuisine as well as the loyal enthusiast who wants authentic eats. The friendly staff is happy to explain the drinks, the *mossab* (that covered dish on each table used as the communal serving plate), and even the restrooms (men's and women's facilities are in different parts of the restaurant).

As is traditional, dishes are served with *injera*, the fermented pancake-like bread used to ladle food, such as the *yebeg wat*, a dish of tender lamb cubes stewed in a spicy *berbere* sauce. Ras Dashen even offers a warm and creamy bread pudding made with *injera*, spices, and flax seeds. An ample offering of signature drinks and hard-to-find beers are poured at the full bar.

Rosded

Thai

C5

2308 W. Leland Ave. (bet. Lincoln & Western Aves.)

Phone: 773-334-9055
Web: N/A
Prices: 🍴🍴

Lunch & dinner Tue – Sun
Western (Brown)

This Thai fave has seen quite a bit of traffic in its day, as evidenced by the lived-in feel of the tiny, eleven-table dining space. But we get it. Belly-pleasing dishes keep the place packed for lunch and dinner, while maintaining a hearty take-out business to boot.

Soups, noodles, rice dishes, curries, and salads are offered in vast varieties on the menu; as are yummy mains like flaky catfish fritters, battered and deep fried, smothered with a glaze of sweet chili sauce and fragrant Thai basil; or Rama Chicken with curry-peanut sauce. Try the *pad prik khing*—curried green beans with a choice of meat; or smoky, tender pork satay, marinated in flavorful yellow curry, grilled, and served with dipping sauce and a zesty cucumber salad.

San Soo Gab San

K o r e a n

C3

5247 N. Western Ave. (bet. Berwyn & Farragut Aves.)

Phone: 773-334-1589   Lunch & dinner daily
Web: N/A
Prices:

 A neighborhood joint that appeals to locals and visitors, this Logan Square standby attracts large groups, thanks to the grill-top tables offering do-it-yourself feasts and lived-in décor.

A meal commences with a mammoth parade of *banchan* (small complimentary dishes); expect several types of kimchi, sesame oil-flavored vegetables, cold noodle salads, and even a steaming bowl of savory soup. The sheer number served forgives a few misses in quality. The generous menu includes all the classics like *dol sot bi bim bap* and *bulgogi*. Try giant *mandoo* accompanied by a pungent, spicy dipping sauce, as well as char-broiled chicken in a smoky-sweet glaze. San Soo Gab San is open almost all night, perfect for a boozey Korean barbecue feast with friends.

Spacca Napoli

P i z z a

D5

1769 W. Sunnyside Ave. (bet. Hermitage & Ravenswood Aves.)

Phone: 773-878-2420   Lunch Wed — Sun
Web: www.spaccanapolipizzeria.com   Dinner Tue — Sun
Prices: Montrose (Brown)

Lines out the door aren't unusual at this Neapolitan-style bistro, which takes its pizza very seriously. In fact, the bistro's pizza ovens were built by third- and fourth-generation artisans from the old country, and owner Jon Goldsmith is a certified *pizzaiuolo*. Important soccer games often play on the TV here, thereby furthering the authentic aspect.

The menu, of course, is built around twelve varieties of pizza along with a selection of antipasti (marinated anchovies) and desserts (spumoni), which are good, but not the centerpiece. Try the classic *Margherita*, made with *fior di latte* mozzarella, fresh basil, and olive oil, and charred just right, so it is crispy, but not too smoky. A decent wine list and authentic espresso round out the offerings.

Sun Wah BBQ

Chinese ✕

5039 N. Broadway (bet. Argyle & Winona Sts.)

Phone: 773-769-1254
Web: www.sunwahbbq.com
Prices: ⊜⊜

Lunch & dinner Fri – Wed
🚇 Argyle

Sun Wah recently moved around the corner to newer, cleaner digs but the food thankfully remains the same. These kind folks have made the decision about what to order as easy as can be. As the name of the joint suggests and the meats hanging in the front windows imply, focus here is on the barbecue. The ambience isn't much and the rest of the menu hit-or-miss, but these inconveniences are worth it for the succulent, expertly prepared, Chinese-style barbecued meats.

Moist soy sauce chicken is distinctive with hints of five spice; barbecued pork is smoky and salty beneath a deep pink glaze; and juicy duck has perfectly crisp skin over a rich layer of fat. Go for the combo plate with all three plus a slab of gnaw-worthy pork ribs.

The Thai Grill & Noodle Bar

Thai ✕

1040 W. Granville Ave. (bet. Kenmore & Winthrop Aves.)

Phone: 773-274-7510
Web: www.thaigrillchicago.com
Prices: ⊜⊜

Lunch & dinner Tue – Sun
🚇 Granville

In the ground floor of the Sovereign apartment building, Thai Grill & Noodle Bar sports a more contemporary (and less clichéd) take on the typical Thai eatery. Amid the grey walls, striped zebrawood tables, and dark banquettes, diners will find locals and families enjoying good renditions of Thai standards and sipping bubble teas (with those tapioca "bubbles").

Diners who are new to Thai cuisine, or just shy about the heat of their food, should not fear as these dishes are friendly to western palates. Even the spicy fish–a fillet of sole with a blend of Asian eggplant, beans, basil, kaffir lime leaves, and chilis–highlights flavors rather than overwhelms with heat. Traditional dishes run the gamut from five different curries to pan-fried noodles.

Chicago ▲ Andersonville, Edgewater & Uptown

Thai Pastry & Restaurant

Thai 🍴

4925 N. Broadway (bet. Ainslie & Argyle Sts.)

Phone: 773-784-5399
Web: www.thaipastry.com
Prices: $$

Lunch & dinner daily
🚇 Argyle

Just south of Argyle Street, in the heart of the city's Little Saigon district is this Thai marvel, standing out among many Vietnamese restaurants. This storefront is brighter and less cluttered than most of its neighbors—the lime colored walls surround cases of, as its name suggests, Thai pastries.

There are pre-packed *klong-klang, a-kare*, taro custard, curry puffs, and many others. But pastry is not the only dessert here: quarts of local favorite, Village Creamery ice cream are available for take-out, which many customers do with the pastries, too. But this neighborhood mainstay is worth coming it for pre-dessert savory dishes. Don't miss the traditional *panang* curry, sweetened with coconut milk and seasoned with kaffir lime and good quality chicken.

Couverts (🍴... 🍴🍴🍴🍴🍴) indicate the level of comfort found at a restaurant. The more 🍴's, the more upscale a restaurant will be.

North & Northwestern Suburbs

North & Northwestern Suburbs

EVANSTON

Evanston is the suburb that even city-dwellers love. As is the case in any major metropolis, sometimes the suburbs fall victim to urban one-upmanship, but Chicago's first stop over the northern border lures city folk with its lakefront charms and foodie finds. Additionally, Evanston is home to Northwestern University and the Woman's Christian Temperance Union, resulting in an incongruous mash-up of college-town hangouts and odd liquor laws.

A HOTBED FOR GOODIES

Evanston's Central Street is a swath of quaint boutiques and cafés. Serious foodies stock up at the famed **Spice House** for their incredible spectrum of high-quality and unique spices, seasonings, rubs, and mixes. All these flavors will certainly inspire and nurture your inner Grant Achatz. It's also a solid choice for housewarming gifts.

Nearby on Central Street is **Rose's Wheatfree Bakery and Café**. A rare and relevant establishment, they've garnered a giant following, all of whom come routinely for a treasure trove of gluten-free goodies including breads, cookies, cakes, cupcakes, and muffins to take home. Also sought after is the café menu of pizzas, salads, and sandwiches. Moreover, they

carry the beloved Tennessee-style Grampa Boo's Basting and Barbecue Sauce for some thrilling at-home grilling.

Evanston and the tony North Shore are also known for their **Clandestino Supper Club**. A sort of roving, underground dinner party, each gathering welcomes a small group of diners to a secret location for a themed menu (like *The Cicero Menu; The Haunted Menu;* and *A Day in the life in Brazil*) prepared by local chefs with local ingredients to create a world of tastes.

DOG DAY DELIGHT

On the other side of the spectrum and shunning all things gluten-free and highbrow is **Wiener and Still Champion**, a hot dog stop where National Corn Dog Day is celebrated with the works (sans ketchup). When ordering, remember that the Chicago dog is a specific thing: a steamed, all-beef hot dog with yellow mustard, Day-Glo relish, chopped onion, tomato wedges, pickle spear, sport peppers, and celery salt on a poppy seed bun. That neon relish is made with sweet pickles and dyed a bright green (sort of like the Chicago River on St. Patrick's Day).

Dunk their deep-fried pickles into sauces that reach as high as "truffle-mushroom" or as low as "bacon-bacon." Other delights may unveil chargrilled burgers, chicken, fish, dippin' dogs, and meatless options all of which may (and should!) be accompanied with a side of crunchy and "Somewhat Famous Fries."

For a more retro-experience, approach the iconic **Superdawg**, with its dancing hot dogs in spotted gear. This family-owned and operated drive-in will make you feel as if you've just entered the set of *American Graffiti*. With its super-menu of super-dogs (made with pure beef), burgers, sandwiches, beverages, and soda fountain specialties including floating scoops of ice cream in bubbling root beer, this is as much a family tradition as it is a landmark since 1948.

A Slice of Americana

True fast foodies pay homage to the golden arches at the McDonald's Museum in Des Plaines. The building is a re-creation of the original store, with views of fresh potatoes being peeled and root beer drawn from a barrel by a uniformed crew of mannequins, fashioning a diorama that is as visually authentic as it is weird.

It is no surprise that Chicago has its fair share of highway fast food stops. After all, the concept was virtually invented here when the Fred Harvey company (which Hollywood immortalized in Judy Garland's *Harvey Girls* film), went from catering to railway passengers to motorists. It partnered to build the visually imposing series of mid-century "oases" stretching over the Illinois Tollway now catering to modern-day travelers.

ETHNIC ENCLAVES

In such a diverse urban center, it is no wonder that other ethnic enclaves are also thriving. Along Devon, you will find one of the country's larger South Asian communities. This corridor of South Asia showcases authentic restaurants, *desi* diners, shops, and grocery stores serving a mainly Indian and Pakistani clientele. Come for tandoori and leave with a sari! Presenting everything Japanese under one roof is **Mitsuwa Marketplace** in Arlington Heights. This enormous and extensive supermarket carries everything from top notch beef, sushi, and sashimi to Japanese baked goods, books, and cosmetics.

Journeying from South Asia to the Middle East and closer to Park Ridge, Des Plaines, and Niles, find an array of ethnic supermarkets filled with Greek and Middle Eastern specialty items. The influence of a massive Mexican population is found here as well within deliciously authentic tacos, tortas, and other foods at the many taquerias and casual restaurants dotting these sprawling suburbs.

With fast food forgotten, end a day here at **Amitabul**. This fusion Korean restaurant prepares scrumptious, healthy, and "simply vegan" foods that include a host of tasty dishes and refreshing drinks. Also proffered are Buddhist delicacies with organic vegetables, nuts, and spicy sauces for a vegan-friendly meal that, somehow, couldn't be more American. It is truly a gem that transcends traditional tastes.

North & Northwestern Suburbs

233

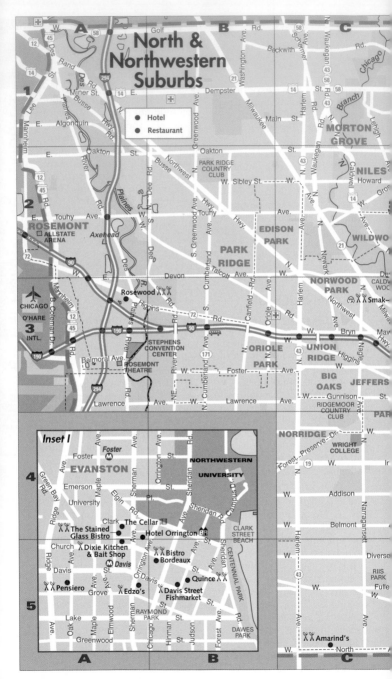

North & Northwestern Suburbs

Legend:
- ● Hotel
- ● Restaurant

MORTON GROVE

NILES

WILDWO

ROSEMONT
ALLSTATE ARENA
Axehead

PARK RIDGE COUNTRY CLUB

EDISON PARK

PARK RIDGE

CHICAGO O'HARE INTL.

Rosewood

NORWOOD PARK

Smak–

STEPHENS CONVENTION CENTER

ROSEMONT THEATRE

ORIOLE PARK

UNION RIDGE

BIG OAKS

JEFFERS

RIDGEMOOR COUNTRY CLUB

PAR

NORRIDGE

WRIGHT COLLEGE

Inset I

Foster

EVANSTON

NORTHWESTERN UNIVERSITY

The Stained Glass Bistro

The Cellar

Hotel Orrington

Dixie Kitchen & Bait Shop

Davis

Bistro Bordeaux

Quince

Pensiero

Edzo's

Davis Street Fishmarket

CLARK STREET BEACH

CENTENNIAL PARK

RAYMOND PARK

DAWES PARK

RIIS PARK

Amarind's

234

Amarind's

C5

6822 W. North Ave. (at Newcastle Ave.)

Phone: 773-889-9999
Web: www.amarinds.com
Prices:

Lunch Tue – Sat
Dinner Tue – Sun

Amarind's corner location and turret-like entrance is a favorite of Oak Parkers and others looking for affordable, solid Thai food in a family-friendly environment. Weekday specials and accommodations for kids keep tables filled day and night. A bright and pleasant décor dotted with Thai artifacts, tapestries, and artwork set the scene.

Start with deliciously filled chive dumplings served with a dipping sauce of soy, chili, and black vinegar. Follow with spicy grilled pork loin coated in a savory marinade of lemongrass, shallot, garlic, scallion, mint, lime juice, and chili paste (note that if you like things spicy, ask your server to alert the kitchen). Accompany tasty dishes like these with a cold glass of sweet and creamy Thai iced tea.

Angin Mamiri

Indonesian 🍴

E2

2739 W. Touhy Ave. (bet. California & Washtenaw Aves.)

Phone: 773-262-6646
Web: www.anginmamirichicago.com
Prices:

Lunch & dinner Tue – Sun

According to its hospitable owners, this is the only spot for Indonesian in Chicago—and in the entire state of Illinois. But finding it may take a few attempts; only a small hanging oval sign marks the spot. Once here, step into a welcoming space, bedecked in colorful masks and bronze birds perched on pale green walls, and find yourself amidst a world of authentic deliciousness.

Get started with *siomay bandung* (tofu stuffed with ground fish, topped with peanut sauce, served with potatoes, wontons, and a molasses-like sweet soy), before trying the intoxicating, spice-packed *coto makassar* soup; or silky beef *rendang* stewed to tender perfection in coconut milk. The multi-layer cake soaked in sweet milk and spices (*kue lapis legit*) is absolutely divine.

Bistro Bordeaux

French

618 Church St. (bet. Chicago & Orrington Aves.), Evanston

Phone: 847-424-1483	Lunch Sun
Web: www.lebistrobordeaux.com	Dinner Tue – Sun
Prices: $$	Davis

Bistro Bourdeaux hits that American ideal of the classic "French" bistro right on *le nez*. The old-world ambience is created thanks to details such as smoky mirrors, ancient pots and pans hanging on hooks, pressed-tin ceilings, and the list goes on. The service is well timed, and the prices just right for a night out.

Just as the décor meets the "Frenchified" brasserie expectations, so, too, does the food. The onion soup is classically done in an American style, with caramelized onions and a blend of rich melted cheeses; and the bone marrow crusted beef is perfectly cooked, served with crispy, crunchy breadcrumbs and herbs. Desserts meet expectations, too. You won't find a berry coulis bathing your *ile flotante* in Lyon, but in Evanston, it's just fine.

Café Marbella

Spanish

5527 N. Milwaukee Ave. (bet. Bryn Mawr & Catalpa Aves.)

Phone: 773-853-0128	Lunch Sun, Tue – Fri
Web: www.cafemarbella.com	Dinner Tue – Sun
Prices: $$	

The unassuming new location of this tapas spot is perfect for large groups who want to pass around plates, tasting a little bit of everything. The décor is understated, with red clay tile floors, brick archways, and simple booths, all the better to allow diners to focus on the authentic food.

The restaurant's Chef/partner Virgilio Trujillo has cooked in some of the city's favorite Spanish-style kitchens, including La Paella and Arco de Cuchilleros, and it shows as the tapas are done quite well here. Look for classics like gazpacho *Andaluz*, *gambas al ajillo*, and *piquillos con atún*. Tortilla *Española* is cooked as if the kitchen were in Spain, not on the northwest side, while sautéed Rioja-style chorizo lounges among large, buttery, tender white beans.

Campagnola

F1

Italian

815 Chicago Ave. (at Washington St.), Evanston

Phone: 847-475-6100
Web: www.campagnolarestaurant.com
Prices: $$

Dinner Tue – Sun
Main

Who says you have to head downtown for a night out on the town? Campagnola is proof that the suburbs can do sizzle. From its sultry soft lighting to its exposed brick walls and banquette seating, Campagnola seems to be designed with a tête-à-tête in mind.

The subdued sophistication of the dining room is echoed in the kitchen, where the chef ensures that the best designs are indeed simple. You won't find a high-falutin carte filled with adjectives describing fancy ingredients or fussy cooking techniques. Instead, this menu, where dishes like halibut Livornese and linguine with lemon zest and shrimp headline, is all about simplicity. From start to finish, Campagnola satisfies with every beautiful bite.

The Cellar

A4

International

820 Clark St. (bet. Benson & Sherman Aves.), Evanston

Phone: 847-425-5112
Web: www.thecellarevanston.com
Prices: ⊜⊜

Dinner nightly
Davis

The Cellar bombasts (and rightly so) an international small plates nosh-fest, where a killer list of brews and a cozy-hip vibe make it a beloved destination among locals and Northwestern University faculty. Sister to The Stained Glass Bistro 'round the corner, this is the more casual sibling—though it's every bit as cosmopolitan.

Tasty bites fall under three categories: "European," "American," and "Worldwide;" jumping from juicy micro-burgers, smothered in blue cheese on a brioche bun; and lobster coconut curry; to crispy fish tacos with spiced *crema*. Ales hail from around the country and globe spotlighting local breweries like Metropolitan Brewing Co.; and traversing the U.S. (Three Floyds, Dogfish Head) and Europe (St. Bernardus Tripel Ale, Belgium).

Davis Street Fishmarket

B5

Seafood

501 Davis St. (at Hinman Ave.), Evanston

Phone: 847-869-3474
Web: www.davisstreetfishmarket.com
Prices: $$

Lunch Tue – Sun
Dinner nightly
 Davis

The mystery has finally been solved, and Nemo has been discovered! He's at the Davis Street Fishmarket. Maybe you won't find the clown fish here after all, but you will find practically every other kind of fish at this Evanston treasure that has been serving up the sea (and regulars) since Madonna's peak in the mid-eighties.

Open up the dictionary to "seafood restaurant," and you'll likely find this spot, where polished woods, sea themed fabrics, and, yes, the customary oversized fish tank, proudly show off the nautical theme. As expected, it's all about the ocean on the menu: from steamed lobsters and raw bar selections to grilled fish, it's a mermaid's paradise. The warm and friendly staff makes sure even those with sea legs feel right at home.

Dixie Kitchen & Bait Shop

A5

Southern

825 Church St. (bet. Benson & Sherman Aves.), Evanston

Phone: 847-733-9030
Web: www.dixiekitchenchicago.com
Prices:

Lunch & dinner daily
 Davis

Kitsch and college campus combine at this paean to southern food. The inexpensive prices and considerable portions have made it a favorite of budget-driven students, so be prepared to wait for a table.

Meals start with a cornmeal griddle cake and progress to plates of flavorful fare like fried chicken, jerk catfish, crayfish étouffée, Dixie ribs, jambalaya, and other classics from south of the Mason-Dixon line. The catfish Po'boy is perfectly fried without a touch of oiliness, layered on a French roll with lettuce, tomato, and remoulade. The rich gumbo is deliciously swimming with shrimp, chicken, and andouille sausage.

Desserts like peach cobbler or pecan pie sweeten the deal and their breakfast makes for an over-the-top start to any day.

Edzo's

A5

1571 Sherman Ave. (bet. Davis & Grove Sts.), Evanston

Phone: 847-864-3396
Web: www.edzos.com
Prices: 💰💰

Lunch Tue – Sun
🚇 Davis

Burger shop plus nearby college campus usually equals one thing, but Edzo's somehow takes the formula and gets a different answer. Yes, this close to the Northwestern University campus, Edzo's attracts a lot of students and faculty. And, yes, the menu is burgers, fries, and shakes. But this isn't just a shack—there's plenty of room for dine-in eating.

And perhaps a burger is a burger is a burger. But these are some burgers. Order yours as a single, double, or triple, then pick your cheese and toppings—how about pepperjack and hot *giardiniera*? Or there's always the crowd-pleaser: the patty melt. Side your burger with some heavy-duty fries; buffalo, truffle or loaded fries top the list. A spicy Mexican chocolate milkshake rounds out the decadence.

Hema's Kitchen

E3

2439 W. Devon Ave. (bet. Artesian & Campbell Aves.)

Phone: 773-338-1627
Web: www.hemaskitchen.com
Prices: $$

Lunch & dinner daily

Bustling Devon Avenue is the go-to neighborhood for Indian and Pakistani vittles, music, movies, clothing, and other delights. And Hema's Kitchen is one of the stalwarts of the area, a favorite of locals (so much so, a second location opened in Lincoln Park), despite the fact that there is no shortage of restaurants from which to choose.

The menu, by Hyderabad native chef Hema Potla, includes some old favorites and twists on the classics. The chicken roll is basically an Indo-wrap, with a kebab rolled in butter-brushed *paratha*, along with verdant green chutney. Lamb *rogan josh* is a mouthwatering curry; sweet, nutty, spicy, and tart, seasoned with cardamom, cloves, and other spices. And pistachio *kulfi* is a creamy, sweet ending to a spicy meal.

Lou Malnati's

Pizza

E2

6649 N. Lincoln Ave. (bet. Avers & Springfield Aves.), LIncolnwood

Phone: 847-673-0800   Lunch & dinner daily
Web: www.loumalnatis.com
Prices:

 Lou Malnati got his start in Chicago's very first deep-dish pizzeria. In 1971, he opened his own, and it's been golden ever since. With 30 locations around Chicago (the original is a bit of a time warp), Lou's remains family-owned and operated with great food and devoted service.

Check their website for a vast menu of pizzas, pastas, and other Italian classics. Portions are colossal: begin with the stuffed spinach bread–that great Chi style garlic, spinach, and cheese combo with tomatoes stuffed into bread–and you'll struggle to stay upright. Try the "Lou" pizza: buttery pastry-like crust crowned with spinach, mushrooms, and sliced tomatoes then doused in sauce and slathered with cheese. Bonus: you can buy their famous dough online.

Oceanique

F1

Seafood

505 Main St. (bet. Chicago & Hinman Aves.), Evanston

Phone: 847-864-3435   Dinner Mon – Sat
Web: www.oceanique.com
Prices: $$$$ Main

 If you have to ask what kind of food one can expect at Oceanique, you may need to get your head checked, or at least your eyes. After all, the name pretty much says it acutely—straightforward French influenced seafood. Located not far from Evanston's Ridge historic district, Oceanique opens its arms to a steady stream of shoppers and residents. It's all in the family as well, since Chef/owner Mark Grosz shares the reins with his wife (who regulates the front), and his son (who manages the acclaimed wine collection).

The chef gussies up his seasonally inspired dishes with sauces and spices. In addition to plentiful seafood, there are mighty meat, poultry, and vegetarian choices. Can't decide? Go for the three- or six-course chef's tasting menus.

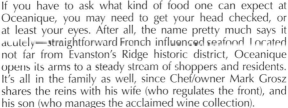

Pensiero

A5

Italian

1566 Oak Ave. (bet. Davis & Grove Sts.), Evanston

Phone: 847-475-7779
Web: www.pensieroitalian.com
Prices: $$$

Dinner Tue – Sun
Davis

Va Pensiero got a makeover and now the lower level of the Margarita European Inn houses Pensiero. This is one Evanston eatery that doesn't get overrun with Northwestern students. Rather an adult crowd dines here, appreciating the upscale (albeit dated) setting and perceived refined service.

The new Pensiero isn't particularly inventive, but serves solid, flavorsome Italian fare that's generally crowd-pleasing. A plate of grilled calamari with green olives, tomato, cannellini beans, tomato, and celery leaf is a simple and light way to start, and the calamari is cooked just right. Pastas are unreliable but a lemon soufflé cake with its caramelized, torched meringue top is the perfect ending, thanks to its tangy-sweet flavor combination.

Quince

B5

Contemporary

1625 Hinman Ave. (bet. Church & Davis Sts.), Evanston

Phone: 847-570-8400
Web: www.quincerestaurant.net
Prices: $$$

Dinner Tue – Sun

Quaint Quince is housed in The Homestead in Evanston. The kitchen may have passed through some hands, but the dining room preserves its intimacy and charm with a bookshelf-framed fireplace, mauve walls, and cream banquettes. As if that weren't enough for a romantic tryst, windows overlooking a tree-lined street bestow floods of light on good lookin' groups.

Mindful servers present patrons with shining details on the kitchen's contemporary and classic combos. Herbs–from the on-site garden–star in superb dishes like delicate octopus atop arugula, smoky chorizo, and garlic purée; and roasted pork medallions paired with gnocchi, squash blossom, fennel, and apple. It would be ungodly to skip the inspired and beautifully prepared sweet corn panna cotta.

Renga-Tei

Japanese

3956 W. Touhy Ave. (at Prairie Rd.), Lincolnwood

Phone: 847-675-5177
Web: N/A
Prices: $$

Lunch Mon & Wed – Fri
Dinner Wed – Mon

Striking bamboo-paned, paper covered windows jazz up a clean, brick façade; the building stands out amidst its bland, strip mall neighbors. Inside, expect waves of smiles and attentiveness from the mature staff in stylish 60s up dos, and a spacious, clean space flecked with showy Japanese kitsch. Snag a seat at the sushi bar, where fresh fish–still kissed with the smell of the sea–gets handled with expert care. Slices of gorgeous abalone or Santa Barbara sea urchin make for excellent sashimi; and dishes like *tonkatsu* (tender, panko-crusted pork cutlets) keep things traditional.

A refreshing twist on the spicy tuna roll is a welcome change– hand chopped tuna, tossed with spicy chilis, then rolled with rice and nori and topped with a touch of sauce.

Rosewood

Steakhouse

9421 W. Higgins Rd. (at Willow Creek Dr.), Rosemont

Phone: 847-696-9494
Web: www.rosewoodrestaurant.com
Prices: $$$

Lunch Mon – Fri
Dinner nightly

The Windy City loves its steakhouses, and nowhere is it more apparent than at this independent restaurant that has been thriving for more than two decades amid the popular chains near O'Hare. Inside the serene space, coffee-colored leather chairs and wood paneling create a classic Rat Pack vibe.

Succulent USDA prime steaks get top billing here, such as the 16 oz. Kansas City strip, cooked perfectly to order. Spend the extra dollars on a peppercorn, Cajun, blue cheese, or horseradish crust on any steak for an added indulgence. French onion soup, smoked salmon on flatbread, shrimp cocktail, mashed potatoes, and baked apples round out the menu. Fresh seafood, like the banana-crusted tilapia, is a good option for those who want something different.

Sabri Nihari

Indian

E2

2502 W. Devon Ave. (bet. Campbell & Maplewood Aves.)

Phone: 773-465-3272   Lunch & dinner daily
Web: www.sabrinihari.com
Prices: ⊕⊕

On a stretch of Devon Avenue filled with halal meat stores, fabric shops, and Indo-Pak groceries, find this bright restaurant with an air of formality and satisfying Pakistani cuisine. Whether eating somewhere that serves only *zabiha* meat (slaughtered in strict accordance with the Islamic faith), is of importance to you or not, this spot is well worth a visit (easiest to arrive by car or bus).

The signature beef *nihari* dish is de-boned and braised in a thickened brown sauce, served with slivers of jalapeño peppers and ginger root. A *biryani* may feature caramelized onions and chicken cooked until tender, topping tasty basmati rice. Classic *dal*, *haleem*, kebabs, freshly made naan, and other Pakistani favorites round out the affordable menu.

Shokran Moroccan Grill

Moroccan

D4

4027 W. Irving Park Rd. (bet. Keystone Ave. & Pulaski Rd.)

Phone: 773-427-9130   Dinner Mon – Sat
Web: www.shokranchicago.com   Irving Park (Blue)
Prices: ⊕⊕

Judging by the ordinary façade, commercial surroundings, and hovering highway, you may be tempted to pass right by. But, oh, the delights that would be missed! Arabic for "thank you," Shokran is a scrumptious spot for homemade Moroccan, where rich silk fabrics billow from the ceiling; framed mother-of-pearl artifacts hang on burnt sienna walls; and hookah pipes and copper chargers bedeck the room.

Brace yourself for the luxurious couscous royale—melt-in-your mouth braised lamb; tasty and moist merguez; tender zucchini, rutabaga, carrots, and chickpeas sublimely snuggled into fragrant, fluffy couscous. Satiate the sweet tooth with handmade cookies—from almond pastries to biscotti-like *fekkas*, each morsel is fresh and irresistible. Thank you, Shokran.

Smak-Tak 🐶

Polish ✕✕

C3

5961 N. Elston Ave. (bet. Markham & Peterson Aves.)

Phone: 773-763-1123   Lunch & dinner Wed – Mon
Web: www.smaktak.com
Prices: 💰💰

♿ Knotty pine paneling, wood chairs, and a small fireplace transform the tiny Smak-Tak into a ski cabin-like getaway. This kitchen cooks up some of the city's best Polish food, which is saying a lot given the plethora of Polish eats in the area.
Portions are huge, and while the staff happily packs up leftovers, diners should plan their ordering so they can try a little of everything. Do not skip the amazing *pierogi*. Versions include cheese and potato, sauerkraut and mushrooms, sweet cheese, blueberry, plum, cherry, or strawberry, and all are tossed in melted butter with sour cream on the side. Potato pancakes served with applesauce; meat-stuffed cabbage; hearty hunter stew; and grilled old Polish-style kielbasa are other stomach-busters.

The Stained Glass Bistro

American ✕✕

A4

1735 Benson Ave. (bet. Church & Clark Sts.), Evanston

Phone: 847-864-8600   Dinner nightly
Web: www.thestainedglass.com
Prices: $$

♿ Sharing a kitchen with The Cellar (its sister restaurant around the corner), this is the more upscale, globe-trotting elder, where international inflections spruce up a modern American menu, in a sexy, urban-chic space. Roasted free range Amish chicken cozies up next to toothsome Moroccan couscous; tender pork belly is served up with coconut custard; old-fashioned crab cakes get a sweet corn *arepa* and chive oil; and miso-glazed Scottish salmon nestles next to bamboo rice, baby bok choy, and watermelon radish salad.
In the mood for just a little wine? You're in luck—over thirty wines by the glass are offered, changing on a daily basis. Try the "Wine Sampler," three different half glasses, for a dash of variety.

Taste of Peru 😊

F2

6545 N. Clark St. (bet. Albion & Arthur Aves.)

Phone: 773-381-4540   Lunch & dinner daily
Web: www.tasteofperucom
Prices: $$

Yes a cliché, but don't judge a book by its cover. Sure, it is located in a generic strip mall and is flanked by a Laundromat and nail salon, but look past Taste of Peru's lackluster location and less-than-appealing exterior, and you'll certainly be rightly rewarded.

Inside, it's kitschy Peru, but you're not here for the aura. You're here for the fiery and funky food that draws everyone from gourmands to Guy Fieri. Chat up the passionate owner– who will give you a quick education in Peruvian cuisine–as you inhale generous portions of ethnic comfort food like *papa rellena* (mashed potatoes stuffed with tender steak), and *cau cau* (honeycomb tripe stew). The owner keeps his cooking secrets close to the chest, but that's ok, since you'll be back again soon.

Tub Tim Thai

D2

4927 Oakton St. (bet. Niles Ave. & Skokie Blvd.), Skokie

Phone: 847-675-8424   Lunch & dinner Mon – Sat
Web: www.tubtimthai.com
Prices: 🍝🍝

A casual stop in suburban Skokie, this Thai find is as accommodating as they come. The setting is pleasant, with dark wood furnishings and pastel walls showcasing a revolving display of artwork typically for sale.

The affordable menu is equally accommodating and the kitchen delights with tasty recipes and quality ingredients. Diners can request the level of spice desired; but if it's not hot enough, there are pickled chilis, chili paste, and chili powder on the table. Choices run the gamut of the traditional Thai options such as shrimp dumplings; spicy basil chicken; pad Thai; and sweet coconut rice with mango for dessert. Tub Tim Thai is never a splurge, but lunch is a particular bargain with an appetizer, salad, and main course for under $10.

Viceroy of India

E2

2520 W. Devon Ave. (bet. Campbell & Maplewood Aves.)

Phone: 773-743-4100

Web: www.viceroyofindia.com

Prices: ⬤⬤

Lunch & dinner daily

A walk down Devon Avenue is like a daycation to India. Each storefront is packed with saris, Bollywood videos, snack shops, restaurants, and other retail businesses offering up a taste of home to Chicago's enormous Indian population. Streets are packed (and, as a result, parking sometimes a challenge) most nights, making for great people-watching.

Viceroy of India is a favorite among the many options on Devon both because of its small café, for sweets and take-out, and its upscale dining room, which accommodates large parties. A reasonably priced lunch buffet; a particularly good *dosa* served with coconut-based chutney; and fragrant lamb *saag* are a few of the draws. The tamarind rice, with its nuts and herbs, has a perfect sour, yet fragrant, note.

North & Northwestern Suburbs

Bib Gourmand 😊
indicates our inspectors'
favorites for good value.

South,
Southwest &
Western Suburbs

South, Southwest & Western Suburbs

With perhaps a few high-profile exceptions (here's lookin' at you, President Obama's Hyde Park), the neighborhoods of the city's west and south sides and the west and south suburbs rarely make the pages of traditional visitors' guides. Instead, they're saved for residents who work and live in these city environs.

Feeding Families

While it's true that these neighborhoods may not have the museums, hotels, or 24-7 service of those more centrally located, they are a foodie's dream, with lesser-known groceries, take-out joints, and ethnic eateries. Back in the day, some of these neighborhoods, including Back of the Yards, once home to the famous Chicago Stockyards, changed the food industry.

Today the Marquette Park neighborhood where, in 1966, Martin Luther King, Jr. brought his civil rights marchers, may seem questionable after dark. But it is worth a ride for no reason other than the mighty mother-in-law. No, not visiting a relative. That's the name of **Fat Johnnie's Famous Red Hots'** best dish: a tamale, a kosher hot dog, chili, and (processed) cheese on a bun, handed through a window.

The rest of Marquette Park (near 63rd St.) features predominantly Mexican storefronts, taquerias, and other food vendors.

Film buffs love the fact that Marquette Park (the 600-acre actual green space, not the neighborhood) was featured in the iconic movie *The Blues Brothers*.

Eating in Eastern Europe

Closer to Midway International Airport, near Archer Heights, is a concentration of Eastern European shops mixed among classic Chicago-style brick bungalows. One favorite is **Bobak's Sausage Company**, with its 100-foot-long meat counter. Shopping here is entertainment in and of itself. Buy a hot lunch to eat on the spot or sausages to take home.

For a bigger and better taste of Chicago, you can also choose to buy from their bulk-pack items, retail-pack items, and imported specialties. Want to try this at home? They also proffer a list of recipes. For a more Polish and Lithuanian take on deli dishes, try Evergreen Park's **AJ's Meats**.

Ireland in Chicagoland

Nearby Beverly is the hub of the city's Irish bar scene, something many people first discover during the raucous South Side Irish St. Patrick's Day parade. But all year long bars serve corned beef, cabbage, and plenty of cold beers. Beverly's Pantry sells cookware and teaches locals how to use it in a series of ongoing classes. Non-food attractions in Beverly include a number of Frank Lloyd Wright houses and other significant architecture (not to mention a real castle).

Farther north and closer to Lake Michigan, cerebral hub Hyde Park attracts Obama fans, academics, students, and more architecture buffs. Professors and students at the University of Chicago crowd the surrounding cafés, eateries, and bars geared towards the smarter set.

SUMMER SNACKING

During summertime, don't miss the wonder of a five-flavor ice cream cone from the **Original Rainbow Cone**, a Chicagoland staple since 1926. Housed in a pretty pink building, the original menu may also unveil a range of splits, shakes, and sundaes; as well as a decadent carte of ice cream flavors such as black walnut, New York vanilla, and bubble gum-banana.

CHICAGO'S BELOVED BITES

Those without any heart or cholesterol problems ought to try the beloved breaded steaks from **Ricobene's**, which has several locations on both the south side and in the south suburbs. Ricobene's also caters to the beefy best in everyone by serving up that Chicago classic deep-dish pizza pie alongside other decadent dishes like rich barbecue specials, Italian-esque

sandwiches, Chicago-style hot dogs, and char-broiled burgers. Suburban Oak Park may be more famous for past residents like Ernest Hemingway and Frank Lloyd Wright, but nonetheless, foodies care more about vinegar-maker Jim Vitalo. His amazing, subtle herb-infused **Herbally Yours** vinegars are sold at the **Oak Park Farmer's Market** on Saturdays in the summer.

GRAZING THROUGH THE MIDDLE EAST

Suburban Bridgeview, home to Toyota Park, where the Chicago Fire soccer team plays, is one of the region's best stops for authentic and fine Middle Eastern fare. Throughout this area, you'll find restaurants outfitted with grills and bakeries galore; visit scores of centrally-located stores, and be sure to take home snacks like pita, hummus, and baba ghanoush; as well as fresh groceries for a night of magnificent Middle Eastern eating.

It would be a sin to end your meal without a taste of sweet, so after you've consumed your fill of falafel and the like, move on to sweet respites in this Middle Eastern Corridor. Visit **Elshafei Pastries** for some flaky baklava and other pistacchio-pocked delights.

For more saccharine satisfaction, sojourn at **Albasha Sweets** and **Nablus Sweets**. These sugary sweet options will leave you smiling for the rest of the evening. Can there be any other way to end such fresh, fun, and fine fare?

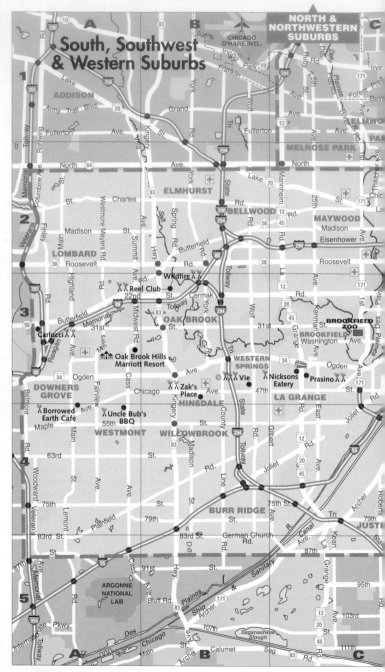

South, Southwest & Western Suburbs

CHICAGO O'HARE INTL.

ADDISON

ELMWOOD PARK

MELROSE PARK

ELMHURST

BELLWOOD

MAYWOOD

LOMBARD

Wildfire

Reel Club

OAK BROOK

BROOKFIELD ZOO

BROOKFIELD

Carlucci

Oak Brook Hills
Marriott Resort

WESTERN
SPRINGS

Vie

Nicksons
Eatery

Prasino

DOWNERS
GROVE

Zak's
Place

LA GRANGE

Borrowed
Earth Café

Uncle Bub's
BBQ

HINSDALE

WESTMONT

WILLOWBROOK

ARGONNE
NATIONAL LAB

BURR RIDGE

JUSTI

252

LAKE
MICHIGAN

● Hotel
● Restaurant

N

F1

F2

GRANT
PARK

SOLDIER FIELD

MEIGS
FIELD

McCORMICK
PLACE

BURNHAM
PARK

F3

La Petite
Folie

Noodles Etc

JACKSON
PARK

SOUTH
SHORE

F4

PULLMAN

F5

D

E

F

PORTAGE
PARK

Foster
St.

Gunnison
Oak
Dr.
Park
Narragansett
Central
Rd.

Lawrence
Elston
Ave.
Irving
Park

LAKEVIEW
Belmont
Ave.
Clybourne

Sheridan
Ashland
Clark
Lincoln
Broadway

D1

Milwaukee
Cicero
Ave.
Pulaski
Kennedy
Kimball
California
Kedzie

Fullerton
Grand
Ave.
Armitage
Ave.

HUMBOLDT North
PARK
Ave.
St.
Blvd.

Division
Augusta
Ave.
Ave.

XX Cucina
Paradiso

OAK
PARK
St.
COLUMBUS
PARK
Expwy.

Western
Damen
Ashland
Chicago Ave.
Ave.
Grand
Lake
St.
Madison
Roosevelt
CHICAGO

XX Shokolad
Division
Ave.

D2

Ridgeland
Oak
Park
RWYN
CICERO
St.
St.

Douglas Blvd.
Ogden
DOUGLAS
PARK
18th
Rd.

Michigan
LaSalle Blvd.

Cormak
31st
Central
Rd.
Ave.
26th
Ave.
Kedzie
Ave.
California
Ave.

Ryan

F3
US CELLULAR
FIELD
XX Nana
Han 202 XX

D3

Pershing
STICKNEY Ship &
Sanitary
Chicago
46th
St.
Stephenson
Ave.
47th
St.

Canal
Expwy
Archer
Kedzie
California
Pershing
4/th
SHERMAN
PARK
Garfield

Halsted
State
Ave.
Cottage
Martin
Shore

Archer
55th
Ave. MIDWAY
INTL.
63rd
65th
St.
St.

50th
CHICAGO
LAWN
63rd
MARQUETTE
PARK
71st
Marquette
Rd.
Pulaski
Kedzie
Ave.
Western
Ave.
Ashland

ENGLEWOOD

Blvd.
55th St.
X Noodles Etc
Midway
Plaisance

La Petite
Folie

D4

BRIDGEVIEW
Harlam
State
St.
Rd.

X Vito & Nick's
Pizzeria
Columbus

79th
AUBURN
87th

Voennces
King
Luther
Grove
67th
Story
Jeffrey
Island

Al Dawadi Grill X

OAK
LAWN
St.
Hwy.
St.
Ridgeland

EVERGREEN
PARK

95th
Beverly
103rd
111th

Halsted
Ave.

D5

294
SW Tollway Ave.
43

Cicero
Ave.
Pulaski
Ave.

253

Al Bawadi Grill

D5

Middle Eastern

7216 W. 87th St. (bet. Harlem & Oketo Aves.), Bridgeview

Phone: 708-599-1999
Web: www.albawadigrill.com
Prices: $$

Lunch & dinner daily

Housed in a former fast food joint on busy 87th Street, Al Bawadi Grill doesn't exactly shout, "peaceful oasis," but the owners have done a lot with what they've got. Water fountains, faux palm trees, and etched glass set the scene for the kind, hospitable service. A colorful pile of pickled vegetables as well as a smoky eggplant salad are brought to the table for diners to enjoy while they peruse the grill-centric menu.

Hummus is velvety and artfully presented, dotted with olive oil, chilis, and sumac accompanied by warm pita. The Al Bawadi mixed grill includes three kinds of kebabs–shish, *kefta*, and chicken kebab–accompanied by grilled onion, tomato, and two styles of rice. Wash it all down with a freshly squeezed juice or smoothie.

Borrowed Earth Café

A4

Vegetarian

970 Warren Ave. (bet. Highland Ave. & Main St.), Downers Grove

Phone: 630-795-1729
Web: www.borrowedearthcafe.com
Prices: $$

Lunch & dinner Tue – Sat

This suburban stalwart is as earnest as they come. The environmentally friendly dining room cleverly encourages diners to learn to appreciate a raw food way of life. The aesthetic is more Woodstock than Gwyneth Paltrow, but the food is good enough for any health-conscious Hollywood celeb.

Enjoy a guiltless lasagna made with thin sheets of zucchini, juicy tomatoes, grated carrots, loads of creamy pesto, and fluffy cashew "ricotta." It arrives with a side of kale-licious salad: kale, hemp seed, and cabbage tossed with the house dressing. For even more of the leafy power green, try the addictive and delicious kale chips. Blueberry mango cheesecake is a revelation and easily surpasses run-of-the-mill dairy cheesecakes, minus the guilt.

Carlucci

Italian ✗✗

A3

1891 Butterfield Rd. (off I-355), Downers Grove

Phone: 630-512-0990
Web: www.carluccirestaurant.com
Prices: $$

Lunch Mon – Fri
Dinner nightly

Live in the Windy City long enough and you will end up celebrating a promotion with co-workers, niece's high school graduation, or another milestone at Carlucci's. The suburban office park setting doesn't help raise expectations from the outside; but inside, the space is warm and welcoming, and the service attentive and professional.

The food is equally surprising. The *petto di pollo ripieno*, a breaded chicken breast stuffed with ricotta, prosciutto, and peas, is so tasty you may need to refill your bread basket so you don't miss a drop of its lemon butter sauce. Ingredients in the tasty *insalata Genovese*–romaine, black olives, cherry tomatoes, and tuna–are individually seasoned before being tossed together. For dessert, treat yourself to bread pudding.

Cucina Paradiso

Italian ✗✗

D2

814 North Blvd. (bet. Kenilworth & Oak Park Aves.), Oak Park

Phone: 708-848-3434
Web: www.cucinaoakpark.com
Prices: $$

Dinner nightly
🚇 Oak Park (Green)

An awning-covered sidewalk welcomes the arty Oak Parkers from the neighborhood to relax and dine in this comfy restaurant surrounded by brick blocks of charming boutiques. Inside the dining room, vintage posters set the mood.

On Mondays half-price wines pack 'em into the bar, and throughout the week this is a solid choice in the neighborhood. Service is spotty but the food tastefully prepared. The kitchen does a fine job on the classic, country Italian menu. Chicken pistachio is served with a red pepper cream and a balsamic sauce, pan-fried with a pleasant, crisp exterior; the sauce on the pasta shells, tossed with sausage, onions, peas, marinara, and basil has a nice, gamey essence. Sides are worthy including the grilled asparagus and white polenta.

Han 202 😊

F3

Chinese XX

605 W. 31st St. (bet. Lowe Ave. & Wallace St.)

Phone: 312-949-1314
Web: www.han202restaurant.com
Prices: 😊

Dinner Tue – Sun

Visit Han 202 and be pleasantly surprised by its sparkling clean, chic-minimalist décor. The dining room is replete with red-stained wood tables, each topped with a lotus blossom votive; and the partially open kitchen offers a peek at an orderly staff churning out creatively prepared Chinese cuisine. Han 202 only offers a prix-fixe menu which is uniquely ambitious at a very reasonable price. Perhaps begin with blue crab wonton soup, whose plump, silky dumplings are both delicate and chock-full of crab; and incredibly tender filets of Mongolian beef in a sweet-salty brown sauce showcase fine product, expertly prepared. Meals end of a refreshingly light note and may include a selection of sorbets for dessert.

La Petite Folie 😊

F4

French XX

1504 E. 55th St. (at Harper Ave.)

Phone: 773-493-1394
Web: www.lapetitefolie.com
Prices: $$

Lunch Tue – Fri
Dinner Tue – Sun

Consistently considered one of area's best restaurants, La Petite Folie is tucked into a tree-lined courtyard of the Hyde Park Shopping center. Inside, find an unpretentious décor accented by a curved wood bar and cordial service.

The surroundings improve even more as the kitchen cooks up classic French fare made with the best seasonal, local ingredients available. Bargains can be found at lunch, perhaps featuring a three-egg omelet filled with duck sausage and onion confit; or the chopped shrimp in light tomato-cream sauce folded into handmade crêpes. Dinner can be a bargain, too, during the $32 three-course prix-fixe, available from 5:30-6:30 P.M. daily. Classic salads and flaky dessert tarts are sure to please even the most ardent francophiles.

Nana

F3

3267 S. Halsted St. (at 33rd St.)

Phone: 312-929-2486

Web: www.nanaorganic.com

Prices: $$

Lunch & dinner daily

A precious find on an unassuming street, Nana is a modern magnet for diners who live by fresh, local, and organic eats, but who don't wish to spend an arm and a leg for the pleasure. Bridgeport locals and others gather for Nana's sincere, clean, and Latin-inspired preparations, and to check out the art (dotting the white walls) and jewelry on sale.

The spicy *chilaquiles*–served with a side of eggs, any style–are elevated beyond their usual "leftover tortilla" status thanks to a zingy tomatillo cream salsa. The owner's *mama*, also the pastry chef at north side favorite, Café 28, makes the delicious desserts. Her cherry and peach cobbler, for example, is topped with a brown sugar-cinnamon crumb dome, spiced up with jalapeño, and packs a surprising punch.

Nicksons Eatery

C3

30 S. La Grange Rd. (bet. Calendar & Harris Aves.), La Grange

Phone: 708-354-4995

Web: www.nicksonseatery.com

Prices: $$

Lunch & dinner Mon – Sat

Make sure you're starving (and have rescheduled your appointment with the cardiologist) before heading to Nicksons Eatery, as this charming spot in downtown La Grange, celebrates country American cooking. Tin ceilings, homely wood floors, and a cowhide-covered banquette lend a barn-like aura to the dining room.

The Baca family, which includes husband and wife Nick and Carson (thus the name), and brother Rick, run the show with fingerlickin' good food. Tasty Texan brisket tacos, pan-seared pork chops, pork ribs, and soft shell crab Po'boys—this is country cooking with a gourmet slant. Those crispy sweet potato fries will hook you! In the sweet vein, key lime pie, double chocolate pecan fudge, and old-fashioned root beer floats offer a slice of Americana.

South, Southwest & Western Suburbs

Noodles Etc.

F4

1333 E. 57th St. (bet. Kenwood & Kimbark Aves.)

Phone: 773-684-2801
Lunch & dinner daily
Web: www.noodlesetc.com
Prices: ⬯⬯

A grade-A attraction for University of Chicago students and faculty, this pan-Asian eatery serves its carb-friendly fare in an inviting space with counter seating, booths, and traditional tables. The affordable menu, casual setting (think: paper napkin-rolled flatware), generous portions, and decent selection makes this an obvious pick for the college crowd. Service is prompt, even when tables are packed.

As is expected from its name, the menu includes a wide variety of noodles including udon, ramen, *pho, pancit*, lo mein, *tom yum*, and plenty of other Asian versions of the dish. There's also a sizeable offering of starters in portions best suited to sharing.

Sure, it's not authentic, but everything here is tasty, well-made, and a very good value.

Prasino

C3

93 S. La Grange Rd. (bet. Cossitt & Harris Aves.), La Grange

Phone: 708-469-7058
Lunch & dinner daily
Web: www.eatgreenlivewell.com
Prices: $$

The fact that Prasino has a "smoothie sommelier" should be the only clue you need to realize that this is not your average suburban restaurant. Prasino (from the Greek word for "green") is all about being eco-friendly. Light fixtures are made from recycled wine boxes and information about the reclaimed wood furniture is available to interested diners.

Ingredients are organic, sustainably grown, and locally-sourced whenever possible. The concept is so green it features a Natura filtered water system, an alternative to all those bottles. In some dishes like the poached artichoke with a creative béarnaise, or banana bread with pistachio ice cream, the quality shines through. Others, like the deconstructed crab salad are too complicated for their own good.

Reel Club

B3

Seafood ✕✕

272 Oakbrook Center (off Rte. 83), Oak Brook

Phone: 630-368-9400
Web: www.reel-club.com
Prices: $$

Lunch & dinner daily

Shopping in the behemoth Oakbrook Center could work up an appetite for almost anyone. Reel Club, a Lettuce Entertain You offering at the mall, gives weary shoppers and locals a great alternative to the staid food court.

The menu is focused on seafood, including Sunday's seafood buffet; but there are plenty of American standards such as salads and surf-and-turf. The ahi tuna burger is fresh and tasty, slathered in a lemon-ginger aïoli and served on a toasted brioche with fantastic hand-cut fries. The seafood gumbo is so savory and satisfying it could make a meal on its own, but finish with a Mounds Bar, paying homage to the classic candy bar, as decadent as it sounds. A pre-selected flight of five wines offers a well-priced sampling with entrées.

Shokolad

E2

Eastern European ✕✕

2524 W. Chicago Ave. (bet. Campbell Ave. & Rockwell St.)

Phone: 773-276-6402
Web: N/A
Prices: ⊜⊜

Lunch & dinner Tue – Sun

Ukrainian, Russian, and Eastern European dishes are comfort food to much of Chicago's population, and diners come to Humboldt Park's Shokolad to indulge their cravings in a bright, casual setting. Must tries include the potato and cheese *varenyky*, the Ukranian answer to the Polish *pierogi*, and the *pelmeni*, tender, spiced ground pork dumplings.

Sure, cheesecake lollipops aren't authentic Eastern European treats, but these dark or white chocolate covered cheesecake rounds are favorites of regulars. In fact, they may be responsible for introducing many people to Shokolad. Highlighting the prowess of the pastry department, there's a bakery show case with sweets to take away.

Regulars tout the Sunday brunch, by far one of the best around.

Uncle Bub's BBQ

A4

Barbecue

132 S. Cass Ave. (at Dallas St.), Westmont

Phone: 630-493-9000   Lunch & dinner daily
Web: www.unclebubs.com
Prices: 💿

Suburban Westmont is known for just three things: being the former home to Blues legend Muddy Waters, being the current home to Beanie Baby-maker Ty, Inc., and Uncle Bub's BBQ. This large roadhouse serves hundreds of barbecue fans every day. They order at the counter (next to the big ol' bucket o' hot peppers.) Their favorite is the chicken, served smoked and grilled with an extra zigzag of Bub's secret sauce on top. The rub makes the chicken moist and smoky, and it pairs well with the classic corn bread (shaped into a mini loaf) and green beans. All Bub's meats (pork, chicken, and beef) are slow-cooked at temps no more than 210 degrees. Meaty homemade chili hits the spot, as does the lucious chocolate cake with buttercream frosting.

Vito & Nick's Pizzeria

E4

Italian ✗

8433 S. Pulaski Rd. (bet. 84th & 85th Sts.)

Phone: 773-735-2050   Lunch & dinner daily
Web: www.vitoandnick.com
Prices: 💿

When in Rome, do as the Romans do. When in Chicago, eat pizza. Since 1949, Chicagoans have been eating Vito & Nick's pizzas, made from a recipe that remains a family secret. Pies are available in two sizes (12" or 14"), with toppings like cheese, sausage, pepperoni, anchovies, shrimp, sliced beef, and *giardiniera*. Sausage is the way to go, and you can add an egg on Fridays. Sick of pizza? Hearty plates of spaghetti, ravioli, and *mostaccioli*, with or without meatballs or sausage, round out the menu and you can start with a crisp salad or one of the fried appetizers. Like many Great Lakes locales, on Fridays there is an all-you-can-eat fried smelt special.
Want this taste at home? Order a partially cooked pie to finish in your own oven.

Vie ❀

Contemporary XXX

B3

4471 Lawn Ave. (bet. Burlington Ave. & Elm St.), Western Springs

Phone: 708-246-2082 Dinner Mon – Sat
Web: www.vierestaurant.com
Prices: $$$

Linca Bergonia

Vie has a suburban exterior with a city-chic interior. The sophisticated space stars polished concrete floors, blue-gray walls and seats, and large, abstract black-and-white photographs depicting rural routines. With a handsome bar, thick linens, and fresh flowers, the vibe at Vie is that of a special occasion place; and the well-trained staff reiterate this with wise recommendations, attentive service, and witty banter.

The kitchen's passion for locally sourced and seasonally suitable ingredients manifests itself in a menu that details the farm provenance of its produce—some dishes are even paired with a local beer from Goose Island. The cocktail and wine collections also score well, proffering unique selections by the glass and creative concoctions.

The season leads the dishes naturally, like a garden fresh amuse bouche of melon with lemon-thyme vinaigrette, or ricotta-stuffed, fried squash blossoms atop dragon tongue beans mixed with crispy ham and squash ribbons. Whitefish fritters are laced wih spring onion shavings and a smoky paprika aïoli; and the rich rhubarb galette–made creamy with pink peppercorn ice cream–provides an enticing burst of tart, spicy, and sweet flavors.

Wildfire

Steakhouse ✗✗

232 Oakbrook Center (off Rte. 83), Oak Brook

Phone: 630-586-9000
Web: www.wildfirerestaurant.com
Prices: $$$

Lunch & dinner daily

This 1940's-inspired steakhouse has a cozy vibe, despite the location looking out at the mall parking lot, and the crowds who pack these tables. The music playing in the background and the low lighting contribute to the attractive ambience.

A chain-owned shopping mall restaurant might not have been high on the "must eat" list; but like its partner company Lettuce Entertain You is wont to do, Wildfire exceeds expectations. The menu bulges with sandwiches, salads, and pizzas at lunch; with steaks and seafood added at dinner. Each entrée, like the filet mignon, is cooked tender and to order. High-quality, lean meats add to the pleasurable experience. The classic steakhouse creamed spinach is heavy on the cream and seasoned with butter and nutmeg.

Zak's Place

American ✗✗

112 S. Washington St. (bet. 1st & 2nd Sts.), Hinsdale

Phone: 630-323-9257
Web: www.zaksplace.com
Prices: $$

Lunch Mon – Fri
Dinner Mon – Sat

You could go home after work, fire up the stove, and make yourself a meal, but why bother when you could just pull up a seat at Zak's Place? Any restaurant named after a gone, but not forgotten, beloved pet is sure to comfort and charm. It is American bistro-style to a tee with delicious dark woods, exposed brick walls, pressed-tin ceilings, and a dash of ductwork thrown in for good measure.

Like the décor, which mixes a little old and new, the menu presents a wide array of inventive choices. Elk sausage and pork *arrollado* prove that this kitchen is a serious contender, while red velvet panna cotta shows off a quirky side. Of course, there's also seared tuna salad and a French onion soup for traditionalists who like their bistro standards.

Where to Stay

Conrad

521 N. Rush St. (at Grand Ave.)

Phone: 312-645-1500 or 800-266-7237
Web: www.conradchicago.com
Prices: $$$

Grand (Red)

283
Rooms

28
Suites

Conrad

It starts with a great location. The city's business and theater districts are close by, while the parks and shores of the lake are a few minutes East, but what makes the Conrad Chicago stand out is its appeal to label lovers—the hotel is adjacent to Nordstrom and the high-end shops of The Northbridge Shopping Center.

It continues with no expense spared in-room treats. The Conrad spoils its guests with a seemingly endless stream of luxury amenities: Pratesi sheets, Acca Kappa bath products, Bose surround sound, 42" Plasma televisions, free WiFi and Ethernet access. Services are equally plentiful, and include indulgent options like bath butlers and pillow menus. If your credit card got more of a workout than your stroll down the Magnificent Mile gave you, the hotel's fitness center is available 24 hours a day.

And it doesn't end there. The hotel has three inviting and distinct venues. Rendez-Vous has a casual sophistication perfect for light meals or drinks (try the signature chocolate martini), while the Restaurant at Conrad steps it up with Midwestern-focused cooking. Open during warmer months, The Terrace is a sure bet for cozy outdoor enjoyment—movies are even shown on Sundays.

Chicago ▶ River North

dana hotel and spa

 E2

660 N. State St. (at Erie St.)

Phone: 312-202-6000 or 888-301-7952
Web: www.danahotelandspa.com
Prices: $$

Grand (Red)

194
Rooms
22
Suites

dana Hotel and Spa

Get to know dana. This boutique hotel certainly has its number on you, that is if you're a young, discerning traveler with a penchant for fine living and high-priced tech toys. The dana hotel perfectly complements its creative, art gallery-filled neighborhood. It captures the essence of industrial chic with stone, wood, and natural design elements. The calling card of this design philosophy—exposed ductwork and piping— is found throughout the hotel in the lobby and private accommodations.

Rich, hand-hewn Jarrah wood floors make a striking statement in the guestrooms, but it is the floor-to-ceiling windows that are the unmistakable star. Exposed concrete and unfinished support pillars show off the signature style, but oversized showers capped off with rain showerheads and pillow-topped beds ensure that you can be cool and cosseted at the same time. Hipsters will find plenty to add to their gadget wish lists after a stay here –the Zeppelin-Bowers & Wilkins sound systems sync to guests' MP3 players for a state-of-the-art sound.

From the modern and spacious spa and the rooftop Vertigo Sky Lounge to the seasonal Asian café, Aja, the facilities are all top-notch.

Chicago ▶ River North

267

Felix

D2

111 W. Huron St. (bet. Clark St. & LaSalle St.)

Phone:	312-447-3440 or 877-848-4040
Web:	www.hotelfelixchicago.com
Prices:	$$

Chicago (Red)

225
Rooms

Spa

Hotel Felix

Is Al Gore hiding somewhere? He may not be camping out here, but the Hotel Felix would certainly warm his heart. This innovative boutique hotel was the first hotel in Chicago designed to meet the specifications of Silver LEED certification. From design elements (carpets are made from recycled materials; floors are cork and bamboo) to practices (paperless front desk; eco-friendly cleaning products), the Felix takes eco-conscious living very seriously.

The rooms and suites perfectly complement the hotel's relaxed modern sophistication. The soft earth tones and simple furnishings are the very definition of urban living.

Cast your worries aside—this is not a hippie commune by any stretch. It doesn't just do good, but it looks good too at this chic, contemporary hotel. Take a seat in the inviting lobby bar (with a working fireplace) and discuss carbon footprints over cocktails or dine on market-influenced American cuisine at the well-received Elate Restaurant (which also provides room service). The Spa features a comprehensive variety of treatments, all guided by the healing properties of plant and flower extracts.

The best part? It doesn't take a lot of green to stay here.

Chicago ▶ River North

The James

55 E. Ontario St. (at Rush St.)

Phone: 312-337-1000 or 877-526-3755
Web: www.jameshotels.com
Prices: $$$

 Grand (Red)

191
Rooms
106
Suites

The James Chicago

It is not surprising that The James has a loyal following with European travelers and stylish young professionals. A great location in River North coupled with a trendy atmosphere make this hotel the perfect package.

It is chic from top to bottom in that Californian/Scandinavian minimalist way. Blonde woods, simple lines, and contemporary furniture all effortlessly create the understated look. Thankfully, the staff eschews that "too cool for school" philosophy found in other hotels that resemble the James.

Standard rooms outfitted with platform beds and wet bars give a taste of the scene, but the lofts, one-bedroom apartments, and penthouse, with more space and better views, are certainly worth the splurge. The accommodations come with plenty of goodies; bathrooms are stocked with Kiehl's products and wet bars feature full-sized bottles.

The business lounge is a boon for corporate visitors (work spaces are not included in all rooms), while the lower-level fitness center and spa have all of the modern updates. Guests develop a special soft spot for David Burke's buzzed-about Primehouse, since the restaurant sends up freshly baked cookies nightly to all guests.

Chicago ▶ River North

269

Palomar

505 N. State St. (at Illinois St.)

Phone: 312-755-9703 or 877-731-0505
Web: www.hotelpalomar-chicago.com
Prices: $$

 Grand (Red)

238
Rooms
22
Suites

Hotel Palomar

Just like its guiding force, the World's Fair, the shiny new Palomar Hotel brings innovation, style, and panache to Chicago. Situated in the heart of River North, this 17-story hotel is one of the latest Kimpton properties to hit the scene. Enter through the glass doors, glide past the chic living room-style lobby, and let the elevators whisk you away to a cosmopolitan and contemporary world.

Bright couches, deep-colored drapes, and carpets covered in big red blossoms create a dramatic look in the rooms and suites alike. Bathrooms continue the modern chic style with cream marble tiles, dark wood finishes, and stainless steel fixtures. The pièce de résistance at the Palomar is its 17th floor sundeck, pool, and fitness center, where you can sunbathe, swim, or sweat with a skyscraper view.

In-room spa services, complimentary morning coffee, and an evening wine hour are among the niceties this hotel extends to its guests. Don't miss Sable Kitchen & Bar's inventive New American food and glamorous setting evocative of the sexy 1940s. All this and you can bring your biggest four-legged friend too, since the Palomar doesn't discriminate against larger pets.

The Peninsula

108 E. Superior St. (bet. Michigan Ave. & Rush St.)

Phone: 312-337-2888 or 866-382-8388
Web: www.peninsula.com
Prices: $$$$

Chicago (Red)

257
Rooms

82
Suites

Mark Wieland

From the elegant lobby to the ultra-luxe guest rooms to the top-notch spa and restaurants, The Peninsula delivers an all-around exceptional experience. No detail is overlooked, and it all looks and feels very plush from oversized marble soaking bathtubs, to bedside electronic panels controlling everything from lighting to temperature.

The FSPA Spa and fitness center offers a temple of serenity in the heart of the Gold Coast. The pool, surrounded by glass and offering jaw-dropping views, is quite simply the best in town, while the fitness center is *the* place to sweat and be seen. The luxury quotient also extends to the hotel's many dining selections and glorious beverage offerings. The Peninsula bar is truly fantastic and exudes a dark, luxurious, and clubby ambience. Hugely raved about and regarded as one the best "scenes" in Chicago, the bar is buzzing and lively on weekends. Ritzy crowds flock here to savor some seriously divine cocktails along with a wonderful selection of light bites.

Whether sipping on afternoon tea in the lofty lobby, noshing on flaky croissants at Pierrot Gourmet, or hitting the hotel's hot spots (Shanghai Pavilion and Avenues), it's all very posh here.

Chicago ▶ River North

SAX

E4

333 N. Dearborn St. (bet. Kinzie St. & the Chicago River)

Phone: 312-245-0333 or 877-569-3742
Web: www.hotelsaxchicago.com
Prices: $$$

Chicago (Red)

333 Rooms

21 Suites

Andrew Bordwin

Bring your lover and leave your work behind when you check into the SAX. Now a member of the Thompson Hotel group, this hot lair is located in Marina City, defined by its two iconic Bertrand Goldberg-designed buildings (yes, the ones known as the corn cobs). It is on the north bank of the Chicago River and is surrounded by parks, shops, and restaurants located within this multiplex.

The SAX has you at first glance. The lobby has a classy bordello, hip vampire look (think lots of crystal and 18th century-style red velvet upholstered chairs). The guestrooms are identical in spirit to the lobby and are decorated with the same romantic and fresh vibe, though softer colors are also used.

Many guests play hard at the SAX, where entertainment comes in many forms. There is a 10-pin bowling alley for a little retro fun and a sixth-floor lounge powered by Microsoft, but the Crimson Lounge is the jewel in the crown. It is the happening haunt where bright young things gather for VIP bottle service and DJ or live music. Don't worry if you're not a night owl, since not all of the fun happens when the sun goes down. Bin 36 is an inviting spot to sample wine and small plates all day.

Chicago ▶ River North

Trump International Hotel & Tower

F4

401 N. Wabash Ave. (bet. Hubbard St. & the Chicago River)

Phone: 312-588-8000 or 877-458-7867
Web: www.trumpchicagohotel.com
Prices: $$$$

Grand (Red)

229
Rooms
110
Suites

Bill Haber

Go big or go home seems to be Donald Trump's mantra, and the Trump International Hotel & Tower shows off these principles in all of its glorious, shimmering style. The hotel, part of a 92-story mixed use tower, stands out among the Loop's skyline for its curvaceous, elegant design of sleek stainless steel and tinted glass. It grabs your attention, but there's nothing flashy about the well-heeled sophistication peddled here.

Bright with large windows, the Italian limestone-clad lobby has a surprisingly intimate character. The highly professional staff handles everything in a seamless manner. Trump Attachés or personal concierges offer the highest level of personalized attention.

The Donald's own gold-loving style is never evident: the guestrooms and suites are the very definition of cool and contemporary with grey, black, and soft brown color schemes. Whether it is Bose clock stereos and iPod chargers on the bedside tables or Miele cooktops and Bernardaud china in the kitchenettes, the accommodations showcase the world's leading brands.

From the guestrooms and the 14th-floor health club to Sixteen's dining room, the real VIP here is the show-stopping view.

Chicago ▶ River North

273

Westin River North

E4

320 N. Dearborn St. (bet. Kinzie St. & the Chicago River)

Phone: 312-744-1900 or 877-866-9216
Web: www.westinchicago.com
Prices: $$$

🚇 Chicago (Red)

407
Rooms

17
Suites

♿

🛴

🛎️

🐕

The Westin Chicago River North

It may be located across from the legendary House of Blues, but guests at the Westin aren't singing the blues. Instead, they're whistling a happy tune, thanks to a good night's sleep in one of the many spacious and comfortable rooms and suites. This mod marvel enjoys an ideal location. Sitting at the edge of the river, the hotel is a convenient base; it is a business traveler's favorite perch—they flock here as much for the conferences held in the more than 28,000-square-feet of meeting space as they do for the restaurants and accommodations.

The 407 guestrooms and 17 suites are appointed with a subtle sophistication. Clean, simple furnishings crafted of polished woods and soft, muted colors are used to create a restful and relieving atmosphere. Westin's signature Heavenly beds make you want to jump right in, while the Heavenly Bath with therapeutic spa showers is certain to wake you up or wind you down.

Some of the best features of the Westin are its three distinctive entertainment venues. Ember Grille is a carnivore's dream with fire-roasted entrées and prime steak; Kamehachi Sushi Bar serves Japanese delicacies; and Hana Lounge is just right for catching up over cocktails.

Affinia

166 E. Superior St. (at St. Clair St.)

Phone: 312-787-6000 or 866-246-2203
Web: www.affinia.com
Prices: $$

Chicago (Red)

215 Rooms

Affinia Chicago

The Affinia Chicago, bookended by the ever-popular Gino's East restaurant and a new condo tower, is terrifically located, near a prime stretch of Michigan Avenue. The bright lobby, with large windows, white terrazzo floors, and stainless steel accents is the first sign that this hotel subscribes to the clean and uncluttered look.

The rooms echo the lobby's look with ivory color schemes and simple furnishings, while the bathrooms get a little crazy with metallic orange-toned wallpaper and black granite-topped vanities. Affinia also offers a host of comforts. Pick one of six styles from the pillow menu or enjoy an "experience kit" (walking tours with loaded iPods and stayfit kits with equipment and DVDs).

This hotel is in the thick of it (you'll hear street noise even 18 floors up), but that's why you want to be here. Another reason is the food. C-House, run by celebrity chef, Marcus Samuelsson, is all-out fantastic. The menu is seafood and chops with tasty sides that are a gourmet riff on classics. With a bellini in hand, head up to the C-View rooftop bar and lounge. Not only does this heavenly haven offer a great scene, but it also boasts a magnificent bird's eye view.

Chicago ▶ Streeterville

The Allerton

701 N. Michigan Ave. (at Huron St.)

Phone: 312-440-1500 or 877-701-8111
Web: www.theallertonhotel.com
Prices: $$

🚇 Chicago (Red)

359
Rooms

84
Suites

♿

🛗

🧑‍💼

Nathan Kirkman Photography

Relive a part of Chicago history while staying at The Allerton. This Gold Coast landmark was built in 1924 and was one of the first high-rises on North Michigan Avenue. With a beautiful Italian Renaissance design, intricate stone details, decorative brickwork, and iconic neon signs, this vestige is an architecture and history buff's dream.

Regarded as a gorgeous getaway, The Allerton represents a welcome departure from the modern towers that line the Magnificent Mile. But there's nothing stuffy or antique here: checkerboard terrazzo flooring sets a stylish tone in the lobby, though it is in the rooms and suites where the design really gleams. From the white tufted leather headboard to the Lucite cube bedside lamps, it is art deco all the way.

Each evening, this inviting home-away-from-home hosts a complimentary wine hour for guests to mingle and munch. Other trappings include a 24-hour health club and the sleek M Avenue Restaurant and Lounge with its upscale dining and comfortably chic setting. The lobby-located flightboard displaying airport departure times and accompanying printer kiosk is certainly one of the most convenient gestures.

Inn of Chicago

A2

162 E. Ohio St. (at St. Clair St.)

Phone: 312-787-3100 or 866-858-4430
Web: www.innofchicago.com
Prices: $$

 Grand (Red)

339
Rooms
20
Suites

Scott Thompson Photography

If you have Champagne taste but a beer budget, the Inn of Chicago is just the place for you. It may be a half-block away from the Magnificent Mile, but you don't need a lot of moolah to stay at this value-oriented hotel that offers the same coveted neighborhood without the sticker shock.

The Inn of Chicago has enjoyed a long history—first opening in 1928 as the Hotel St. Clair—but this space is rooted firmly in the present with its modern design and high-tech amenities. It may not be pricey, but this hotel does not skimp on the extras—large screen plasma televisions, dazzling views, and large walk-in showers are among the standard offerings. All guests are welcomed with open arms, but business travelers are especially well cared for here, with conference rooms, a business center, fitness center, and WiFi throughout the hotel.

Though the hotel does not have its own restaurant, the Lavazza coffee shop hits the spot with pastries and sandwiches and the InnBar is the in-place for a post-work or post- sightseeing signature cocktail. Of course, the hotel's pièce de résistance is the 22nd floor Skyline Terrace, which opens during warmer months and showcases stunning city views.

Chicago ▶ Streeterville

InterContinental

A2

505 N. Michigan Ave. (bet. Grand Ave. & Illinois St.)

Phone: 312-944-4100 or 800-628-2112
Web: www.icchicagohotel.com
Prices: $$

🚆 Grand (Red)

717 Rooms

75 Suites

♿ 🚲 🏊 ✍️ 🐕

InterContinental Chicago

Like an aging starlet with a story to tell, the historic InterContinental has lived many lives. Like old photographs or letters, there are several signs of the hotel's former incarnations—there is even a blue Majolica-tiled pool complete with terra-cotta fountain of Neptune that was the training site of Olympic athlete Johnny Weissmuller.

Don't be put off—just because it revels in its history doesn't mean it ignores modern needs. 24-hour room service is timely, the business and fitness centers are convenient, and the dining choices are enjoyable. The exquisite lobby is the showpiece of the InterContinental. They just don't make grand entrances like this anymore and this magnificent four-floor rotunda with handcrafted mosaic tiles of onyx and marble is worthy of attention. Though not as grand, the accommodations are decorated in the same old-world vein.

InterContinental spices up the old with the new at its dining establishments. ENO is a unique concept managed by the master sommelier and offers flights of wine, chocolate, and cheese from around the world. Their take-home gifts make wonderful souvenirs. Zest, the hotel's main restaurant, has a modern American flavor and feel.

Chicago ▶ Streeterville

Allegro

 B2

171 W. Randolph St. (at Wells St.)

Phone: 312-236-0123 or 800-643-1500
Web: www.allegrochicago.com
Prices: $$

 Clark/Lake

452
Rooms
31
Suites

David Phelps

Not on the A list? Check in to the Allegro Hotel and you'll certainly feel like a very important person! Adorned in a slick Hollywood Regency manner, the vibe here is relaxed, fun, and young. Part of the Kimpton hotel chain, the Allegro has that cool boutique-esque ambience, yet it offers the top-notch amenities of a hotel chain.

Brush up on your geometry before heading to the rooms and suites at the Allegro, since geometric patterns are everywhere. From the silver and white wall paper to the royal blue carpets to the decorative pillows, it is pattern play throughout. The accommodations have a stylish blend of old Hollywood glamour and contemporary dazzle.

Kimpton is known for its many amenities, so expect extras like evening wine receptions, complimentary morning coffee, and no fee/no restrictions pet policies. From KimptonKids programming and in-room spa services to well-equipped fitness facilities, state-of-the-art conference and meeting rooms, and eco-friendly practices, the Allegro lives up to its promises. Relive the days of the three-martini lunch at the Encore Lunch Club & Liquid Lounge or settle in to a comfy booth for some yummy Italian food at 312 Chicago.

Chicago ▲ Loop

Burnham

 C3

1 W. Washington St. (at State St.)

Phone:	312-782-1111 or 866-690-1986
Web:	www.burnhamhotel.com
Prices:	$$

 Washington

103
Rooms
19
Suites

Burnham

Hotel Burnham has pedigree and panache. A historic landmark built in 1895 as one of the first skyscrapers and former home to corporate giant Reliance, the building has been reworked, revamped, and reinvigorated with a dramatic décor. Hotel Burnham is part of the Kimpton chain, but this property has a fiercely independent spirit and delivers a well-rounded, first-class experience.

From caged elevators and mosaic-tiled floors to mailbox slots on the guestroom doors (there's no delivery—they're sealed shut), traces of the building's past add a distinct charm and unique flavor. There's nothing sedate about these accommodations, where regal guestrooms pop with sensational bursts of color and patterns. It's all very fancy, with gilded furnishings and tasseled silk canopy beds, but it's good to be king. Even the closet has a few surprises with leopard- and zebra-patterned bathrobes.

The customary amenities (fitness center, business center, concierge staff) are here, but the unusual touches are most memorable (try parenting a goldfish during your stay). There is also 24-hour room service, but the enjoyable atmosphere at Atwood Café is worth leaving your room.

Chicago ▶ Loop

Fairmont

D2

200 N. Columbus Dr. (bet. Lake & Water Sts.)

Phone: 312-565-8000 or 800-526-2008
Web: www.fairmont.com/chicago
Prices: $$

State/Lake

622
Rooms

65
Suites

Fairmont Chicago, Millenium Park

The Fairmont has always enjoyed a fantastic location convenient to Michigan Avenue and Millennium Park, but thanks to an infusion of $50 million and the artful eye of renowned architect David Rockwell, this hotel now sizzles with a fresh style. The look is very mod and the lobby could double as the latest "it" spot, but there is substance behind this style with Fairmont's superior comfort and plush amenities. The rooms and suites are a study in upscale modern design, where earth tones set a soothing slate, interesting patterns (zebra-striped carpets, bamboo leaf-inspired pillows) inject an upbeat flavor, and artist Warwick Orme's floral artwork captures the eye. Comforts abound, and Fairmont even offers allergy friendly rooms (PURE) and a dedicated floor for corporate travelers (GOLD).

Arla is the hotel's all-day dining spot and is known for its Asian fare, but the Fairmont really has guests at "hello" with its impressive lobby capped off by an outpost of ENO, where 500 varietals of wine (60 types by the glass!), 35 different types of cheese, and artisanal chocolates await gourmands. Overdid it on the Camembert? Head straight for the 11,000 square-foot fitness center and spa.

Chicago ▲ Loop

Hard Rock

D2

230 N. Michigan Ave. (at Water St.)

Phone: 312-345-1000 or 866-966-5166
Web: www.hardrockhotelchicago.com
Prices: $$

State/Lake

370 Rooms

11 Suites

Hard Rock Hotel Chicago

It is likely that you know the Hard Rock shtick. Like a laid-back Smithsonian for rock and roll memorabilia, the Hard Rock has made its name by sharing the hard-living rock star lifestyle with diners and hotel guests, but the Hard Rock Hotel Chicago strays a bit from the standard and shows off some local pride. Housed within the historic Carbide & Carbon Building, the Hard Rock mixes its expected look with art deco architecture. This fun and upbeat hotel offers reasonable prices for the cool vibe and central location.

The guestrooms take the rocker lifestyle quite seriously. If the celebrity costumes displayed in the hallways doesn't clue you in, the rock star-themed artwork certainly will. Dark colors and low lighting are ideal for late night revelers, though business travelers might have trouble getting work done.

The sleek and modern lobby is home to two popular establishments—the Base Bar, where cocktails are mixed with organic ingredients, and China Grill, another popular chain known for its hip quotient and fusion family-style upscale food. In case you don't already have one of the ubiquitous Hard Rock t-shirts, you can pick one up in the lobby's Hard Rock store.

Hotel 71

71 E. Wacker Dr. (at Wabash Ave.)

Phone: 312-346-7100 or 800-621-4005
Web: www.hotel71.com
Prices: $$

State/Lake

285
Rooms
22
Suites
&

It's not your age, the year, or even your shoe size, Hotel 71 is named for its E. Wacker Drive address. This modern hotel enjoys a spectacular riverfront setting near the pedestrian riverwalk and directly across from Trump Tower.

With a 24-hour fitness center packed with state-of-the-art cardiovascular and weight training machines, an entire 6th floor dedicated to business needs with meeting and boardrooms, and a convenient business center, Hotel 71 is a natural choice for business travelers.

Less is more as far as design goes at Hotel 71. The sleek, modern design is soothing and warm. Tan, brown, and golden hues run throughout the public and private spaces, while the guest accommodations add plaid patterns and animal prints as interesting accents. The guestrooms are spacious and equipped with ergonomic chairs, large bathrooms, and complimentary in-room coffee. From mini-stereos to three telephones, electronics are plentiful. Those wishing to take in the sights should be sure to book rooms with river views.

While you won't be able to jump into the Batmobile, the top floor ballroom with captivating views was used as Bruce Wayne's apartment in the 2008 Batman movie, "*The Dark Knight.*"

Chicago ▲ Loop

Monaco

C2

225 N. Wabash Ave. (bet. Haddock & Wacker Pls.)

Phone:	312-960-8500 or 866-610-0081
Web:	www.monaco-chicago.com
Prices:	$$$

State/Lake

172
Rooms

20
Suites

David Phelps

Hats off to the Hotel Monaco Chicago, another one of the shining stars in the Kimpton chain. Housed in a former hat factory near the Chicago River, it is within walking distance of the Loop, Michigan Avenue, shopping, and the theaters, but it doesn't rely on its location alone.

Everything about this property speaks to its gracious style and demeanor. The staff, from the first greeting by the doorman to the efficient and helpful front desk clerks, seems genuinely concerned with guests' comfort. The lobby is tastefully appointed with a romantic modern European style and is elegant without being stuffy.

Stripes and diamond patterns create a pleasing modern style in the guestrooms and suites, but it is the river and city views that particularly stand out. Rooms are even furnished with cushioned window nooks, known as meditation stations, for relaxing and day-dreaming with a view. Many of the amenities found at other Kimpton properties, such as in-room spa services and goldfish companions, are offered here as well. It's the little things like free Starbucks coffee in the mornings, nightly wine hours, and pints of ice cream on the room service menu, that endear this hotel to its guests.

Palmer House

17 E. Monroe St. (at State St.)

Phone: 312-726-7500 or 800-445-8667
Web: www.palmerhousehiltonhotel.com
Prices: $$

🚇 Monroe

1584
Rooms
55
Suites

Sammy Todd Dyess/Palmer House

It doesn't get any more legendary than the Palmer House. This great-granddaddy of Chicago hotels was built 13 days before the great fire of 1871; it was then rebuilt and reopened in 1873 as the world's first fireproof hotel. Back when a nickel got you a vaudeville show, the lobby was a true spectacle. Despite a massive nip and tuck, some things never change, and the lobby remains a serious scene.

Palmer embraces the Old World: the ceiling, painted with Greek mythological characters, was restored by the same craftsman who worked on the Sistine Chapel. Italian marble, gilded candelabra, grand staircases—it's like a page was ripped from the grand lobby handbook. Where else can you sleep where Mark Twain, Liberace, and Charles Dickens once laid their weary heads?

If walls could talk—the Palmer House has seen and done it all. Electric lighting, telephone, and elevator service were all pioneered here. At every turn the hotel honors its history, and yet, guests are never asked to forsake today's comforts. From the indoor pool, fitness center, and spa, to conference facilities and two restaurants, the Palmer House lives as comfortably within the 21st century as it did in the 19th.

Chicago ▲ Loop

The Wit

 C2

201 N. State St. (at Lake St.)

Phone: 312-467-0200 or 866-318-1514
Web: www.thewithotel.com
Prices: $$

 State/Lake

238
Rooms

60
Suites

The Wit Hotel Chicago

There's definitely a bit of whimsy at the Wit Hotel. Just listen to the sound piped in to the hallways—it's chirping birds by day, crickets by night, and roosters in the morning. Even the wake-up calls are unusual—when was the last time you were greeted by Al Capone's voice?

This hotel is definitely not your grandfather's Doubletree, though it is in fact managed by it. Instead, it is ultra-modern in both design and décor. The rooms and suites pack a punch with orange chaise lounges and plentiful high-tech amenities. Widescreen TVs are loaded with movies and music channels, while suites come with complete kitchens.

Boasting three bustling spots, dining is definitely not an afterthought at this hotel. Cibo Matto, which translates to "crazy food" in Italian, has a sleek vibe and seriously good Italian cuisine, while State & Lake heats up the local scene with its American cooking. ROOF—the 27th floor indoor-outdoor space complete with fire pits—is *the* place to be. This hot spot with DJs galore draws a young, swank crowd. You may find yourself jostling for space in the elevators with these revelers ready for a big night out, but it's all part of the fun at the Wit.

Chicago ▶ Loop

Blackstone

636 S. Michigan Ave. (at Balbo Ave.)

Phone: 312-447-0955 or 800-468-3571
Web: www.marriott.com
Prices: $$$

🚇 Harrison

328
Rooms

4
Suites

♿

🛏️

🧖

🐾

The Renaissance Blackstone Chicago Hotel

It might be owned and managed by Marriott, but there's nothing cookie cutter about this significant property. First, the location is noteworthy. Walk to Grant Park, Shedd Aquarium, Soldier Field, or the Art Institute, but it's not just the "steps away" status that gives this hotel its pedigree. Since 1910, The Blackstone has been the beloved choice of celebrities and chief executives, hosting every president since William Taft.

While it may be historical, it is certainly not creaky—this thanks to a spot-on face-lift that took the hotel into the new millennium. The Beaux-Arts exterior makes a stunning first impression, but the sizzle resides solely indoors. There is a bit of wit and whimsy in the public spaces: from gilded leather tufted couches, to the 1,400 pieces of original art, The Blackstone puts a fresh spin on classic details. Rooms and suites are truly modern and wear earthy tones; while bathrooms are boldly decked with white-and-black palettes. Staggering views of the lake are a draw.

Mercat a la Planxa is celebrity chef Jose Garces' temple to Catalan cooking. Sip sangria and taste some tapas while soaking up the scene at this white-hot Michigan Avenue spot.

Chicago ▶ Chinatown & South Loop

Blake

B1

500 S. Dearborn St. (bet. Congress Pkwy. & Harrison St.)

Phone: 312-986-1234
Web: www.hotelblake.com
Prices: $$

🚇 LaSalle

158
Rooms
4
Suites

Hotel Blake

Spacious rooms, reasonable rates, and a top-notch restaurant prove that Hotel Blake is indeed worth its salt. Housed within the historic Morton Building (the former home of the Morton Salt Company), this hotel effortlessly blends past and present with its modern style and amenities.

Espresso-hued wood-paneled walls with red accents set a handsome tone in the appealing lobby. The attractive minimalist décor is striking, yet the ambience has a relaxed ease. Wireless Internet is available throughout the public and private spaces, and a glass-walled business center with separate conference room is off the lobby.

The rich chocolate and soft beige color scheme is continued in the 162 guestrooms. The accommodations are large and comfortable. Many amenities, like the large desks with ergonomic leather chairs, have business travelers in mind, but it's not all work and no play at the Hotel Blake. Fine linens dress the beds, pleasing artwork adorns the walls, and iHome iPod docking stations replace alarm clocks, but for a further taste of home, bring along Fido (as long as he is under 20 pounds).

Room service is far from your standard fare here, courtesy of the lobby-located Custom House Tavern.

The Drake

E4

140 E. Walton St. (at Michigan Ave.)

Phone: 312-787-2200 or 800-553-7253
Web: www.thedrakehotel.com
Prices: $$

Chicago (Red)

161
Rooms
74
Suites

It doesn't get more old-time Chicago than The Drake and this esteemed hotel retains its status as one of the finest in the city. Opened in 1920, The Drake oozes with history. The rich and royal all flocked here in its heyday and while today's guests are more likely to be here for business meetings, not state meetings, the hotel maintains its regal presence.

The grand architecture and impressive lobby are a sign of what's to come. Expect old-world elegance in the rooms and suites. Standard rooms are quite small, but all accommodations are well appointed with a traditional design (think antique furnishings, gilded mirrors, and ornate lighting fixtures).

The walls may not be able to talk in this historic hotel, but the Cape Cod Room's bar can show off a bit—Joe DiMaggio and Marilyn Monroe are among the many who have carved their initials in it. Today's guests will do better to save their knives for buttering the scones at the properly elegant afternoon tea at the Palm Court. From its delicate finger sandwiches to its fine bone china, this rite of passage is a tea to make the Queen proud (in fact, Queen Elizabeth did have tea here, along with other royals throughout the years).

Chicago ▲ Gold Coast

Elysian

D4

11 E. Walton St. (bet. Rush & State Sts.)

Phone:	312-646-1300 or 800-500-8511
Web:	www.elysianhotels.com
Prices:	$$$$

Chicago (Red)

38 Rooms

150 Suites

Elysian Hotel

You'll think you've died and gone to haute heaven at this super-luxe hotel. Walk through the cobblestoned motor court that reminds one of a French château, and step a few more well-shod paces into the striking lobby. This seductive space is the very picture of contemporary minimalism. Its striking chandelier and gleaming marble floors are sure to make a lasting first impression.

The glorious good looks extend to the rooms and suites, where champagne and platinum color schemes and tailored furnishings give off a current British sensibility. It is all very glamorous, and the Carrara marble bathrooms (showers come with leg rests for shaving!) are over-the-top gorgeous.

The service is A-plus. Within this palatial establishment, the uniformed staff delivers polished, gracious, attentive, and intuitive service, making guests feel like ladies and lords of the manor. It doesn't end there. Dining is a first-rate affair at two impressive restaurants, while the tucked-away Bernard's Bar has that wood-paneled elegance down pat. Even exercise is elevated to an art form at the spa and health club, where you can unwind with a homeopathic facial after hoofing it on the treadmill, or succumb to a lava shell massage after a swim in the mosaic-tiled pool.

Four Seasons Chicago

D4

120 E. Delaware Pl. (bet. Michigan Ave. & Rush St.)

Phone: 312-280-8800 or 800-819-5053

Web: www.fourseasons.com

Prices: $$$$

Chicago (Red)

176

Rooms

167

Suites

Four Seasons Hotel Chicago

Four Seasons knows how to pour it on. This elegant hotel has it all — white-glove service, impressive facilities, elegant accommodations, fine dining, and a prime location just blocks from Lake Michigan and within a stiletto's throw of some of the world's best shopping.

The guest rooms and suites are outfitted with a fresh, contemporary decor and are crammed with creature comforts. The beds, dressed with dreamy linens and soft colors, are exceedingly inviting; and the marble bathrooms make a grand and glamorous statement. There are plenty of places to put your feet up and relax, but the window seat is arguably the best. Is there anything better than soaking up the scene in a fluffy bathrobe? From the doormen and front desk to the dining and spa staff, the service is seamless and spot on. Dining choices include the elegant signature Seasons Restaurant, serving French and American cuisine, and the more relaxed Seasons Lounge, where buffets, brunch, and afternoon tea are held. There is always the upper crusty ambience of Seasons Bar, perfect for cocktails and conversation.

Stress fractures from all of the shopping? Head straight to the spa for some seriously sophisticated therapy.

Chicago ▲ Gold Coast

Indigo

1244 N. Dearborn Pkwy. (bet. Division & Goethe Sts.)

Phone: 312-787-4980 or 800-972-2494

Web: www.hotelindigo.com

Prices: $$

Clark/Division

163 Rooms

2 Suites

Indigo

There is nothing pretentious about Hotel Indigo. This boutique hotel chain, part of the InterContinental Hotels worldwide chain, is proof that budget doesn't have to be boring. Located on a quiet residential street in the Gold Coast, Hotel Indigo is a breath of fresh air with its summer's dream décor. It is all very beach house on the Scandinavian coast with its white-painted patio-style wood furnishings, white beadboard, gleaming blonde wood floors, and indigo blue and lime green colors.

This hotel has the cottage look down pat, and the upbeat personality extends to the guestrooms. Banish the wintry blues in these mood-elevating, beach shack-style accommodations, where wood floors add a particularly homey touch and walls covered in floral murals bring the outside in. The luscious colors and inviting ambience are surefire mood boosters. Niceties, such as Aveda bath products, flat screen televisions, coffee makers, and free wireless Internet, add a final touch. Though small, the fitness center has the necessary cardio machines and free weights to fit in a workout. Room service is available in the mornings, and the lobby bar/restaurant features light fare throughout the day.

Park Hyatt of Chicago

D5

800 N. Michigan Ave. (at Chicago Ave.)

Phone: 312-335-1234 or 877-875-4658

Web: www.parkchicago.hyatt.com

Prices: $$$$

Chicago (Red)

185
Rooms

13

Suites

The Park Hyatt is the place to stay when you want to sneak a peek at how the other half lives. Situated catercorner to the historic Water Tower on the Magnificent Mile, the Park Hyatt occupies the first 18 floors of a sky-reaching tower, home to some of the city's most exclusive private residences.

Park Hyatt is the A student in the Hyatt hotels chain, and the Park Hyatt Chicago is no exception. It is understated sophistication at its best, offering luxury and comfort to its privileged guests. The contemporary designed guestrooms don't skimp on size or style and offer plenty of conveniences and goodies like high thread cotton bedding, butler service, large safes big enough to hold and charge laptops, and video checkout. The sleek marble and granite bathrooms are equally spacious (oversized tubs, separate walk-in showers) and stocked with deluxe bath salts, Blaise Mautin products, and candles.

From valet parking and turndown to a weekly sommelier-guided wine and spirit tasting, courteous and efficient service is a staple.

The seventh-floor NoMI restaurant and lounge has commanding city views and is populated with everyone from deal makers to ladies who lunch.

Chicago ▶ Gold Coast

Raffaello

E5

201 E. Delaware Pl. (at Seneca St.)

Phone: 312-943-5000 or 800-898-7198
Web: www.chicagoraffaello.com
Prices: $$$

 Chicago (Red)

97
Rooms

73
Suites

Nathan Beckner

Craving Champagne but on a beer (imported, of course) budget? The Raffaello might just be your biggest and best boon ever. This stylish boutique hotel gives you a swanky Gold Coast address without the pomp—and price—of its fussy competitors.

Located next door to the John Hancock Tower, Rafaello is also just steps from Water Tower Place and the shops of the Magnificent Mile. So it goes without saying that this treasure has a prime location, and the hits just keep on coming at this contemporary spot. The soaring ceilings capped off with an oversized chandelier, and the gleaming marble floors of the lobby are a sure sign of good things to come. Rooms are on the smaller side, so upgrades are worth the extra bucks; but the soothing spirit will leave you smitten. Creams, beiges, and dark woods define the current look, and amenities like high-quality bath products and high-tech extras like iPods and iHomes maintain the modern theme. Do business in style in one of the elegant conference rooms, or hit the fully equipped fitness center with spa services.

Never quite made it into the cool click? Book a table at the hotel's restaurant Pelago and you'll feel part of the in-crowd, instantly.

The Ritz-Carlton Chicago

E5

160 E. Pearson St. (bet. Michigan Ave. & Seneca St.)

Phone: 312-266-1000 or 800-621-6906
Web: www.fourseasons.com/chicagorc
Prices: $$$$

 Chicago (Red)

344 Rooms

91 Suites

Ritz-Carlton Hotel Chicago

It just does not get any better than this. The Ritz-Carlton Chicago, managed by esteemed Four Seasons, has one of the city's most coveted locations. Situated at Water Tower Place, the shopping of Magnificent Mile is practically served up on a silver platter for guests of The Ritz-Carlton (and there is also direct access to the indoor shops at Water Tower Place).

Valets graciously welcome guests and then whisk them away to the classically elegant world of the 12th floor lobby. The gentle trickle of the central fountain alludes to the serenity found here. While the lobby shows off a traditional aesthetic, the recently renovated guestrooms and suites are done up with a definitively modern take. Thick, plush geometric-patterned carpets set the tone for the well-appointed (plush furnishings, deluxe amenities) and well-planned (plentiful storage, spacious dressing areas, large desks) rooms, ideal for both business and leisure travelers.

From access to the ritzy Carlton Club, a spa/indoor pool/fitness facility with a seasonal sundeck, to the glass-enclosed Greenhouse with breathtaking Lake Michigan and city views, there are plenty of perks as a guest of this exclusive hotel.

Chicago ▶ Gold Coast

Sofitel

D5

20 E. Chestnut St. (at Wabash Ave.)

Phone: 312-324-4000 or 800-763-4835
Web: www.sofitel.com
Prices: $$$

 Chicago (Red)

382
Rooms

33
Suites

Sofitel Chicago Water Tower

Some of architecture's greatest minds built their masterpieces in Chicago, and the Sofitel continues the city's long-held tradition of innovative design. Imagined by French architect Jean-Paul Viguier, this fantastic structure is comprised of a 32-floor prism of white glass and steel. The result? A new landmark in a city synonymous with stand-out buildings.

Of course, the location just a short walk from the Magnificent Mile and Museum of Contemporary Art doesn't hurt either. Neither does great service, and chic designer guestrooms with plentiful amenities and services.

The hip vibe is immediately felt upon entering the lobby, where towering ceilings and sleek décor set a stylish tone. The guestrooms continue the cool theme with modern furnishings, marble bathrooms, and plentiful creature comforts (Frette robes, complimentary movie channels). From corporate (staffed and self-service business centers) to personal (concierge), needs are met with grace and know-how by an intuitive staff. Grab a book from the charming library and bone up on architecture while enjoying a drink in the lounge/bar or over a delightful contemporary French meal at Café des Architectes.

Sutton Place

21 E. Bellevue Pl. (at Rush St.)

Phone: 312-266-2100 or 866-378-8866
Web: www.chicago.suttonplace.com
Prices: $$$

 Clark/Division

204
Rooms
42
Suites

Mike Dragovoja/Sutton Place Chicago

Sure, some of the interiors are a little dated and it could benefit from a little nip and tuck, but the Sutton Place hotel's location—a few steps from the lake and Michigan Avenue—along with its fine concierge service make it worth stomaching the slightly outdated style. The hotel appeals to mature travelers who appreciate the complimentary downtown sedan service and other easily accessible transportation options just outside the doors, as well as the great value for money.

Sutton Place puts you in the heart of it without the heart attack-worthy price point. The rooms and suites are spacious and feel tranquil. Large double windows look out over the city and many rooms allow for glimpses of the shimmering lake. From large desks to lounge chairs set by the windows, the rooms are comfortable and welcoming.

Business travelers never miss a beat while staying at the Sutton Place hotel. The 4th floor business center and well-equipped conference facilities keep everything humming along. Feeling a little homesick for Mom's country cooking? Head to the Whiskey Bar & Grill. This restaurant has been dishing out yummy comfort foods (burgers, mac and cheese) for over 10 years.

Chicago ▲ Gold Coast

The Talbott

 D4

20 E. Delaware Pl. (bet. Rush & State Sts.)

Phone: 312-944-4970 or 800-825-2688   Chicago (Red)
Web: www.talbotthotel.com
Prices: $$

120 Rooms
29 Suites

The Talbott

Want to feel like a resident of the ritzy Gold Coast? Check right in to the boutique Talbott, a member of the Small Luxury Hotels of the World. This hotel feels like a private residence, and with a location just two blocks from the Magnificent Mile, you can hit the shops and still have energy to walk home.

Inside, The Talbott feels like a classic English estate; dark wood-paneled walls lined with hunting scenes and a roaring fireplace feel straight out of the princely countryside. Far from fuddy-duddy, the hotel displays its sense of humor with a lady bug-dressed cow sculpture scaling the façade. Designed by artist Brian Calvin for the 1999 Chicago Cow Parade installation, the cow adds a serious touch of whimsy to this otherwise traditional hotel.

The accommodations offer a respite from the city pace with their quiet elegance and high quality amenities (Frette linens, Aveda toiletries). While it has been awarded a Green Seal certification for its eco-sensitive choices, guests' comfort is never compromised.

Bice Bistro echoes the hotel's relaxed elegance in its attractive dining room and sidewalk café. A great spot for people watching, Bice also delivers room service to hotel guests.

Whitehall

D5

105 E. Delaware Pl. (bet. Michigan Ave. & Rush St.)

Phone: 312-944-6300 or 866-753-4081
Web: www.thewhitehallhotel.com
Prices: $$

Chicago (Red)

214

Rooms

8

Suites

Gerlinde Frey

Smack dab in the middle of it all sits the Whitehall Hotel. This independent boutique hotel is right in the thick of it, nestled among the shops, restaurants, theaters, and entertainment of the Magnificent Mile and the nightlife of Rush Street. Many of Chicago's major attractions (Millennium Park, Navy Pier) are also just down the road.

This elegant red brick building was once home to full-time residents who occupied apartments, but today's temporary residents are treated to a glorious old-world European style. The lobby is a love letter to the past, with sparkling chandeliers, tufted leather chairs, and elegant wood paneling, and many of the furnishings have been restored to their former grandeur.

The guestrooms and suites have the feel of another era, appointed with four-poster beds, wrought iron headboards, leather-topped mahogany desks, and hand-painted armoires, but the amenities (luxurious Egyptian cotton sheets) are definitely 21st century. The fitness center and fee-based business center are on the smaller side, but offer the basics, while the 2nd-floor meeting rooms are quite large given the hotel's size.

Fornetto Mei brings together the foods and flavors of Italy and China.

Chicago ▲ Gold Coast

Villa D'Citta

D3

2230 N. Halsted St. (bet. Belden & Webster Aves.)

Phone: 312-771-0696 or 800-228-6070
Web: www.villadcitta.com
Prices: $$

🚇 Fullerton

6
Suites

Chuck Gullett

What's that? The genteel townhouse you were crossing your fingers for was willed to another family member? Forget about it. Just book a room at the unique Villa D'Citta, and you'll get the same feel, without the pesky property taxes. It was originally built in 1887, and this B&B was a private residence until 2009. Stately, sophisticated, and just steps from Lincoln Park's main strip, Villa D'Citta is a luxurious and quiet alternative to the anonymity prevalent in larger hotels.

The residential ambience and bed-and-breakfast style lures couples, discerning travelers, and adventurous types who want to really feel at home in the Windy City. And feel at home they do, where guests have run of the place. Totter around the gourmet kitchen, grill on the outdoor deck, or hop into the Jacuzzi—it's all part of the experience. There are just a handful of rooms and suites, all decorated with a modern, slightly masculine appeal. Or, empty out the piggy bank and rent the whole kit and caboodle.

Ralph, the host, and his tiny dog Whiskey, will make you feel welcome from the instant you walk in. From restaurant recommendations to sightseeing, Ralph has you covered.

Chicago ▶ Lincoln Park & Old Town

Majestic

528 W. Brompton Ave. (bet. Lake Shore Dr. & Pine Grove Ave.)

Phone: 773-404-3499 or 800-727-5108
Web: www.majestic-chicago.com
Prices: $

Addison (Red)

48

Rooms

4

Suites

From Iron Hotels of Chicago

Need to find yourself a temporary den while hitting up a Cubs game? Opt for the Majestic. This boutique hotel with just 52 rooms is the closest hotel to Wrigley Field, so you can have your fill of beer and dogs and even stay for extra innings without a long trip home. Just because it's near the ball park doesn't mean this hotel doesn't know how to pour on the sophistication—the intimate space is reminiscent of old world Europe.

Once ensconced inside one of the guestrooms or suites, you'd never know that you're in bustling Lakeview. Instead, it's peace and quiet in an elegant setting. From the mahogany furnishings and landscape paintings that are riffs on Monet to the gold-toned fabrics, the accommodations are clearly inspired by an English country estate. Try to upgrade to a suite since the standard rooms are on the small side.

Guests are treated to complimentary breakfasts, afternoon cookies, and wireless Internet. Don't worry about parking headaches, especially on game day, since the hotel does offer a garage. The amenities are limited, so you'll need to dine in an area restaurant and work out in a local gym. But with a price point and location this good, who cares?

Chicago ▶ Lakeview & Wrigleyville

301

Willows

555 W. Surf St. (bet. Broadway & Cambridge Ave.)

Phone: 773-528-8400 or 800-787-3108
Web: www.willowshotelchicago.com
Prices: $

 Wellington

51
Rooms
4
Suites

&

Broughton Hotels of Chicago

Maybe it's the quaint tree-lined street in the heart of a neighborhood. Maybe it's the designation as a historic landmark (the building dates to 1926). Or, maybe it's just the charming country inn ambience, but the Willows Hotel rightfully boasts a distinctive experience in Chicago.

Just a mile from Wrigley Field and a short walk to notable Lincoln Park and lovely Lake Michigan, Willows invites guests to unwind in gracious European-style comfort. French reproduction furnishings and French-influenced wall coverings add sophistication, while honey, green, and brown color schemes lend an inviting, slightly homey, touch.

The Willows is definitely not for those high maintenance, testy travelers who seek hotels brimming with modern services. There is no business center or exercise facility (though they do provide access to a nearby gym), and a simple breakfast is served in the lobby. If you want manicures and martinis, go elsewhere. But if you are the type who wants to live like a local while stretching out in a comfortable, chichi, and copius guestroom, the Willows Hotel is a sure bet. Besides, who can resist a place that has an afternoon social with freshly baked cookies?

The Orrington

1710 Orrington Ave. (bet. Church & Clark Sts.), Evanston

Phone: 847-866-8700 or 888-677-4648
Web: www.hotelorrington.com
Prices: $$

256 Rooms

13 Suites

Hilton Orrington

The Orrington now is proof positive that everything old can be new (and renewed) again. This hotel first opened its doors in 1925 and has achieved landmark status, but a recent multi-million dollar renovation has brought this elegant hotel seriously up to snuff. The location, not far from downtown Evanston's shopping, dining, and entertainment, is ideal for those journeying on business, pleasure, or visiting nearby Northwestern University. The convenience factor is par none.

Black wood furnishings set against dramatic red and yellow walls, striped fabrics, and clean lines set a modern tone in the range of rooms and suites. The accommodations are well-suited for corporate travelers with ample work spaces and comfortable chairs. The Orrington is dog-friendly. Look out for the bowls of biscuits and water at the entrance. Whether you need to check in to the office (24-hour business center) or check out at the fitness center (24-hour gym), The Orrington has your needs covered.

Three dining options include the Globe Café & Bar for all-day dining with a focus on lighter fare (salads, sandwiches, et al), Futami for Japanese cuisine, and Indigo Lounge for martinis and mixed drinks.

North & Northwestern Suburbs

Oak Brook Hills Marriott Resort

3500 Midwest Rd. (at 35th St.), Oak Brook

Phone: 630-850-5555 or 800-228-9290
Web: www.oakbrookhillsmarriottresort.com
Prices: $$

348
Rooms

38
Suites

Tyson Photo/Oak Brook Hills Marriott

The Oak Brook Hills Marriott Resort is a business traveler's dream. Visit this suburban Chicago resort with the confidence that you won't feel "stuck" at a conference or the like. It's not just about the event and meeting space, though there certainly is a lot of it. This Marriott branch entices guests with an 18-hole golf course, indoor and outdoor pools, fitness center, tennis courts, and easy access to area shopping.

All the rooms and suites are sunny, spacious, and extremely comfortable. From plush duvet covers to ergonomically designed desk chairs, the accommodations treat guests to a wonderful plethora of amenities.

Of course, all of the action takes place outside the rooms. The Audubon certified Willow Crest Golf Course is a definite morale booster. Lessons, equipment rentals, and putting green are all part of this fist class facility. Looking for a way to calm your colleagues? Take them to one of three area spas or hit up the Oak Brook Center or Yorktown Mall. Brought the whole family along for the company conference? Take them to nearby Brookfield Zoo.

Back at the Marriott, there are four restaurants all showcasing American cuisine, and many of them boast scenic views of the golf course.

You know
the MICHELIN guide

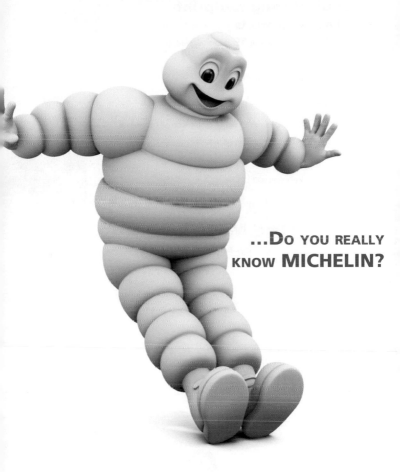

...Do you really
know MICHELIN?

Data 31/12/2009

The world No.1 in tires with 16.3% of the market

A business presence in over 170 countries

A manufacturing footprint
at the heart of markets

In 2009 **72** industrial sites in **19** countries produced:

- **150** million tires
- **10** million maps and guides

Highly international teams

Over **109 200** employees* from all cultures on all continents

including **6 000** people employed in R&D centers

in Europe, the US and Asia.

*102,692 full-time equivalent staff

The Michelin Group
at a glance

Michelin competes

At the end of 2009

Le Mans 24-hour race
12 consecutive years of victories

Endurance 2008
- 6 victories on 6 stages
in Le Mans Series
- 12 victories on 12 stages
in American Le Mans Series

Paris-Dakar
Since the beginning of the event,
the Michelin group has won
in all categories

Moto Endurance
2009 World Champion

Trial
Every World Champion title since 1981
(except 1992)

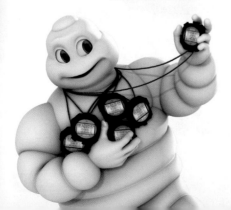

Michelin, established close to its customers

68 plants in 19 countries

- Algeria
- Brazil
- Canada
- China
- Colombia
- France
- Germany
- Hungary
- Italy
- Japan
- Mexico
- Poland
- Romania
- Russia
- Serbia
- Spain
- Thailand
- UK
- USA

A Technology Center spread over 3 continents

- Asia
- Europe
- North America

2 Natural rubber plantations

- Brazil

Our mission

To make a sustainable contribution to progress in the mobility of goods and people by enhancing freedom of movement, safety, efficiency and pleasure when on the move.

Michelin committed to environmental-friendliness

Michelin, world leader in low rolling resistance tires, actively reduces fuel consumption and vehicle gas emission.

For its products, Michelin develops state-of-the-art technologies in order to:
- Reduce fuel consumption, while improving overall tire performance.
- Increase life cycle to reduce the number of tires to be processed at the end of their useful lives;
- Use raw materials which have a low impact on the environment.

Furthermore, at the end of 2008, 99.5% of tire production in volume was carried out in ISO 14001* certified plants

Michelin is committed to implementing recycling channels for end-of-life tires.

*environmental certification

**Passenger Car
Light Truck**   **Truck**

Michelin
a key mobility enabler

Earthmover   **Aircraft**   **Agricultural**

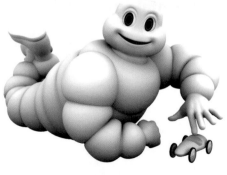

Two-wheel   **Distribution**

Partnered with vehicle manufacturers, in tune with users,
active in competition and in all the distribution channels,
Michelinis continually innovating to promote mobility today
and to invent that of tomorrow.

Maps and   **ViaMichelin,**   **Michelin**
Guides   travel   **Lifestyle,**
                     assistance   for your travel
                     services   accessories

MICHELIN
plays on balanced performance

- **Long tire life**
- **Fuel savings**
- **Safety on the road**

... MICHELIN tires provide you with the best performance, without making a single sacrifice.

The MICHELIN tire pure technology

1 Tread
A thick layer of rubber provides contact with the ground. It has to channel water away and last as long as possible.

2 Crown plies
This double or triple reinforced belt has both vertical flexibility and high lateral rigidity. It provides the steering capacity.

3 Sidewalls
These cover and protect the textile casing whose role is to attach the tire tread to the wheel rim.

4 Bead area for attachment to the rim
Its internal bead wire clamps the tire firmly against the wheel rim.

5 Inner liner
This makes the tire almost totally impermeable and maintains the correct inflation pressure.

Heed
the MICHELIN Man's advice

To improve safety:
- I drive with the correct tire pressure
- I check the tire pressure every month
- I have my car regularly serviced
- I regularly check the appearance
  of my tires (wear, deformation)
- I am responsive behind the wheel
- change my tires according to the season

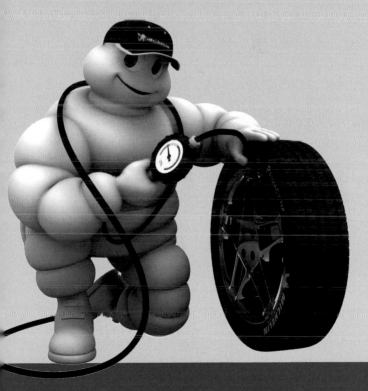

www.michelin.com
www.michelin.(your country extension – e.g. .fr for France)

● Where to **Eat**

⌂ Where to **Stay**

Indexes

Alphabetical List of Restaurants

Indexes ▶ Alphabetical List of Restaurants

319

Restaurants by Cuisine

American

Bin 36	✗✗	20
bin wine cafe	✗	156
Bongo Room	✗	156
Boston Blackie's	✗	47
Breakfast Club	✗	71
Bristol (The)	🐝 ✗	157
Browntrout	🐝 ✗✗	197
Chicago Firehouse	✗✗	91
Custom House Tavern	✗✗✗	92
DMK Burger Bar	✗	200
Duchamp	✗✗	161
Edzo's	✗	240
Eggsperience	✗✗	23
erwin	✗✗	201
Flying Saucer	✗	185
Glenn's Diner	✗	202
Grill on the Alley (The)	✗✗	118
Hearty	✗✗	202
Hugo's Frog Bar & Fish House	✗✗	118
Joe's	✗✗✗	31
Kuma's Corner	✗	186
Lokal	✗✗	166
Lou Mitchell's	✗	77
Lula Café	🐝 ✗	186
Meli Cafe	✗	78
M. Henry	🐝 ✗	221
Mike Ditka's	✗✗✗	120
NAHA	✿ ✗✗✗	33
Nana	🐝 ✗✗	257
Nicksons Eatery	✗	257
One North Kitchen & Bar	✗✗	62
Original Pancake House	✗	122
Over Easy Café	✗	222
Park Grill	✗✗	62
Prasino	✗✗	258
Province	✗✗	82
Red Canary	✗✗	170
Rhapsody	✗✗	63
RL	✗✗	36
Ruxbin Kitchen	✗✗	171
Sable	✗✗	37
Southport Grocery	✗	206
Stained Glass Bistro (The)	✗✗	245
State & Lake	✗✗	64
Sweet Maple Cafe	✗	106
Table Fifty-Two	✗✗✗	128
West Town Tavern	🐝 ✗✗	178
Wishbone	✗	208
Yolk	✗	98
Zak's Place	✗✗	262
Zodiac (The)	✗✗✗	51

Asian

aja	✗✗	18
aria	✗✗✗	58
Chen's	✗	198
Noodles Etc.	✗	258
Opera	✗✗	96
Red Light	✗✗	83
Shikago	✗✗	64
Sunda	✗✗	40
Thalia Spice	✗✗	177
Urban Belly	🐝 ✗	191

Barbecue

Brand BBQ Market	✗	183
Lillie's Q	✗✗	166
Pork Shoppe	✗	189
Smoke Daddy	✗	173
Smoque BBQ	🐝 ✗	190
Twin Anchors	🐝 ✗	148
Uncle Bub's BBQ	✗	260

Indexes ▶ Restaurants by Cuisine

CHICAGO

River North

American
Bin 36	✗✗	20
Eggsperience	✗✗	23
Joe's	✗✗✗	31
NAHA	✿ ✗✗✗	33
RL	✗✗	36
Sable	✗✗	37

Asian
aja	✗✗	18
Sunda	✗✗	40

Chinese
Shanghai Terrace	✗✗	38

Contemporary
Avenues	✿✿ ✗✗✗✗	19
Crofton on Wells	✿ ✗✗	22
Epic	✗✗	24
graham elliot	✿ ✗✗	29
Pops for Champagne	▤	35
Sixteen	✿ ✗✗✗	39
Zealous	✗✗✗	43

Fusion
Japonais	✗✗✗	30
SUSHISAMBA rio	✗✗	41

Gastropub
English	✗	23
Gilt Bar	☺ ✗✗	27

Hawaiian
Roy's	✗✗	37

Indian
Vermilion	✗✗	41

International
Hub51	✗✗	30

Italian
Coco Pazzo	✗✗	21
Osteria Via Stato	✗✗	32
Phil Stefani's 437 Rush	✗✗	34
Prosecco	✗✗	35
Quartino	✗✗	36

Japanese
Ai	✗✗	18
Friends Sushi	✗✗	25

Mexican
Frontera Grill	☺ ✗✗	25
Mercadito	✗✗	32
Topolobampo	✿ ✗✗	42

Pizza
Gino's East	✗	27
Giordano's	✗	28
Pizzeria Uno	✗	34

Seafood
Fulton's on the River	✗✗	26
Shaw's Crab House	✗✗	38

Steakhouse
Benny's Chop House	✗✗✗	20
David Burke's Primehouse	✗✗	21
Fleming's	✗✗	24
Gene & Georgetti	✗✗	26
Harry Caray's	✗✗	28
Keefer's	✗✗✗	31
Smith & Wollensky	✗✗	40

Streeterville

American
Boston Blackie's	✗	47
Zodiac (The)	✗✗✗	51

Contemporary
C-House	✗✗	47
Cité	✗✗	48
Tru	✿ ✗✗✗✗	52

French
Les Nomades	✗✗✗	49

Chinese
New Peking ✗ 204

Contemporary
Chalkboard ✗✗ 198
Sola ✗✗ 206

French
La Creperie 😊 ✗ 203

Greek
Melanthios Greek
   Char House ✗✗ 203

Guatemalan
El Tinajon ✗ 200

Italian
Frasca ✗✗ 201

Mexican
Chilam Balam 🍴 199
Mixteco Grill 😊 ✗ 204

Pizza
Pizza Rustica ✗ 205

Scandinavian
Ann Sather 😊 ✗ 197

Thai
Always Thai ✗ 196
P.S. Bangkok ✗✗ 205
Sticky Rice ✗ 207
Thai Classic ✗✗ 207

Turkish
A La Turka ✗ 196

Vegetarian
Chicago Diner ✗ 199

Andersonville, Edgewater & Uptown

American
M. Henry 😊 ✗ 221
Over Easy Café ✗ 222

Chinese
Mei Shung ✗ 221
Sun Wah BBQ ✗ 227

Ethiopian
Demera ✗ 217
Ras Dashen ✗ 225

French
Bistro Campagne ✗✗ 215
LM ✗✗ 219

Gastropub
Hopleaf 😊 ✗ 218

Indian
Marigold ✗✗ 220
Paprika ✗ 223

Italian
Anteprima ✗ 214
Pizza D.O.C. ✗ 224

Japanese
Blue Ocean ✗✗ 216

Korean
San Soo Gab San ✗ 226

Latin American
La Fonda Latino Grill ✗ 219

Mediterranean
Ceres' Table 😊 ✗✗ 216

Mexican
La Ciudad ✗ 218
Los Nopales 😊 ✗ 220

Pizza
Great Lake ✗ 217
Spacca Napoli 😊 ✗ 226

Southern
Big Jones ✗✗ 215

Thai
Opart Thai House 😊 ✗ 222
Rosded ✗ 225
Thai Grill &
   Noodle Bar (The) ✗ 227
Thai Pastry
   & Restaurant ✗ 228

Vietnamese
Ba Le ✗ 214
Pho 777 ✗ 223
Pho Xe Tang - Tank
   Noodle ✗ 224

331

Starred Restaurants

*W*ithin the selection we offer you, some restaurants deserve to be highlighted for their particularly good cuisine. When giving one, two, or three Michelin stars, there are a number of elements that we consider including the quality of the ingredients, the technical skill and flair that goes into their preparation, the blend and clarity of flavours, and the balance of the menu. Just as important is the ability to produce excellent cooking time and again. We make as many visits as we need, so that our readers may be assured of quality and consistency.

A two or three-star restaurant has to offer something very special in its cuisine; a real element of creativity, originality, or "personality" that sets it apart from the rest. Three stars – our highest award – are given to the choicest restaurants, where the whole dining experience is superb.

Cuisine in any style, modern or traditional, may be eligible for a star. Due to the fact we apply the same independent standards everywhere, the awards have become benchmarks of reliability and excellence in over 20 countries in Europe and Asia, particularly in France, where we have awarded stars for 100 years, and where the phrase "Now that's real three-star quality!" has entered into the language.

The awarding of a star is based solely on the quality of the cuisine.

☼ ☼ ☼

Exceptional cuisine, worth a special journey.

One always eats here extremely well, sometimes superbly. Distinctive dishes are precisely executed, using superlative ingredients.

Alinea	XXXX	135
L20	XXXX	142

☼ ☼

Excellent cuisine, worth a detour.

Skillfully and carefully crafted dishes of outstanding quality.

Avenues	XXXX	19
Charlie Trotter's	XXX	137
Ria	XXXX	124

☼

A very good restaurant in its category.

A place offering cuisine prepared to a consistently high standard.

Blackbird	XX	72
Boka	XX	136
Bonsoirée	XX	184
Crofton on Wells	XX	22
Everest	XXX	60
graham elllot	XX	29
Longman & Eagle	X	187
NAHA	XXX	33
NoMI	XXX	121
Schwa	X	172
Seasons	XXXX	126
Sepia	XX	85
Sixteen	XXX	39
Spiaggia	XXXX	127
Takashi	XX	175
Topolobampo	XX	42
Tru	XXXX	52
Vie	XXX	261

Bib Gourmand

This symbol indicates our inspector's favorites for good value. For $40 or less, you can enjoy two courses and a glass of wine or a dessert (not including tax or gratuity).

Breakfast Specialists

Whoever coined the phrase "Breakfast is the most important meal of the day," must have been from Chicago because this food lover's town, already rich in epicurean traditions, boasts an impressive lineup of eateries specializing in comforting and creative morning meals. Whether you crave fluffy pancake stacks, gooey cinnamon rolls, or heaping skillets of eggs and hash brown potatoes, breakfast in Chicago is uniquely appreciated and delicious. Also special to the Windy City, late risers have as much of an opportunity to fuel up as early birds since many breakfast spots serve well into the afternoon—often until 3:00 P.M.

The following is a list of establishments where our inspectors have experienced a stunning start to their day.

Brunch

Late Dining

Alphabetical List of Hotels

Notes

Notes